This Wheel of Rocks

This Wheel of Rocks

An Unexpected Spiritual Journey

SISTER MARYA
GRATHWOHL, OSF

Riverhead Books

New York

2023

RIVERHEAD BOOKS
An imprint of Penguin Random House LLC
penguinrandomhouse.com

Grateful acknowledgment is made for permission to reprint the following:

Excerpts from *The New Jerusalem Bible*, copyright © 1985 by Darton,
Longman & Todd, Ltd. and Doubleday, a division of Penguin Random House LLC.
Reprinted by permission.

Library of Congress Cataloging-in-Publication Data
Names: Grathwohl, Marya, Sister, author.
Title: This wheel of rocks : an unexpected spiritual journey /
Sister Marya Grathwohl.
Description: New York : Riverhead Books, 2023.
Identifiers: LCCN 2023008409 (print) | LCCN 2023008410 (ebook) | ISBN
9781594487309 (hardcover) | ISBN 9780593713877 (ebook)
Subjects: LCSH: Grathwohl, Marya, Sister. |
Nuns—United States—Biography| Northern Cheyenne Indian
Reservation (Mont.)—Biography. | Christian biography.
Classification: LCC BX4705.G61834 A3 2023 (print) |
LCC BX4705.G61834 (ebook) | DDC 271/.9002—dc23/eng/20230712
LC record available at https://lccn.loc.gov/2023008409
LC ebook record available at https://lccn.loc.gov/2023008410

Printed in the United States of America
1st Printing

Book design by Amanda Little

To Earth's future:

for children everywhere

for the children of every species.

CONTENTS

This Wheel of Rocks

Prologue

The four-thousand-foot ascent up Wyoming State Highway 14 from the Tongue River valley to the first summit of the Bighorn Mountains is a journey back in time.

Along the way, big brown signs tell stories locked in ascending layers of stone. I grab the only paper in the car, a Wyoming map, and scribble notes in the margins as my longtime friend Dorie Green throttles up steep switchbacks. I catch TRIASSIC-PERMIAN 199–299 MILLION YEARS AGO, followed in quick succession by PENNSYLVANIAN, MISSISSIPPIAN, DEVONIAN 360–410 MILLION YEARS AGO, and ORDOVICIAN 443–488 MILLION YEARS AGO. Breathtaking views of the valley open below us at each bend.

Dorie and I talk excitedly about the life-forms that were emerging during those periods. Ideas just as breathtaking as the spectacular views. Dorie, who had distanced herself from organized religion nevertheless, coins the phrase "rock rosary" to express the sequence of life mysteries locked in the rock layers: reptiles, forests, amphibians, fish, bodies of cooperating cells, photosynthesis.

As the mountain reveals the splendor of life's evolution, I find myself asking, "Who are we human beings? Within this array of life-forms, what is our role, our gift to Earth?" These immense questions require a universe or religion. Perhaps a mountain could assist with a nagging smaller question, the question I explore here.

Then near the summit, we abruptly round a cliff. Another sign: PRECAMBRIAN 2.9 BILLION YEARS AGO. GRANITE. And my soul slams into awe.

Earth began forming approximately 4.6 billion years ago. At this cliff we are in the presence of some of the oldest exposed rock on the planet. When these massive slabs were slowly cooling deep underground, life itself had been murmuring forth in mysterious and, perhaps, simple ways for about a billion years.

We find a pull-off. I race back to the cliff and near the sign pick up something small. A stone, heavy for its size, glistens with quartz. I hold it close to my lips.

"You," I whisper, "you witnessed life's genius in creating photosynthesis."

I stand silent, listening. Time stops.

In my hands is a scripture, a stone crying out. I recall that it was a mere two thousand years ago that Jesus said, "If the people are silent, the stones will cry out."

Earth, a rocky planet, cries out. Earth cries out against global mass extinction of species, the destruction of human-caused climate change, and the prowess of militarized and industrialized humanity to poison and destroy Earth's support systems: soil, air, and water. Earth cries out against the suffering we humans cause each other.

Here is my question for the mountain. How do we learn to become contributing members of the pageant of life, of this ongoing story of a communion of species, subjects in their own right?

Is Earth really a communion of subjects, each to be respected with humility, or more like a collection of objects, to exploit for human economic gain and power? Standing on primordial granite, holding it in human hands close to our ears and hearts, we hear the voice of life's early ancestors.

Microscopic beings found ways to absorb energy and replicate themselves.

Billions of years later, can we dare to find ways to participate in the energy of life's communion and invent flourishing human communities that enhance the whole Earth community and, especially, the planet?

As members of the Sisters of St. Francis, Oldenburg, I and others challenge ourselves "to speak a word of hope." Throughout my life, I've heard the cries of suffering Earth. It began when my parents and I visited the tomb of the extinct passenger pigeon in the Cincinnati Zoo. I left feeling sad. As a young adult I became aware of the cries of polluted air and water. More sadness. Gradually I made my way to Crow and Northern Cheyenne elders and children, to college professors and scientists, to geologists and scripture scholars and Earth activists, who taught me to listen to the suffering of Earth and people, and respond in hope by working to reinvent what it means to be human. In these times of extreme destruction, I dare to offer this book as a word of hope and an invitation to transforming action.

Part I

THE ROAD TO PRYOR, MONTANA

1

Inklings

Show your servants the deeds you do;
let their children enjoy your splendor!

PSALMS 90:16

They were inklings, I realize now. Flowing in the material world, they came whispering. I believe they were sent from God. The messages lodged in my soul and mind, tenacious as loss, tenacious as memories of beauty. They had the potential to shape my future.

The earliest was Mom. Mary Jane Seiler Grathwohl often walked, carrying me, around her yard. She stopped to admire tall white lilies, held me to their wide faces to smell them. She wiped yellow pollen off my nose.

Newly wed Jane and Larry Grathwohl bought a home on a dead-end street, Laura Lane, in Norwood, Ohio. They took frequent evening walks, seeking nearby parks where they could take the children they anticipated bringing into their lives. They discovered an Indian mound a twenty-minute walk from their home. Two distinct cultures, named by archeologists Adena (800 BCE to 100 CE) and Hopewell (100 CE to 500 CE), had built hundreds of burial and ceremonial mounds throughout the Ohio valley. What the builders called themselves is unknown. Unknown to Jane and Larry was how the mound would shape my future. To me, Laura Lane was no dead end.

The mound was located on the highest point in our neighborhood. Fenced as a small park, it was one of the few mounds that had been left undisturbed. Norwood had built the town's two water towers behind it.

Whenever it was my turn to suggest the destination of a frequent family walk, I always chose the Indian mound. Its conical grassy hill was almost as high as a one-story house. Maple and oak trees had taken root on it.

It was quiet and cool at the mound, even in the humidity of summer. As we walked around it, Mom reminded us not to climb on it because it was special. "Maybe some people were buried in the mound," she said. "Let's pray for them." My sisters, Regina and Susan, and I stood close to Mom and said the usual Catholic prayer for the dead, "May their souls and all the souls of the faithful departed rest in peace. Amen." We knew the prayer by heart because we prayed it before every meal as Mom and Dad recalled their deceased parents and six sisters and brothers. We extended to these unknown dead the reverence we had for family members.

I realize now that my parents nurtured my sense of wonder here as they encouraged respect for the mound. I learned that *mystery* coupled with quiet and beauty evoked a sense of the sacred. This place wasn't "church" by any stretch, but here in nature and ancient human ritual there was a kind of holy presence and power. It appealed to me, perhaps more than church.

The mound ignited my imagination. I felt an affinity with the people who had built it and must have had their homes in what was now our neighborhood. Back on Laura Lane, walking to school and passing friends' houses, I pictured the children of the Mound people playing under the trees in yards or peeking out from behind the bushes that hedged sidewalks.

In addition, the mound and its people recalibrated my sense of history, gave me a human story *here* that was older than our family stories of grandparents coming to the Ohio valley from German and Alsace-Lorraine regions. It was a story older than America, older than Columbus, and closer to home than stories of the first Thanksgiving and Pocahontas.

All this was a child's small awareness, but it bestowed a respect and reverence for the original peoples of this continent. It hinted at the sacred inherent in nature. It would help guide my life and ministry among the Crow and Northern Cheyenne in their ancestral homelands we call Montana.

Grandpa, Mom's dad, also lived with us in the Laura Lane house. He had lost a leg in an accident at work. Using a cane and an artificial limb, he navigated the house slowly, and often sat out on the front porch. He had an endless supply of peanuts for the squirrel that lived in the tall oak a few feet from the porch steps. My sisters and I sat on the steps, placing a peanut as Grandpa directed at the base of the thick trunk. In a swirl of tail, the peanut disappeared.

Next peanut a few inches out from the trunk. It soon disappeared. A little closer to the steps. Gone. Then I put a peanut on the toe of my shoe. We all sat very still and silent.

Squirrel suddenly leapt from the tree to my shoe, snatched the peanut in his mouth, leapt to my knee, then my shoulder, ran across the back of my shoulders, and leapt from my other knee back to the tree. Wide-eyed, breathless, thrilled, I turned to Grandpa.

"The squirrel ran on me," I shouted to him. I ran into the house to tell Mom. I realize now the squirrel's feet left a trail of prints not only across my shoulders, but in my being. The feel of wild, of squirrel became part of me. And I felt so lucky. It was my first lesson in how to enter into the world of other beings, beings beyond our control.

Every summer, Mom and Dad scraped together enough money to take us all to the Cincinnati Zoo. Over the years, the zoo had gradually evolved from smelly buildings of caged animals to more spacious, sometimes open-air settings that sought to mimic the animals' natural habitats. Monkey Island, surrounded by a deep moat, looked like a playground, complete with hills, a maze of tunnels, trees, and hanging vine swings. Tropical birds flew in large rooms thick with greenery. An alligator lazed in a miniature swamp.

One stone building didn't fit the pattern. It was small, with an orange pagoda-style roof and heavy wooden doors we pulled open slowly. The floor was polished stone. The air was cool and hushed. Light filtered through small windows. It felt almost like a church.

In front of us were two bird exhibits and the birds were all dead. They'd been stuffed and mounted as if in a natural history museum, not a zoo.

Dad and I stood together, looking at three large, lovely birds. Softly blue-gray with rosy breasts, long tapered wings and graceful tails, they resembled mourning doves. Dad told me they were not doves but passenger pigeons and the very last one, Martha, had died in this zoo on September 1, 1914. He pointed to a painting.

"That's Martha," he said.

Dad told me that once there were more passenger pigeons than any other land bird species in the world. There were billions of them. They lived in forests throughout eastern North America and migrated in flocks so large they darkened the sun like an eclipse.

Billion meant very little to me but I could imagine huge clouds of birds obscuring the sun. I could imagine that, although it was only an imagined thought. I realized they didn't exist anymore. Not even one.

I continued to stare at dead stuffed birds. Among them was Incas, the last Carolina parakeet, who died in Martha's death cage on February 21, 1918. These bright green, yellow, and orange birds once numbered in the millions. I tried to apprehend the loss of two entire species. Especially the passenger pigeon. No more passenger pigeons, anywhere. How could this happen when there had been so many?

Alexander Wilson, the father of American ornithology, visited a passenger pigeon breeding area near Shelbyville, Kentucky, in 1806. He documented that it was several miles wide and stretched forty miles through the forest. In a single tree he counted more than one hundred nests. People in the region reported that the songs of passenger pigeons rang through the trees, sounding like hundreds of sleigh bells. In 1813 John James Audubon recorded a migrating flock that filled the sky as it flew overhead without diminishing for three full days.

The Native Peoples of Canada refused to hunt nesting passenger pigeons until the young were able to fly. They attempted to keep European settlers from disturbing the easily approached brooding flocks. Instead, the Europeans armed themselves with guns, clubs, stones, and poles to kill the birds. Deprived of their food supply as Eastern pine, beech, and hemlock forests were destroyed by settlers to clear the land, the birds had learned to eat farmers' peas and oats.

Eventually young pigeon became a table delicacy and market demands drove the constant slaughter of the birds. Throughout the 1870s tons were packed in ice and shipped from nesting areas in the Catskills to New York City. They were sold for about fifty cents a dozen.

Netters using bait could snare up to 250 dozen birds in one grab. Pots of burning sulfur were placed under roosting trees, dazing the birds, causing them to fall to the ground. Hundreds of pigeoners, relying on telegraphed information and traveling by train, followed flocks as far as a thousand miles. At a nesting site near Petoskey, Michigan, pigeons were netted, shot, and clubbed to death at a rate of 50,000 birds a day, every day, for five months. And then the pigeoners went home, changed out of bloody, feathered clothes, and sat down to dinner with their families. In some places, up to 180,000 birds were taken in a single day.

On May 11, 1947, the Wisconsin Society for Ornithology erected a stone monument to the passenger pigeon on a bluff along the Mississippi River that overlooks one of their former flyways. On a bronze plaque below an image of the bird it reads, THIS SPECIES BECAME EXTINCT THROUGH THE AVARICE AND THOUGHTLESSNESS OF MAN. And perhaps through desperation. For farm families struggling to feed themselves, the swarms of feeding pigeons were yet another threat, perhaps even evoking the biblical plagues.

It's possible that no one imagined that such a large multitude of birds would ever disappear completely. But by 1880 their decline was continuous and accelerating. In the 1890s flocks of a few hundred were still being sighted, and then shot or netted. Attempts were made to breed small captive flocks, but failed. The last reported wild bird in Wisconsin was shot in September 1899. The last reported wild bird on the entire continent was shot on a farm near Sargents, Ohio, by a fourteen-year-old boy on March 24, 1900.

Martha died alone in her cage at approximately 12:30 p.m. in Cincinnati, Ohio. She was twenty-nine years old. The continent's symphony of bells fell silent forever.

News of Martha's death shocked the nation. She was frozen in a block of ice and sent by train to the Smithsonian, where she was stuffed and remains today. It was the first time Americans experienced the finality of extinction of a species. People began to realize the importance of conservation efforts to protect wildlife. The country saw firsthand the need for policies and laws to preserve habitat and control rapacious killing of wildlife for sport or food.

I didn't know all this history as a child but, strangely, the extinction of the passenger pigeon became an ache in my heart. In school we learned about the extinction of other birds and animals like the flightless and amiable dodo. I felt sad, even though we were told the dodo was stupid, almost as if it deserved extinction.

Today, most scientists warn that we are currently in a Sixth Great Extinction, caused almost exclusively by human actions: destruction of habitat, economic pressures, overfishing, poaching, and climate change. We live amid a crescendo of extinctions. Knowing this, the sight of Martha and her story returned to haunt me. She was and remains the tangible horror, loss, and evil of human-caused extinction staring us in the face.

When I was twelve, we moved from Laura Lane to a Cape Cod–style house on a quarter acre of land on Blue Rock Road in White Oak, another Cincinnati neighborhood. Mom loved the house. Dad relished the expanse of land. He immediately set about growing grapes for wine and cultivating a large organic garden.

One night in our new home, Mom nudged me awake from a sound sleep. "Judy," she said, calling me by my given name, "come here. I have something to show you." Puzzled, disgruntled, I stumbled behind her into the bathroom. She stood at the window and pulled open the towel curtains she had made. They were white with large yellow butterflies. Unable to afford real curtains, she had designed and made these.

"Look."

We leaned together over the white wicker clothes hamper and peered out the window. There, bright against the night sky, the full moon glowed like an immense lantern, as if alight from within. Our tar-slick garage roof, long needles of the pine tree, metal strands of Dad's grape arbors, and dewy grass all shimmered in its light. Everything was aglow, everything awash with light. Including my mom and me.

"I just didn't want you to miss the beauty," she whispered. "Now we can go back to bed."

She, with Dad, was my best life teacher. After almost fifty years of being a Franciscan Sister, I learned that *beauty* for Franciscan theologians and philosophers is the ultimate and most intimate knowing of God, another name for God, *the* name for God. Saint Bonaventure and Blessed John Duns Scotus teach that the beauty and diversity of creation nourish us through suffering and loss. When we've run out of purpose, when memories of war sicken us, when Earth is attacked with unparalleled savagery for coal, gas, oil, timber, and profit, when poverty runs rampant and extreme wealth for very few soars, when friends betray us, and everyone we love lives far away . . . then, still *beauty* endures, and helps us make it through. Like God.

Mary Jane Grathwohl, my mom, was the first to teach me that. She gave me a method for growing in knowledge of God. Here's what you do. Wake up. Get up. Pull aside any curtains. And *stand there* in the dark, in the beauty.

The following winter, I tore into the kitchen as if driven by the last gales of the snowstorm that had engulfed the afternoon. I saw Dad at his little homemade desk in the corner of the dining room, opposite the kitchen door. I stopped in the doorway; snow from my boots dripped on the blue and yellow linoleum.

"Dad!" I began.

"How was school today, Judy?" he asked, looking up from paperwork.

"Not school, Dad, but the Queen Anne's lace out there on Frey's hillside pasture. You know, right behind the new apartment building."

He nodded.

"Dad, all the winter killed flowers with the snow on them. It's beautiful and I don't want to forget that sight. I'm afraid I will, though."

I was telling him just because he was there. And also because he could still describe in detail many memories from his three trips out west to the national parks. Even though it had been over twenty-five years since he'd been there in the 1930s. Whenever we asked him, he told us about fishing at sunrise from the shore of Lake McDonald in Glacier, the sweat and danger of an all-day hike down into the Grand Canyon, Old Faithful erupting gloriously right on time. How come he remembered it all so well? I waited.

"Here's what you do, honey. It's really easy. Just go back out to Frey's hillside and stand there in the middle of those snowy flowers. Stand there until you can feel them inside you, in your heart. Then you will never forget."

I don't know if I ever really *felt* their beauty inside my heart as the storm passed and the sky cleared into stars. However, whenever I think about that evening, the memory still rises from somewhere within me. Then, though, I simply walked back home in the dark, picking my way down the hill, following light from our kitchen window.

That was my first lesson in contemplative prayer. It's the same practice, whether in a mountain meadow, a hospital room, or a convent chapel. Show up, take time, feel the beauty in your heart.

These varied inklings wove themselves over time into the fiber of my being. We can't know how such whisperings might nuance our destiny, lead us into an unexpected future. They contribute to shaping us into who we are. They will influence how we perceive the world and the decisions we will make. Perhaps only in retrospect do we discover their potency.

I will continue to be mesmerized by Earth's mysteries and beauty, and grieved by human destruction of our home causing intolerable suffering to Earth, people, other animals, and plants. I will eventually be motivated by love to work for Earth's protection and restoration. I would struggle to figure out how God was in this calling I felt so strongly. It wasn't the typical ministry of a Catholic Sister. Could it possibly be within the realm of faith to love God and nature, even deciding to serve nature? It would not be a clear, well-defined path.

Summons

"Come and see."
And so they went.

JOHN 1:39

A s a young man in the 1930s and before he met my mother, Larry Grathwohl dreamed of visiting all the national parks west of the Mississippi River. The youngest son of German immigrants who had fled war and poverty as teenagers in the 1890s, my dad set off seeking beauty and adventure in the wild spaces of America when he was twenty-three years old. His first choice, Yellowstone National Park.

His brother Al and their friend Harry Scholle went with him. Dad, trained in accounting, kept the daily log of their expenses. He'd made his own journal for this, cutting four-inch-wide strips of ledger paper, two pages for each day of their trip. He'd punched holes for ring binders in the top corners of the pages. He'd pasted tiny brown tabs at the bottom of every other page, the day's date on each tab.

On Sunday, July 14, 1935, they left Harry's home on Heywood

Street, Cincinnati, at 3:20 a.m. They drove 687 miles that day to Mason City, Iowa, arriving at 8:00 p.m. Total cost of the day for gas, food, bridge toll, and room rent: $14.29. Fourteen days and 4,362 miles later they would arrive back on Heywood Street.

On the second journal page of each day, he recorded the weather. And mused. The Badlands: "earth and color shaped into awe-inspiring design." The Black Hills: "scenes where a certain feel of peace seemed to fill one." Crossing the Bighorn Mountains: "in clear, cool weather we drove across the plateau of the range on a gumbo dirt road. Then down the other side on the same type of road through Shell Canyon, a wonderful, scenic, but dangerous trip. The road is hardly wide enough for two cars, has very deep ruts, hairpin turns and in some places drops off on the outside as much as 300 feet."

And finally, Yellowstone: "Our first day we secured a cabin at the Lake and attended an evening Ranger talk. On the way back to our cabin we witnessed one of the most beautiful scenes of our lives as we watched the full moon rise out of Yellowstone Lake casting its gleam in a golden bar across the waters." And then home: "We saw the outskirts of fair Cincinnati and arrived to great rejoicing at Harry's home, ending the most thrilling, fun packed, emotion stirring, and impressive two weeks of my poor youthful experience."

Dad occasionally showed to his family his journals and the photo albums he had made of his journeys. He'd spread them across the dining room table and my mom, sisters, and I crowded around him, kneeling on chairs and leaning over the table. Pointing to sepia pictures, he regaled us with stories of watching geysers and waterfalls, hiking deep canyons, seeing herds of wild animals, and walking among the world's tallest trees. I grew up wanting to live there.

Once Mom found me sitting on the front porch steps crying.

"Judy, what's wrong?" she asked as she sat down beside me.

"I don't belong here," I said. "I belong out west, in the places of Dad's pictures and stories. Why did Grandpa and Grandma have to stop here in Cincinnati when they came to America? Why didn't they keep going west?"

"Cincinnati was where they had relatives, and they wanted to be with them," she said.

That didn't satisfy me.

Catholic Rain

Holy, holy, holy, Lord God of power and might.
Heaven and Earth are full of your glory.
CATHOLIC MASS PRAYER

I was living with an inner lightning.

Fortunately, the lightning of sacred living Earth flashed within the steady rain of daily Grathwohl family Catholic practices. You know that rain, stand-under-the-porch-roof rain, fragrant and soft as it mists across your face and cools you on a hot summer afternoon.

This rain bestowed life and helped my parents make sense of losses and joys, suffering and their struggles. It murmured its way into meals, bedtime rituals, even neighborhood socializing.

As I imagined every family did, we said prayers of blessing before every meal. No exceptions for anything, not even picnics or meals in other people's homes. To not pray at mealtime was unthinkable, disrespectful of God and family. Praying at meals wasn't obligation; it was part of the essence of our meals.

Perhaps my parents wanted to slow down the rush of the day by welcoming the presence of Almighty God at the family evening meal. This prayer brought pause to sibling chatter or arguing, Mom's meal preparation and other work, Dad's impatience to get some task finished, and Aunt Rose's frustration with a boss. For a brief moment time stopped, and home became *church*.

These prayers included a blessing of family and food, a Hail Mary and remembrance for the dead, and a petition on behalf of the suffering people of Hungary fighting Communism. Our prayer widened our table beyond the present, taking us back to those who had gone before us and beyond the confines of our home to include global concerns. They were shaping and stretching children's awareness of their world.

This rain included my first night prayer experience as an infant. Dad would prop me on his shoulder and slowly walk around their bed, humming "Song of the Volga Boatmen," popularized by Glenn Miller a few years before I was born. None of the traditional lullabies ushered me into sleep like that deep, rhythmic hum, my dad swaying as he paced. I believe now that I learned the meditative drone of night prayer by hearing it, over and over. Perhaps it was my parents' prayer, too, and not a chore.

Several years and two babies later, Mom tucked us each under blankets and we prayed with her to the angels of God, especially our personal guardian angels who hovered at our shoulders, to care for us during the vulnerability of sleep. She'd turn off the light, telling us not to start talking again or pull the blankets from each other. Sometimes, the prayer worked.

There were even prayers beyond our family. Every week the Catholic neighbors on Laura Lane gathered in someone's house to pray the rosary. We children had to stop playing and join our parents. We grumbled, but when the four sets of parents called for every one of us, we obeyed and marched up the sidewalk as if the school bell had rung to end recess.

We sat together, on porch swings and in winter on living room couches and chairs as we prayed fifty Hail Marys, tied together with announcements of events from the childhood, life, death, and heavenly glory of Jesus and Mary. We were praying for a cure for polio and a distant cousin who had it, for an end to the Korean War, and whatever troubled the working-class families we knew, and most of all, for the conversion of Russia. Then off to play again. Something secure about so many parents continuing to sit together talking while we played until the streetlights came on and it was time for everyone to go home. There was security in Catholic rain.

Parallel to all this, I was also being led into another kind of Catholic prayer. Now I would say it was God-Presence time. Seasoned spiritual guides have called it "learning to sit in the gaze of God's love." At age seven, I knew nothing of that, but that didn't stop God.

This kind of prayer was something I fell into. The first time it happened, I was simply trying to be "good in church." It came to me as I sat with about a hundred other children, waiting my turn to go to Confession, to kneel in a curtained box and whisper my sins through a screen to an unseen priest. He would then say Jesus's words of forgiveness.

I was rather indifferent about doing this. Confession was a chance to get rid of sins, so that if you died you could go straight to heaven. I honestly couldn't imagine doing anything so bad it would land me in hell. Going to Confession therefore entailed drumming up little sins like arguing with my sisters, disobeying my parents, or taking a puff from the neighbor lady's cigarette. Although *that* wasn't on the sin list in my prayer book, it plagued me for weeks because I knew Mom would adamantly condemn such behavior.

That particular "sin" long since forgotten, I'm now back to the ordinary list, trying to recall the number of times for each sin. In the meantime, I sat, waiting. I was last in the long line of seated little children preparing to go to Confession. I daydreamed, imagining that by some miracle the curtained box was really an elevator that would take me to the very top of the cavernous church and I could move aside the curtain and see everything at once. Or maybe it would take me into the basement of the church, probably dark and scary, but something to explore.

I prayed the rosary. I sat and waited. I looked idly at the familiar stained-glass windows. I sat still. I waited some more. I liked being out of school. I liked being in the quiet, cool church.

I have no idea how long I sat there, but during that stillness I got lost in a quiet peacefulness. I found my *self* there and it felt good. I realize now that I inadvertently discovered inner *calm*, and it was sweet, kind, comforting. I was in church, so I assumed the calm was God. God, a Presence, not an image of an old man, father, or judge surrounded by big words like almighty, eternal, or glorious. Just Presence, and close to me.

My second-grade teacher, Sister Hyacinth, startled me when she leaned over the bench to tell me I could go ahead of the line. "You've been so good, sitting here all this while," she said in a church whisper.

I liked being good. I really liked something else more. It was that stillness that came over me, the Presence around and within me. And, I felt a little embarrassed that I hadn't kept up with the line.

Throughout those childhood hours of Catholic rain, I realize now that I discovered another presence of God, my own soul. I would not have been able to name my discovery then. Rather, soul was *felt*, not named or known with the mind or words. I sensed my child's inner self stirring in the whispered rhythms of rosary prayers, in the dreamy night prayers, and in the reliable faithfulness of all that family praying.

Now I know with certitude beyond faith that we can change the prayers, pray in English or other languages, be in the presence of prayer language we don't understand, participate in other cultures' ways of prayer and kindness, suffer through illness or a family crisis, and *soul* remains a reliable guide into authenticity and wisdom. I sense now that soul knows itself and its life within the great compassionate Mystery we strive to name. Soul stirs, rises, grows toward and within the unnameable silence and beauty of God, a mothering watery God, a rain beyond Catholic, beyond any specific religion or creed, a rain that soothes us in suffering and challenges complacency. Soul flowers in this rain of the worlds, of meteor showers, of the cosmos.

4

Chasing the Horizon

The spirit of the Lord fills the whole world.

WISDOM 1:7

T he journey up the Bighorn Mountains began almost fifty years before I got there. As my journey west began, I didn't know that the ancient stone chronicle of the pageant of life even existed. My, dad, however, had been on that very mountain road, chugged over the hidden words in 1935.

There were no brown signs then. Instead he was astounded and unnerved by the spectacular depth of Shell Canyon and the flimsy road that descended the mountain on the opposite side from the summit. His destination was Yellowstone National Park.

For me, that road began in southern Indiana.

My seventh-grade teacher, Sister Francis Leonette, urged me to consider attending the Sisters' high school program in Oldenburg, Indiana, which prepared students to become Sisters. She maintained high standards in her classroom and succeeded in keeping unruly boys on task. I was too intimidated by her to question her conviction when she told me, "You'd make a good Sister and ought to consider that God could be calling you to serve him by entering the convent." Well, I had wanted to become a priest when I was in the third grade but my equally assertive German grandmother, Grandma Grathwohl, told me that it was forbidden for girls to become priests. Only boys. "You, however, could become a Sister."

My eighth-grade teacher, Sister Mary Mark, was more affirming and encouraged critical thinking. I enjoyed exploring answers to her thoughtful questions about math ("Why do you think these geometric equations work?") and religion ("What do the Church dogmas about Mary the Mother of Jesus *really* mean?"). She helped me pace my enthusiasm for staying after school to help with classroom cleanup and sometimes arranging flowers in bouquets for the altars in church. Unlike Sister Francis Leonette, she always made sure I got home before dark and was on time for dinner.

Most significant, I had learned from our Catholic neighbor friends that these Sisters staffed schools in Montana.

Sister Mary Mark contacted Sisters in another convent in Cincinnati who invited some other eighth-grade girls and me to pray with them and enjoy snacks and sodas. I felt honored to be included in this group and to be inside the actual home of the Sisters. Two of the other girls were my friends and it was a fun evening.

The following September, three of us had ordered academy uniforms, packed our suitcases and were in our families' cars on our way to attend classes at the Sisters' academy in Oldenburg as boarders. We joined the Aspirancy program designed for students who aspired to become Sisters and anticipated entering the convent in February of our senior year. Although I wanted to serve God and pray with the

Sisters, I also had my eye on the schools they staffed on the Crow Indian Reservation in Montana.

During my senior year in high school in 1963, on February second, a feast day that commemorated when Mary and Joseph brought Jesus as a young boy to the temple to consecrate him to God, twelve high school classmates and I were ready to enter the convent of the Sisters of St. Francis. Our suitcases were packed this time with the prescribed heavy black shoes and several pairs of black stockings, black slips and robes, toiletries, and no makeup. No family pictures, and of course, no money.

That day I wore the loveliest clothes my family had: Aunt Rose's powder-blue cashmere sweater and matching skirt, and her fire-red coat with a real fur collar. We all expected that I'd live the rest of my life clothed in a black wool dress and starched white collar, a waist-length veil over my severely cropped hair. This time, I was not thinking about living among the Crow and teaching their children in Montana. I was a tight mix of emotions: excitement, fear, and sadness over leaving my family and home.

"Please drive slower, Dad," I said. He told me he already was.

We descended the road, inching past the grocery store, a fried chicken café, and several houses.

Dad then followed the convent's wall to an open gate and turned right at the narrow road into the convent grounds. We saw three acres of manicured wintry lawns, tall trees, cement walks, and stone shrines housing life-size statues of Jesus blessing children, Jesus blessing the world, and, on the hillside beyond the frozen pond, Mary with three shepherd children and a few sheep. On our right was the motherhouse and academy, a labyrinthine building of classrooms, libraries, visiting parlors, kitchens, dining rooms, dormitories, chapels, and a health care wing for aged Sisters. On our left was the three-story rectangular brick building called St. Agnes Novitiate, where young women preparing to become Sisters lived. This year nearly fifty young women almost filled it to capacity.

It was to become my new home.

Dad found a place to park. Mom, Aunt Rose, and my sisters, Regina, Susan, and Monica, climbed out of the car behind me. It felt good to be held tightly within my family as we walked up the steps of the entrance to the novitiate. Dad, leading us, had retrieved my one suitcase from the trunk. The lovely wood-framed door with gleaming cut-glass windows swung open. Sister Estelle, director of the novitiate, welcomed us, smiling.

"Come in, Judy," she said, calling me by my given name. Then she greeted my family, also calling everyone by name. I barely noticed her warmth in the uproar of greeting my other high school classmates and families. Some were already dressed in the black blouses, ankle-length black skirts, and black capes. Black net veils were perched on teenage '60s hairstyles. My friends were now the newest Sister candidates, called postulants. They each looked wonderful, and I couldn't wait to be dressed like them, too.

Here we finally were, inside the novitiate, on our way to becoming Sisters. Here we were, following in the footsteps of Jesus and Saint Francis in a dramatic way. We were forgoing the possibility of marriage and raising our own families. We would learn to live a life dedicated to God alone and to serving youth in the teaching tradition of the Catholic Church. Here we were, ready with the quick generosity of youth, to dedicate our lives to a high calling.

Sister Estelle found a place for my family in one of several parlors. Then she shepherded me out to the hallway. Postulant Peg Maher, who had entered the previous September, seemed to appear out of nowhere and we soon were climbing steps at the far end of the hall to the third-floor dorm for postulants. Up here, silence reigned.

Peg guided me through rows of crisply made beds with stark white spreads. Beside each bed was a straight wooden chair and bed stand. She stopped at my bed. She had already put the postulant blouse, skirt, and net veil I would soon be wearing at the foot of the bed. It was her Sunday outfit and it looked like new. Our own postulant clothing hadn't yet arrived, although we had submitted our measurements on time and Sister Estelle had placed the order well in advance.

Peg stepped out to the hall as I changed into the black blouse, which was several sizes too big for me, and the skirt, secured with the large safety pin she had handed to me with a grin and roll of her eyes. The ample cape fell to my waist. Peg soon returned and declared it'd do. We scrunched the veil over my curls.

"At least you'll be excused from scrubbing pots, floors, and toilets while wearing my Sunday best," she said.

She turned to help me unpack. Personal items such as Grandpa's olive wood rosary, my Bible, and my little address book disappeared into the bed stand. Toiletries were placed on my portion of a shelf in the dorm bathroom. When she spied my razor hidden in a slipper she said, "You won't be needing this anymore."

"I knew we weren't supposed to bring one, but . . ."

She stopped me with a shrug and said, "No one needs to know."

Unexpectedly, a sweet, almost conspiratorial moment of mutual understanding and trust. I felt relief because I had been struggling with a bit of guilt over sneaking a forbidden object into the convent. Peg's quick nonjudgmental response set in motion a sense that the rules here were not intended to be harsh, and that there was room for a little

29

flexibility regarding personal needs. I felt a playful rush of freedom. This time it was over a very small thing, but in the future, it would shed light on other, more important decisions. Even Sister Estelle would one day teach us that there was a legitimate way to allow for personal choice in certain rare circumstances.

We packed Aunt Rose's soft cashmere sweater and skirt and my white silk slip and pretty dress shoes into the suitcase. Back downstairs, I hurried to rejoin my family, who shared my excitement. We stood together for pictures. I gave the suitcase back to Dad. I sat down with them in the ill-fitting clothes and talked with them and nearby friends.

Sister Estelle was soon moving through the hubbub and telling us it was almost time for prayer. We all stood. My family and I hugged and we said good-bye to each other and then I was watching them walk out the door of shining windows and down the long sidewalk to our car. I felt my throat tighten.

After the last family left, thirteen new postulants turned to follow Sister Estelle in a quiet huddle to the novitiate chapel. We found the page for Saturday evening prayer in the book of psalms. Then, as did new young Sisters more than a hundred years ago on this very land, we began to pray.

"Our help is from the Lord," our leader chanted softly.

"Who made heaven and earth," we answered.

Fifty-five years later, I wonder about my motivations back then. A romanticism about Catholic Sisters, their graceful robes and veils, their mysterious and holy life behind convent walls? Genuine inspiration based on their dedication to God? Admiration for teachers, most of whom were skilled and caring, who encouraged my gifts? Anticipation of someday living and serving people in distant and beautiful places?

Perhaps all of us who became postulants that cold February day in the early 1960s carried a mix of these motivations through those doors. Perhaps none of us did. I would eventually discover to my surprise that some were escaping unfortunate childhoods, some were seeking to become educators, some simply wanted to pray a lot. We would soon discover that becoming a Sister entailed household chores: cleaning, food preparation, dishes, laundry. These were tasks our mothers and grandmothers did, for the sake of their children and husbands. We, of course, were doing them for God and for the other Sisters.

My mom had dreamed of becoming a nurse when she grew up. Instead, she had to take a job as a stenographer immediately upon high school graduation. Her father had lost his job after his leg was amputated. My dad suppressed his dreams of moving to northern Ohio to follow a job offer and a career in financing. Instead, he and Mom stayed in Cincinnati and accepted his mother into their home. He worked in his brother's dry-cleaning shop, laboring over vats of chemical solvents. Mom said he started swearing and smoking after he took that job.

No wonder they insisted to my sisters and me that we could become whatever we wanted. Little girls' dreams were important, I'd learned early on, and all you had to do to fulfill them was study hard in school. Except for priesthood. I believed in the holiness of the Catholic Church and wanted to be part of that as much as possible. Above all, I thought I mostly wanted to serve God.

On August twelfth of the year we'd entered, we postulants were formally accepted into the Sisters of St. Francis. We were given the official dress of the Sisters and Sister names. I was pleased to receive the name Marya, Hungarian for Mary, which echoed my mother's name, Mary Jane. For my feast day I chose the Visitation, which commemorates when Mary hurried off into the hill country of Judea to visit and assist her elderly pregnant cousin, Elizabeth. It spoke to me of Mary's spirit of adventure and service.

We immediately began a year of intense prayer and study as novices. I embraced all the prayer. Its simplicity and beauty appealed to me. The psalms we chanted three times a day inspired me.

Our studies included the history of the congregation, sacred scripture, and what it meant to be followers of Jesus and St. Francis. We primarily studied the Holy Rule of the Sisters, learning the obligations of the vows we would be taking in two years, as well as the traditions and customs of the congregation, many of them dating back almost a hundred years.

The spiritual teachings and practices we learned that year emphasized a detachment from the things of the world and a focus on God alone. There wasn't a joy of soul in this for me. As a result, I felt a need to always be on guard, protecting some inner value and gift I couldn't name. Some other attraction was welling up in me. I couldn't articulate it but I felt at odds with the program, uneasy and critical. I projected my sadness and dissatisfaction outward to what I perceived as the glacial slowness of my community's renewal and modernization, which had been mandated by the teachings of the Second Vatican Council.

And then I made a discovery that turned out to be the first of a series of five revelations. They would gradually expand my faith and bring an inner peace I had never expected. The first was almost accidental, the second grew out of reading books I'd kept without the necessary permission, and the last three Sister Estelle taught in her daily classes. They became my most vivid memories of that year of study. They influenced my thinking, faith, prayer, and ultimately ministry. They all referred to nature.

During this year, several novices left the novitiate and returned home. One of my high school friends and also a novice, Sister Daria, questioned me after I had spouted off once again about the shortcomings of what I felt was the community's slow response to the directives of the Second Vatican Council, published in October 1965 as *The Decree on the Adaptation and Renewal of Religious Life*. "If you're so dissatisfied, why don't you leave?" Bewildered, I had no straightforward answer.

And then, it seemed, I received word from God.

Twice a week we climbed creaking wooden stairs to the choir loft that floated, unsupported, over the entrance to our convent chapel. I was assigned to the back row of altos, with other tall novices. We stood for an hour, perched on wooden benches. Sister Mary Gloria, whom we adored for her kindness and enthusiasm, presided from the pipe organ bench. She danced across the pedals as well as multiple layers of keyboard, directing us periodically with an up flung hand. The pipe facade soared above us. We were almost at eye level with Franciscan saints whose images gleamed in the stained-glass windows just under the long, domed chapel ceiling. In the company of Crescentia, Colette, Agnes of Assisi, Bernardine of Siena, Philip of Jesus, and Francis Solano we sang, breathed, sang. Really sang. Repeated difficult phrases over and over.

At the time, the songs, responses, and chants for official Church ceremonies like the Mass were in Latin. Thanks to years of studying Latin in high school, I generally caught the drift of what they meant, but the more exact, deeper meaning of what I was singing eluded me. I decided to carry the hefty hymnbook back to the novitiate. I knew there was a Latin/English dictionary in the novitiate study room.

Our days were scheduled from morning to night. I had little time for my task. Translating Caesar in high school Latin class had been like solving a riddle. I had enjoyed a sense of accomplishment whenever meaning leapt at long last from a lengthy, convoluted sentence. Ignoring the lights-out rule in the novitiate, I decide to slip into the study after night prayer, when the rest of the building fell dark and silent.

Although the pages were tissue paper thin, the songbook was at least two inches thick. Passed from novice to novice over many years, the light blue *Liber usualis* was well-worn. It fell open easily. I began working on the opening chant for the upcoming feast of Pentecost, which commemorated the inrushing of the Holy Spirit as wind and fire upon Jesus's gathered disciples and Mary.

Word by word I wrote the English below the Latin. "The whole world . . . the Spirit of the Lord . . ." Easy. I was abruptly stopped by the stubborn knot of the multisyllabic verb *replevit*. I conjugated it, pulling out the root. Aha, I found it in the dictionary. "Fills." I'd expected something like blesses or enlivens or creates. Fills! "The Spirit of the Lord fills the whole world." I put down my pencil and stared into quiet darkness, enthralled.

In one sense, there was nothing new about this. I'd recited by heart since elementary school that God is everywhere, filling and directing the world. This is standard Catholic teaching. Most significantly, God dwells within the heart of every person. On the other hand, I didn't remember ever learning that dogs, canaries, African violets, squirrels, and other wild animals were also filled with God. Or that God's Holy Spirit filled the air, seas, and soils.

But that night, under a dim lamp in that hushed building, new meaning leapt from fragile pages. God's Spirit fills humanity, and all that exists. No exceptions. The text is from the Bible, book of Wisdom, chapter 1, verse 7. Fills. I felt a rush of comfort, of validation, having discovered words from scripture that resonated with my innate love of nature. I didn't know then, but this scripture would enliven the motions of my soul, lifelong.

Shortly after our formal acceptance as Sisters into the community, we began college courses, studies of the Gospels and Epistles of the New Testament. The priest-teacher, Franciscan Father Vincent Kroger, was knowledgeable and always prepared: class after class of precise theological meanings.

I barely paid attention as I paged through the letters of Saint Paul looking for favorite hymns to the Cosmic Christ, passages I had discovered in high school and in the essays by Pierre Teilhard de Chardin, the French priest and scientist. I had no clear, theological idea of what they really meant, of how Jesus of Nazareth became the Cosmic Christ, or what "cosmic" meant, for that matter. It was those nature images that resonated.

"Christ is subjected to the One who has subjected everything to him, *so that God may be all in all*" (1 Corinthians 15:28; italics mine.). All creation, rocks, plants, and animals: filled with God through Christ, who permeates the oneness of the universe. I liked this. It echoed my earlier discovery in the book of Wisdom. And Ephesians 1:10, "God brings everything together under Christ, everything in the heavens and on earth." All creation, the whole evolving universe, brought together as one body, the Body of Christ.

In high school, along with Shakespearean sonnets I could still recite, I had memorized the cosmic hymn to Christ in Saint Paul's letter to the Colossians: "Christ is the image of the unseen God, the first-born of all creation, for *in him were created all things in heaven and on earth*: everything visible and everything invisible . . . *in Christ all things hold together*, . . . and through him God reconciles *everything to himself*, everything in heaven and everything on earth" (Colossians 1:15–20; italics mine.). Everything.

As we studied the Epistles in the novitiate, I continued to ponder the insights I'd gained from reading essays by Teilhard de Chardin. My friend Barbara Fritsch had gotten magazines that published excerpts of Teilhard's essays from her mother. June Fritsch assiduously read them at her kitchen table piled with her family's dishes. Barbara and I pored over the same magazines at a table in the hushed academy reading room.

A geologist, paleontologist, and trained theologian, Teilhard (1881–1955) was not an easy read. He created words to express his novel effort to integrate faith with science, especially evolution. I struggled to comprehend words like "cosmogenesis," and terms like "Christ as Omega Point" and "evolution as biospiritual." Still, I persisted. I had been inspired by Teilhard's devotion to the natural world and the universe as a vast, "living" organism to which human beings belong, and all of which is evolving toward fulfillment in Christ.

Now, in the novitiate, as Christmas approached, we had permission to write our parents, family members, and friends. We could even make suggestions for what gifts they could give us. I asked Mom and Dad for a recently published book of Teilhard's writings: *The Divine Milieu: An Essay on the Interior Life*.

After a four-month separation, we had a warm reunion on Christmas Day in a beautifully decorated parlor of the novitiate. My classmates' families were all there, too, and once again the place was noisy.

We exchanged gifts. I gave my family Christmas pencil drawings I had copied from old cards, with quotes from the Christmas gospels. They gave me the usual hand lotion, cards, stationery, and stamps. And the book. I was excited to unwrap that book. And because I feared Sister Estelle might withhold permission for me to keep it, I secretly took it up to the dorm and hid it under my mattress. I eagerly read it at night by flashlight, perched on a stool in a shower stall.

Teilhard was not on the list of authors that novices were encouraged to read. Catholic authorities in Rome had thwarted his prestigious academic appointments and forbidden the publication of his works until after his death. He died in New York City in 1955. His essays were collected by devoted friends and colleagues and first published as books in French in 1957, and later in English.

He would become one of the most influential Catholic thinkers of the twentieth century. His writings were eventually received by theologians and made their way into the deliberations of the Second Vatican Council. On the book jacket under his handsome photo, he was acclaimed as "a great man of science and a great soul," "one of the most spiritually and secularly erudite of our time" who "takes his place amongst the foremost of the world's great thinkers."

Teilhard's writings about science and God gave me an antidote to the otherworldly spirituality that characterized faith life of the times and the daily prayer and spiritual practices of the convent. For him the inner reality of all matter was radiant with Christ. He labored faithfully to show how scientific evidence of an evolving universe was consistent with Catholic thinking and theology.

Perched on that stool, I labored over his words, struggling to grasp his obscure insights. I wrote notes in the back pages of the book. Teilhard taught me that light from the beginning of creation streamed forth as increasingly complex relationships, from molecules to galaxies, planets to life. For Christians, this is manifest as Christ. I began to realize that the God I loved shines forth as Christ in creation. My young life as a Sister, as a novice, was in Saint Paul's lovely words in Colossians 3:3, "hidden with Christ in God." It gradually dawned on me that to be enthralled by the night sky, to follow evolution's trajectory, to revere and even love Earth and nature that surrounded me, was indeed to meet, follow, and revere Christ. This became my personal, overriding belief.

It followed then that to care for or harm creation was to care for or harm Christ. To participate in the majesty and struggle of creation was to participate in the cosmic evolution of Christ. I enthusiastically accepted what Teilhard wrote about all this: "Nothing is profane to those who know how to see."

I came to understand that the "kingdom of this world" we'd left and were encouraged to "despise" in novitiate classes could not possibly refer to God's creation. Of course, I could accept despising the *sins* of the world, like killing, stealing, and committing adultery, like widespread poverty and nuclear war, but not the world in its entirety. It, after all, is Christ. And through Christ, God fills and reconciles everything.

At the time I had not read or even heard of Rachel Carson's *Silent Spring*, published a year before I entered the convent. I was ignorant of the disastrous effects of widespread use of chemicals in agriculture, although Dad insisted on having an organic garden in the backyard. He convinced Mom and his family that his vegetables, melons, and berries were healthier for us than those from the store. They definitely were larger and more flavorful. Organic also meant that my sisters and I spent time picking caterpillars and other insects off plants one by one.

On occasion during study times, I sent myself out on forbidden walks into the neighboring countryside. I squeezed through the rusted convent cemetery gate behind the gravestone of our revered founder and, hidden by trees and bushes, hurried along the edge of the Oldenburg town cemetery to a life-size stone and cement crucifixion scene: Jesus dying on the cross, Mary his mother and Saint John standing at his feet, and Saint Mary Magdalene kneeling. I climbed onto the platform, pulled my long skirts around my feet, and leaned against Mary. Here, refreshing breezes of summer, brilliant hillsides of hardwood forests in autumn, fall of snow in winter, and the tender comfort of spring embraced and soothed me. The land dropped into Harvey's Branch Creek below the cemetery. I relaxed into the solace of affection for land and solitude. Here, I saw and felt the intimacy of God's Holy Spirit filling the world.

One evening in chapel as I waited for the prayers to begin, I wrote in my prayer journal, "Lives dedicated to the love of God must now find ways to embrace God's world. Faith demands that we plunge into the world's suffering and uncertainties. Faith is not intended to box us in but rightly understood, expands our minds and hearts to God and to the needs of today's world." I was inching my way into finding a place for love of nature in my life as a Sister of St. Francis.

Once a week we dove eight hundred years deep into our congregation's founding vision by studying the lives of Saint Francis of Assisi and his most faithful disciple, Saint Clare of Assisi. Through story after story I discovered how bold and innovative they were. Francis insisted on the absolute nonviolence and peacemaking of the gospel message, even when he was personally attacked. He and his companions carried no weapons, refused to participate in feudal wars and the Crusades, and were to own nothing that had to be defended. "Preach the Gospel," he said, "using words only when you have to." Owning nothing, being poor like Jesus and rich in God, was his overriding passion, his source of freedom and joy. It opened his heart to all people, and, as I discovered one day, to all creation.

This particular class, Sister Estelle gave us copies of a prayer or song Francis had composed toward the end of his life: the Canticle of Creation. I was somewhat familiar with it and joined the others in praying it aloud. It soon became almost routine. We prayed aloud so many prayers. This was yet another one.

"Be praised, my Lord, through our Brother Sun, and Sister Moon and Stars." Followed by praises of God through Brother Wind and Sister Air and every kind of weather, and our sister Mother Earth, who sustains and governs us. And then, suddenly, I *knew.* This was not metaphor for Francis. It was real brotherhood and sisterhood with all that is, the entire cosmos, elements, Earth, plants, animals. I repeated my insight to myself. Not metaphor. He really meant this, felt it, knew it himself, this relationship of brotherhood and sisterhood that defines all that is. And more, this brotherhood and sisterhood praises God.

I felt it now, too, sitting there in Sister Estelle's class. I felt the meaning of Francis's song. It enlivened my heart. Francis was celebrating a profound brotherhood and sisterhood, not just with other people, but also with the rest of all creation. I sensed this could make a huge difference in just about everything. I sensed this was very important, if not for everyone else, certainly for me.

I had no idea of how this new awareness would expand and grow as I learned later the relationships Crow and Northern Cheyenne had with Earth and all beings. And after that, when I studied cosmology and evolution, especially the evolution of life. It swirled around inside me with the insights I was gaining from reading Teilhard, although I wasn't making clear connections then. I couldn't imagine the implications of this awareness for prayer, or how I would live my life, or how I would view ethics or politics or economics. Over time, this sisterhood and brotherhood of all creation, celebrated as praise by Francis of Assisi, would become the core value of my life as a Sister of St. Francis, as *his* sister.

Francis's Canticle struck at the heart of our utilitarian relationship with God's creation, with planet Earth. To be family with all creatures, even air and water, themselves praising God with us, demanded relationships of respect, care, and restoration, not destruction. That year, 1963, unknown to me, the Clean Air Act was passed by Congress. We didn't celebrate that in our Franciscan community. Would I have seen a connection with Francis's prayer?

In addition, extinction of species within this web of relationships became inherently wrong. No wonder I'd felt so keenly the loss of the passenger pigeon as I stood before the exhibit in the Cincinnati Zoo that honored the memory of Martha. Even as a child, did I have some sense of relationship, and that it was wrong for people to hunt and kill birds to extinction?

Connecting Francis's mystical insight with environmental activism and political awareness was all well into the future. That afternoon in the novitiate classroom, I simply knew something dramatically new, about *everything*. It was a very quiet moment, but it obliterated everything else Sister Estelle taught that day, including why she had us pray the Canticle.

Somewhere in the course of that year of prayer and study, Sister Estelle began a class by saying we were all called to become saints. That seemed beyond me and I didn't want to get caught in the impossibility of trying to become a saint. She went on to remind us that we all have had "holy cards" with pictures of saints on them. Often these little cards depicted the saint holding whatever was their focus in ministry or holiness, like the rosary or a model of a church, or a child or the Bible. Then she said something that shocked me and that I have treasured throughout my entire convent life: "You are to aim to be pictured as saints holding the globe, because you as Franciscans are meant to love the whole world."

Throughout the novitiate year I had struggled with wariness toward convent life and its rules. I never confided this to Sister Estelle. She may have been able to help me clarify what was truly stirring in my heart. I sensed that something other than dedicating my life to God was summoning me, some other life purpose. Whatever that mysterious call was, I was confident Montana was the essential first step.

In the 1960s there was a fairly wide gap between a young Sister's personal aspirations and the congregation's policies and procedures for the annual assignments. Reverend Mother and her four-Sister General Council assigned Sisters to the schools the community staffed. They sought to match each Sister's gifts and skills with the needs of the schools. Because faculty members lived together in a small local community, they also carefully considered the compatibility of the Sisters assigned to these local houses. It was a daunting task, viewed more with apprehension by young Sisters awaiting their first assignment. Despite Sister Estelle's insistence that God's Holy Spirit guided Reverend Mother and her Council, I doubted the Holy Spirit's ability to tell them to send me to Montana.

August 13, 1964, I was among twenty second-year novices who were kneeling before the altar in our little chapel. We had completed the year of spiritual practice and study of our way of life as Sisters of St. Francis. Sister Estelle led us in prayer, asking for the grace to willingly accept God's will for us for the coming school year. She then read one by one, slowly, our names and where we were being assigned. My assignment: a rural school in St. Wendel, Indiana, a village northwest of Evansville. I burst into tears. I had never heard of the place.

I lived and taught there three years, tutored by an excellent principal, Sister Julitta, and three other seasoned teachers. I enjoyed being part of this little community of Sisters, especially the friendship of Sister Joan Miller. Surrounded by farms, I learned the seasons of plowing and planting, weather worrying, and harvesting. We prayed daily for farmers and favorable weather.

When Reverend Mother Marie visited, I asked to be assigned to Montana. She replied that while she appreciated my desire, the distance would be too difficult for my parents. I was then assigned to Kansas City, Missouri, to teach in a school there. Our students were African American. Surrounded by asphalt and high-rise urban housing projects, I learned the daily challenges of families beset by racial prejudice, severe economic inequality, and substandard housing. I was tutored by another highly skilled principal, Sister Myra, and five seasoned teachers. I especially enjoyed the friendship and stalwart wisdom of Sister Angela Williams.

But I was blind to the significance of the work that Dr. Martin Luther King was doing at the time. We Sisters watched the nightly news together with its mix of reports on the Vietnam War and on marches in US cities for racial equality and freedom. I didn't attempt to learn about or support local civil rights efforts. Photos of nuns and priests marching in protest of racial injustice bewildered me. I didn't grasp the importance of King's Dream for ourselves, our students, their families, and the country.

Although I was genuinely inspired by the Vatican II mandate to read and respond to the signs of the times, *how* to do that in these spe-cific circumstances eluded me. I didn't know how to examine my own prejudices and assumptions about American social structures. I was blind to white privilege and how it shielded me from the suffering of many people. I stayed entrenched in the usual response to poverty: set up charitable programs and bring about change through education. I didn't venture beyond the safety of the convent and school. I didn't read Dr. King's speeches. I didn't realize his life was in danger.

And then the civil rights movement marched right onto our play-ground.

When Dr. King was assassinated on April 4, 1968, our Kansas City neighborhood erupted in protests, looting, and fires. The Na-tional Guard arrived and patrolled our playground at night, the single streetlight glinting off their helmets, weapons, and the hood of their jeep parked in front of the convent. Their bullhorn jolted us awake. One of the Sisters opened her window and shouted for them to leave. Sister Myra hastened to hush her.

Parents asked us to keep their children inside after school until they could come to pick them up. A police radio announcing the cur-few blared into our Good Friday church service. We attended the Eas-ter Vigil celebration at a safer parish in the suburbs. We left early to get home before curfew. Easter's promise of new life seemed irrelevant.

The diocesan Office of Catholic Education offered a Saturday workshop called "Identifying Racial Injustice and Prejudice." When we arrived we were handed a questionnaire. Did you ever feel you needed to dress up, fix your hair, and put on makeup to go to the gro-cery? Did you ever have to worry about being in a crowd of people who wouldn't respect you, or help you if you got hurt or sick? Were you ever afraid of the police? Did you ever feel judged by your appearance or how you talked?

These questions jolted me out of my privileged sleep. Through them I caught a glimpse of another America. An America I didn't experience. I didn't expect it would be a lifelong process of waking up.

We kept teaching. When the neighboring Christian Brothers High School was closed, we moved into its building. We soon filled it with almost three hundred students. Our athletes filled the hall-length trophy cases with awards.

I taught fifth grade and junior high science classes. From my third-floor classroom whose windows overlooked the parklike Paseo Boulevard I caught glimpses of a wider horizon, a bigger sky ablaze with sunset above the city. Pigeons wheeled with unexpected grace.

A new priest arrived who was a lifelong birder. He knew birdcalls. He identified the nasal *preet* of nighthawks fishing for insects in the humid evening air of late spring. We listened for the wing booms of males. Once we packed our small church with students from all the Catholic schools in the city for an October Mass in celebration of Saint Francis. Father Terrence Rhodes silenced the restless, noisy congregation with opening songs of robin, cardinal, wren, blue jay.

Every summer, Sister Angela and I left Kansas City for classes at Marian College in Indianapolis. Myra, seeing her extraordinary talent, encouraged Angie to study art and she made steady progress. I flipped from science to sociology to theology, amassing credits but far from what qualified for graduation. To my surprise, instead of teaching I was assigned to full-time study at Marian for the 1973–74 academic year.

The English Department head, Sister Rosemary, encouraged me

to pursue a major in literature. All those science classes provided a minor. After graduation in 1974, I remained on campus for the summer to take a required teacher training course in children's literature. Our instructor, Sister Phyllis Marie, was the principal of St. Charles Mission School in Pryor, Montana.

I didn't try to get to know her. I never asked about her school. I was unhappy and preoccupied, wrestling with my next assignment, a suburban school in Springfield, Illinois. I felt trapped, dull of soul. A visit to Springfield with the principal in early June confirmed my unease. The neighborhood was full of white picket fences and manicured lawns. It was a wrong obedience for me. But I didn't see any alternative.

And then one afternoon on campus Sister Phyllis Marie stopped me on the sidewalk in the sunshine, in front of the college auditorium and administration building. I offered to help her with her armload of children's books. She refused and said, "Marya, we need a teacher for our combined first, second, and third grades at our school in Pryor. I like your enthusiasm for teaching. I hope you will consider asking for a change in your assignment for this year. I hope you'll consider coming to Montana."

She was the very voice of God.

Yet events got complicated. A new Reverend Mother and Council had been elected that summer. They were deluged with tasks of congregational leadership in the tumultuous renewal of Vatican II. Would they even know that I existed and have the time to consider my request?

My friend Sister Norma was among those elected. I decided to start with her. I pleaded my cause for Montana. I emphasized that I needed to serve among people who were economically poor in order to fulfill my vows and live my life as a Sister. Sister Phyllis also made an appointment with one of the new Council members.

The change in my assignment would entail finding someone for the Springfield school and then finding someone to fill that person's assignment. And so on. At least five Sisters' lives got rearranged that July. But the voice of God prevailed. In August 1974 I was on my way to Montana.

Part II

FOREVER LAND, FOREVER SKY

APSÁALOOKE HOMELAND

Introduction

I arrived in Crow homelands generally unaware of the history of European and US contact—especially from the standpoint of the Crow. I had a vague sense of the founders' perspective and policies regarding the original inhabitants of the continent. I knew European nations had claimed and fought over, bought and sold huge swaths of land that did not belong to them. My history books taught that US acquisitions of Louisiana and of Hawaiian and Alaskan lands were all part of our nation's Manifest Destiny. This concept had the odd notion that having a flag and putting it on a patch of soil claimed the right to that land. It was then declared owned by the country that paid that person to be there.

I came to Crow homelands in 1974 calling it Montana. But I would slowly discover I had a lot to learn. And be forgiven for. At best, I could claim to have come with an open heart and a genuine desire to serve the people, and God.

Pryor, a Crow community in south-central Montana, would not

only open its heart to me, sharing stories, but also entrust me with the education of its children. Me, a white-skinned woman with decidedly German DNA.

As time passed, families even welcomed me into their homes for birthday celebrations and meals. I was invited to pray with women in the sweat lodge and join in other sacred ceremonies. I began to sense there was extraordinary depth of soul and kindness of heart in this hospitality and generosity. I felt shy and humbled as I met with parents for report cards, waited at the door of a family home, drove up a muddy lane to the sweat lodge. I was being welcomed.

"We've been standing up to the US government for hundreds of years," Beaver Two Moons of the Northern Cheyenne Nation said during a ceremony to pray for and protect me as I prepared in 1994 to protest the 1962 US blockade of Cuba. "Welcome." It was as if we shared a common ground. He gave me instructions on how to protect myself if we were confronted by police or US Justice Department officials. He asked a circle of respected women and men to pray for me.

"You can be like an ambassador for us. Maybe what people learn from you about our ways could help them," Charles Little Old Man of the Northern Cheyenne Nation said when I asked his permission to share my experiences with a group of friends in Indiana.

Diversity is one of the strengths of our nation. Understanding and living within diverse communities is demanding. I lived among Crow and Northern Cheyenne for almost twenty years, and gradually made my ignorant way as a teacher: careening, stumbling, dancing, talking, listening, and praying. Learning.

What I experienced and learned from them helped me so very much. And maybe it could even help others. Most important, maybe it could help Earth, help redefine the prevailing, destructive human-Earth relationship.

Everything I learned, however, was absorbed through the lens of my culture, religion, and worldview. I write my experience from my limited perspective. Gradually, what I learned broke through my mostly unquestioned assumptions about the validity of Catholic teachings and the prevailing American culture. In addition, I began to see that this strange system of Crow and Northern Cheyenne people living on reservations and America having all the rest of their homeland in a vastly different light.

Living there, I recalled how, as a child, I used to "see" Indian (as I called them then) children behind bushes and trees in my Cincinnati neighborhood. I thought they were children of the builders of the so-called Indian mound. This imposing earthen mound had been preserved as a park near our neighborhood. I sensed even then that other people had lived in the place I called home. Or, perhaps these children were Shawnee, the people who were here when the Europeans arrived and stole just about everything.

After I moved to Crow country, I gradually began to feel awkward about the history that got me there. What could I do to participate in healing more and perpetuating injustice less? Then I heard a strong Crow voice coming out of the past.

"Education is your most powerful weapon," Chief Plenty Coups (1848–1932) told his people. "With it, you are the white man's equal. Without it, you are his victim. Study, learn, and help one another."

I wanted to learn to obey this vision of Plenty Coups, the last Crow chief, to the best of my ability, with all my heart. That determination set my feet firmly on an uncharted spiritual journey, at once exhilarating and unsettling. I would slowly learn and embrace the life-changing implications of his teaching. It would eventually shift the trajectory of my faith commitment as a Sister of St. Francis into an unexpected direction. I would be educated by my students and by the people who welcomed me.

5

Baáhpuuo

Shooting Arrows at Rock

I lift up my eyes to the mountains.

PSALMS 121:1

Inside the Billings, Montana, airport terminal, Sister Phyllis and an older Sister I didn't know waved to me from behind the gate. "This is Sister Pauline," Phyllis said. "She teaches art and is an excellent cook."

They helped me collect my luggage. I had moved my whole life from Illinois in two suitcases and a steamer trunk packed with teaching supplies, winter clothes, and an old pair of ice skates, which had been shipped ahead. Phyllis told me the trunk was already in my classroom.

We stepped from the air-conditioned terminal into a blast of dry heat. I squinted into the glare, toward the snowy mountains I had seen from the plane, floating in the distance above Billings and the wide Yellowstone River valley. "Those are the Beartooths," said Phyllis. "Welcome to Montana."

Together we stashed the luggage into a dusty blue van already crowded with groceries and a battered red cooler. "It's an hour's drive to Pryor and in this heat we have to keep the meat and eggs on ice," Phyllis explained. In minutes we were out of Billings and crossing the river. The water was clear, not thick and murky like every waterway near my Cincinnati home.

"You may see a bald eagle in the trees," Phyllis said.

One paved road leads to Pryor. Beyond the river, it climbed out of the Blue Creek valley onto a high plateau planted in alfalfa and winter wheat. From this vantage point we counted five mountain ranges: the Beartooths, the Crazies, the Big Belts, the Bighorns, and the Pryors. In one hour I saw more mountains than in my whole life.

About a half hour out of Billings, high on the plateau, Phyllis announced that we had just crossed onto the Crow Reservation. When I'd agreed to come here, I'd only vaguely realized I'd be living on a reservation. I knew next to nothing about the reservation system and what it entailed for non-Crows to live there. I decided this was something I would ask the Sisters about.

Within a few minutes, we dropped down a long hill into the Pryor Creek valley. Lined by tall gray-trunked cottonwood trees flashing waxy green leaves, the road followed the creek south. Phyllis and Pauline named the families whose isolated homes we were passing: Round Face, Spotted Bear. We passed two prosperous-looking ranches operated by whites who leased the land from Crows, then the Baptist church down a dirt road off to the right, and, rounding a bend, we were suddenly among the few buildings that were the town of Pryor, Montana.

Phyllis drove through Pryor slowly, avoiding a knot of pedestrians and a child on a bike, all in the middle of the road. She pointed out the storefront post office and clapboard grocery whose sign, "Pryor Trading Post," was just this side of readable. Through unwashed windows I saw sparsely stocked shelves.

"Their prices are inflated. We never shop there," she said. Pauline recalled that in the fifties when the Sisters didn't drive, she'd go into Billings every week with the pastor, holding the small brown paper sack of change from the Sunday collection to buy food for the Sisters, the priest, and children's school lunches. "Sometimes we'd put raisins into the hamburger to stretch the meat," she said without further comment.

The Indian Health Service clinic was a white metal trailer behind a high chain-link fence, an attempt to deter break-ins for the drugs that were not supposed to be kept there overnight. Across from it sprawled a modern cement block building, the public school. In the yard, dust blew around swings and a slide.

Next, a square white frame building was the newly established Plenty Coups High School, named after the last chief of the Crows. We passed a few houses and a gas station with two signs: CLOSED and COLD POP. "Open on occasion," Phyllis said.

We left the straggle of buildings behind in the dust of a gravel road that faced the Pryor Mountains. Ahead of us, the valley poured wide open to those mountains ten miles away. What is it that thrills me to anticipate living so near mountains? Scriptures about God's dwelling, about mountains being a source of help and strength? Obvious beauty? They filled my eyes. "How small your eyes," wrote the Persian poet Rūmī, "yet they can hold a whole sky of stars." Or a mountain range.

The Pryors are old, pushed up by the pressure of colliding continental plates hundreds of thousands of years ago. They shaped the entire southwest horizon, constant, round, and strangely inviting. "See the wide breach?" Phyllis pointed to an opening in the long slopes, one side crowned by three prominent limestone buttes. "That's the Gap, home of the Little People. We'll take you there tomorrow. Those three buttes are called the Castle Rocks. People climb them to sit within stone circles in the summer sun and fast from food and water for several days, praying for themselves, their families, the tribe, and all peoples."

Years later I would learn that a cliff at the entrance to the Gap is revered as the home of the Little People. To this day, people leave gift offerings in crevices in the cliff: beaded necklaces, coins, medals. Another show of respect was to shoot arrows there. The region and town are called Baáhpuuo in Crow: Arrow Rock.

We were entering the valley. "What's that?" I twisted in my seat to get a better view of what looked like a massive buffalo. It turned out to be a metal silhouette.

"Oh, that's Plenty Coups State Park," said Phyllis. "The two-story log house in those cottonwood trees was Chief Plenty Coups's home. You can see the small round museum from here, too. He led his people peacefully into the twentieth century. He was invited to Washington, DC, for the state funeral of the Unknown Soldier and dedication of the tomb on November 11, 1921. He placed his eagle feather headdress and his coup stick, between them representing up to one hundred acts of bravery, at the tomb. He was there representing all Native Americans when he did that."

Later when I visited the museum, I learned he'd left those esteemed gifts at the tomb saying, "There might be an Indian's bones buried in there." When he saw Mount Vernon, he got the idea that his home and land in Pryor could be a good place for all Crow families to come and enjoy themselves. The state of Montana went along with the idea and established the park. Plenty Coups is buried there along with his wife, Strikes the Iron, and their two adopted daughters.

He was baptized Catholic and came to Mass at the mission. A Roman Catholic Crow chief. I would learn that he made every effort to model for his people the white man's ways, convinced that would help guarantee their survival. He farmed, sent his children to school, and started a store in a one-room log cabin.

As we continued past the park, Phyllis emphasized the importance he gave education.

Within minutes we were approaching St. Charles Mission Catholic School. I wished Phyllis would drive slower. Too much to absorb. I suddenly missed my mom, my friends, the Sisters at Oldenburg, anything familiar.

She didn't, of course. By the time we were rumbling across the metal bars of a cattle guard and into the school and parish property, my stomach was a knot of shyness, self-doubt, and fear. There was so much I didn't know about Crow culture and history, reservation life, the needs of the children I'd be teaching.

Grass kept green by a phalanx of sprinklers surrounded a yellow cement-block school building. The attached round church was sided with lovely red and tan stone that Phyllis said had been quarried from the mountains. We passed two small houses along a drive that curved behind the church-school building. The pastor, Father Chester Poppa, lived in the first. Two volunteer teacher aides, Dan and Paul, would soon move into the second. Phyllis said they were driving from their homes in Kentucky and Illinois.

Home, the Sisters' convent, turned out to be a prefabricated building that until five years before had been the school. It was the last of three houses along the drive. We stopped in front of it, a long gray building with green trim and a small enclosed porch.

Dolores, the other Sister of our little community, opened the door and welcomed me warmly, gently. We unloaded the groceries into the kitchen and found space for my suitcases in my tiny bedroom. Phyllis proudly said they'd just bought the bright yellow sheets for me, thinking I'd like them because I was young. There was no bedspread.

"You unpack while we help Pauline get supper ready."

I hefted the bigger suitcase onto the small desk below the window, opened it, and began putting things in drawers. In no time Dolores called me, and we sat down to Pauline's roast beef, mashed potatoes, gravy, and homemade apple pie. Framed by the dining room window, the Pryor Mountains were amber and deep blue in the sunset.

That first night I was wide awake in my room, one of four created from a classroom. Someone walked by my open door. Except for her footfall and the occasional hum of the refrigerator, I heard nothing: no traffic, no sirens, no voices. A cool breeze found its way through the open window. I would learn to expect this grateful coolness every night and by morning would be pulling a light blanket over the yellow sheet printed with flowers big as saucers. I pushed my eyes shut.

Next morning as I walked across the parking lot to church for the daily Mass a tall, barrel-chested man approached. "I'm Fred Gone, maintenance man and bus driver. I'm Gros Ventre from up north." I'd never heard of the Gros Ventre tribe. "It's French for 'big belly.' Trappers first met us when we were camped along a big bend in the Missouri River. I guess that bend looked like a big belly to them. So that's what they called the place and us."

I grimaced at that.

He related all this dispassionately, but later Phyllis explained to me how hard it is on people to be known by names given them by outsiders. She told me every tribe, including the Crow and Northern Cheyenne, has a name for themselves in their own language. Obvious, you'd think, but new information for me.

"My wife, Sylvia, who's Crow, is head cook for the school," Fred continued. "My two daughters, Lucy and Bertha, are here, too, today. They can help you unpack things in your classroom."

I shook his offered hand. The mystique of what I'd read of Squanto, Sitting Bull, Cochise, and Geronimo hung around in the sunlight. "What are you up to?" he asked, noting Phyllis was gassing up the van at the nearby pump. Suddenly I noticed we had our own gas pump.

I told him of our plans to drive through the Gap into the Pryor Mountains, where we would eat a picnic lunch. "The Sisters spoke of a campground up there somewhere. I hope we have good weather."

Quick nod, straight face. "There's no such thing as good weather, Sister. Or bad weather, either. Only weather. I hope you enjoy it. Looks like sun and hot to me."

I spent most of Mass distracted by how well I'd been schooled to judge the weather by my needs, by its intrusion into holiday plans or danger to travelers. "Only weather," he had said. What world does he live within? I asked myself. A world that can accept weather simply for what it is.

Responding to the Mass prayers, I wondered if I could stop using words that indicate a judgment of weather: no more *mean* storm or *wicked* frost or *nasty* Mother Nature who could ruin a holiday. Throughout seven years in Pryor, I would struggle to befriend the blizzard that isolated us indoors for days, relentless winter winds that froze pipes and cut off our water supply, and a spring storm whose floods tore out the bridges and access to Billings.

"You, sent out beyond recall, go to the limits of your longing," the poet Rainer Maria Rilke wrote. Some kind of longing brought me here. I lingered at the church door after Mass ended, waiting for the Sisters.

"Hurry," said Phyllis, "I'll take you on a tour of the school. Pauline's already begun packing our picnic." I noticed deep circles under her eyes. Was she tired? Or ill? I later learned she came home every afternoon from school for a nap and regularly spent an overnight in a Billings hospital for treatments. But today, she led me down the long hall to the last door. "This is your classroom. Soon it will be filled with first, second, and third graders." She turned abruptly, saying, "Time to go on that mountain picnic."

6

The Classroom

God saw all he had made,
and indeed it was very good.

GENESIS 1:31

ll but one of your five first graders speak Crow. In addition,
several of your fifteen second and third graders speak primarily Crow. For some, Crow is probably their first language,
the one spoken in their homes," Phyllis had told me. "That's why we
have this reading program called DISTAR. It's designed for students
who speak English as their second language."

Ignorant of the challenge this presented, I turned my attention to
preparing for the first week of school. With nine years of elementary
school teaching experience behind me, I thought I could figure this
out. I located teaching materials I'd brought and piled them on my
desk. One pile for each grade: first, second, third. The manuals for the
DISTAR reading program were indeed unusual. They weren't even
books but were handheld flip charts with one word printed boldly on

each shiny page. I pored over these strange teacher guides with their meager directions. Phyllis had said that previous teachers had refused to use the program, believing it was so unconventional it would hopelessly confuse students.

Although dramatically different from any other reading program I'd seen, I found that it did make sense to me. The alphabet was taught as sounds, rather than letter names. Because knowing the names of letters wouldn't help a non-English-speaker pronounce them. Long vowels had the line over the letters. Short vowels had no marking. Silent letters were omitted from words. Digraphs like "th" and "ch" were taught as sounds along with the alphabet. The two letters were joined together so they looked like one character.

Every reading class, while the second graders were tutored by the aide, Chester Turns Plenty, and third graders worked on a project I'd planned for them, my five first graders sat in a circle of chairs around me. They had quickly memorized the alphabet by sounds. Next, they learned a word on the flip chart I held by slowly saying aloud the sounds as I pointed to letters one by one. Then I'd prompt, "Say it fast." And when they did, the laboriously sounded-out word suddenly became a word they recognized. "Mom," they'd exclaim triumphantly. Then they'd copy the word in their notebooks and draw pictures of their moms.

Several months into the school year Fred Gone stopped me in the hallway. "Gerri, our granddaughter, read to us last night from a paper you sent home with her. She just started first grade and she's already reading." He was all pride and excitement.

"She really pays attention and works hard in class," I said. I was as thrilled by Gerri's progress as he was.

I was enthralled by the lilt in my students' English. Their words fluttered around me like little birds. When they wanted to tell me about something that had happened on the playground, they got their pronouns mixed up, interchanging "he" and "she," and rarely using "it." I had a hard time following their stories and would lose track of whether they were talking about a girl or a boy, even when they started the story with a girl's name. All this led to endless questions from me, bewildering them. But the little birds were patient and didn't seem to mind repeating.

I asked Chester Turns Plenty, a fluent Crow speaker, about these mix-ups. He explained that Crow had no "he, she, or it" pronouns. Sylvia Gone and Dorothy Spotted Bear, the cooks, further explained that the Crow didn't really need those pronouns. Somehow the listener "just knew" from the sentence. They said that they had just one word for third person singular. I concluded it was something like the English "you." When we use that word, we also "just know" from the sentence.

I've pondered this often since then, and the difference in worldview and consciousness it would make to have no "he, she, or it" words. Especially, no "it." We use "it" to refer to animals and plants. That usage puts these other life-forms beneath us because "it" infers something less than the other two pronouns. "It" is an object, a mere thing, that can be used and exploited for our purposes. Forest, river, soils, the air, wild animals, farm animals: the list has no end. All soulless "its." Imagine trying to refer to another person or God as "it," and you get a sense of how powerful this word is. Imagine what the use of "it" allows us to do to nature. Imagine having no "it" concept in language or thought.

The opposite of "it," I gradually figured out, was "Respect."

One day, during prayers in the little round St. Charles Mission Church, it dawned on me that we actually had this "no 'it' concept" embedded in our Franciscan tradition. Saint Francis of Assisi had even added "familial affection" to his awareness of no "it." He, in his prayer-poem Canticle of Creation, praised God for all other creatures, all humans, animals, and plants. He called all these beings our brothers and sisters. He included Earth, air, weathers, fire and water, the sun, moon, and stars, even death, in his cosmic vision of universal brotherhood and sisterhood. By contrast, in the "it" world, we keep forgetting that we are all relatives and that we depend on everybody else. We forget that in fact we are doomed without them.

As I thought about this absence of "it" in Crow language and worldview, in addition to the Franciscan perspective, I remembered the insight and joy I'd experienced from translating that Latin phrase from the Bible when I was a novice: "The Spirit of the Lord fills the whole world." Fills! Fills all that is. Book of Wisdom 1:7. It followed that no creature or element filled with the Holy Spirit could possibly be a soulless thing. In addition, every Sunday, Catholics sang a scripture-based hymn that declared Earth is full, like heaven, of God's glory. Crow language and culture showed me how a whole people could name and live what I believed as biblical, Franciscan, and Catholic teachings and traditions. These beliefs, obviously, had little to no influence in American culture, law, and economics.

There was more to learn. Some of it starkly challenged my accepted-as-normal cultural and economic systems.

Day after day in my classroom, I noted the unique ways the children used English words when they spoke to me. At first, I found it disarming and creative. However, I slowly discovered they were introducing me to another way to see the world. And that intrigued me.

"Teacher, what should I do?" Bobcat Turnsplenty, a first grader, asked. He was small, shy, and usually soft-spoken. In class, I watched him as he worked to absorb what I had said, then translate my words into Crow in his mind, figure out his response in Crow, and then translate that back to English before he said anything. He'd left his desk and interrupted the reading group I was teaching. His voice was almost shrill.

"Look," he said, holding his pencil in front of my face. "The wood part grew over the writing part. It's busted up."

Delia Spotted Bear, a third grader, came over to help. She led Bobcat back to the pencil sharpener. "Here's how it works," she said as she showed him what to do. "It will fix your pencil" was all he needed to hear as he started grinding away.

I watched, thinking about that. The wood part grew.

A few weeks later, his brother, Darrell, let out a howl of pain on the playground. I rushed toward him as he hobbled over to me, bleeding from a gash to his shin.

"That rock bit me," he said, trying mightily not to cry.

I stood by his side as he bravely let the nurse at the clinic stitch his wound. A rock bite is no small thing. Respect means "Be careful when in the company of rocks."

Later, at a gathering of newly arrived volunteers and teachers, the junior high science teacher from another reservation school told me about his first lesson. He began by saying that, drawing on several years of teaching experience, he'd found this to be an exercise that students enjoyed. He'd been confident that his Crow and Northern Cheyenne students would handily complete it.

"Fold your paper in half long-ways. Now, at the top of the left-hand side write this word: Living. At the top of the right-hand side write: Not Living. Okay, now let's go outside and fill in the columns. List everything you see that's living on the left and everything that's not living on the right."

Out they went and scattered across the schoolyard. Some walked toward the Tongue River, shallow and slow this time of year. Others climbed a low hill to look down on distant cattle ranches.

"Most of them had everything written on the 'Living' side," he told me. "Clouds, sky, cottonwood trees, rocks, circling buzzards, mud, the sun, fish, grasshoppers, even the Tongue River. I couldn't figure out how to explain to them how wrong they were. Every way I tried to explain nonliving made no sense to them."

So I told him about how pencil wood grows and rocks bite.

I added that I was beginning to realize that my language and worldview had, unknown to me, been like a brick wall around me, defining, blocking, and limiting my understanding of the world. And as I learned about Crow language and culture, it seemed as though bricks were being chiseled out of the wall. These openings revealed new vistas and deeper understandings about nature and the world. They felt true, beautiful, and holy, even.

This really changes things, we agreed.

Sometimes it got painful. For everyone.

The St. Charles School lunch program had the same rules I'd carefully enforced in the other government-funded, Catholic-influenced school where I'd taught: students should try everything served and then eat as much as they can. That way each child gets a balanced meal and little is wasted. That's important to Catholic Sisters, most of us having heard throughout childhood about the starving children around the world.

St. Charles School cooks had devised an ingenious system to curtail inevitable, irresolvable teacher-student confrontations over food. Students could tell the servers how much they wanted of each item: one bean, half a potato, two pieces of lettuce, four peas. My job was to make sure they ate what they had requested.

And then one fateful day Nathan, who was never difficult in class, refused to eat a small piece of fish. He continued to refuse to eat it as we sat through the entire recess period after lunch. He resolutely shook his head when I offered to have it reheated. The bell rang for classes to resume.

I was beginning to feel cruel and unreasonable. Which, in fact, I was. That's what happens when usually kind Sisters have rules to enforce. At least he wasn't crying.

Then Dorothy Spotted Bear, one of the head cooks, came over and sat down next to me. She had finished serving and putting food away. She put her lunch tray on the table.

"Sister," she said, "fish is medicine to Nathan's family. It's their medicine animal. They can't eat it. If they do, it will make them sick. We forgot about that when we gave him some and he was too shy to say something."

She apologized to Nathan, telling him we were sorry he didn't get to play. "Are you hungry?" Quick shake of his head. "Okay, now go ahead and shoot a few baskets before you go to class."

"Medicine?" I asked after Nathan left.

"Yes. Someone in his family long ago had a dream or something about a fish that let them know fish would always help and protect them. So out of respect they never eat fish," she finished as she picked up Nathan's tray.

I took the tray, wanting her to finish her lunch. Together we watched the little third grader bounce a ball skillfully, miss the basket, and then run down the gym to class.

"I don't think I can possibly be a good teacher for our kids," I said, almost in tears, to Pauline one day in the kitchen after school. "Many days after school, I feel like crying. I'm used to being competent, sure of myself. I liked teaching. I don't feel that way here. Something's all wrong with how I do things. I'm really sorry."

She'd put a meatloaf and potatoes in the oven and we were peeling and grating carrots, chopping celery and tomatoes, tearing lettuce leaves for the salad. Beets were boiling on the stove.

"You're in a different world, Marya, like being in a different country. It's hard to comprehend that because we're still in America, but in many ways, this is not the America we know. I made some serious mistakes when I first came, even though I had learned a lot about cultural differences from my years in China. I don't remember what started it all anymore, but one day I upset a child so much that he bit me in the cheek."

I gasped. Not mild-mannered Pauline who never raised her voice.

"Yes, I got quite a bruise." She shook her head with a wry smile, remembering. "Take it easy. You'll learn. It just takes a while, and the kids know you care about them."

Dolores walked in and sat down. It was her week to set the table. She'd overheard us from the living room where she'd been reading the newspaper.

"It took me awhile, too. The kids are smart and they want to learn. What you need to do is teach yourself to talk slower. Give them time to think in their own language. Let them help each other. Try to get into their world and way of thinking. We have some books about Plenty

Coups, Pretty Shield, and Crow history you might like to read. Relax. And remember to smile."

I had noticed that Dolores smiled a lot.

And then conflict with Catholic dogma and other teachings emerged. I learned the Crow creation story as part of my orientation to their culture. I noticed how benevolent it was, that humans were made from mud, collected from the bottom of a lake by a courageous, deep-diving duck. The newly formed people woke up on a raft and soon came to shore. The Creator of all Earth did not forbid anything to the people. They did not commit an original sin.

I was steeped in Catholic doctrine that the first humans had been forbidden the fruit of a certain tree and sinned, been driven out of paradise as punishment, and had to be redeemed. This first, original sin tainted every child born into the world. Or so I believed. In a creation story with no original sin, how could people need redemption or Jesus? How was I supposed to teach about Jesus? A creation story without original sin was almost unimaginable to me.

One year at Christmas, a Crow woman, Dora, was teaching the volunteer teachers and me some of the carols in Crow. We practiced every week for a month. The plan was that we would teach the children these Crow carols for the Christmas program and Midnight Mass. I enjoyed working my tongue around complicated but rhythmic Crow words. Dora seemed to enjoy coaching us and explaining the deeper meanings of the words we were learning. Practice sessions were playful and fun.

One of the songs we were learning was "Away in a Manger."

Dora told us that the Crow word used to describe the "Little Lord Jesus" meant "pitiful or helpless." She continued, "We have no word for Lord, you see. Jesus was just like us, when we're born. People," she

71

explained generously, "in our belief are not born into this world filled with sin or a weakness to do wrong things. Instead, we are just pitiful and helpless. We need a lot of care and teaching so that we grow up into good-hearted persons. The goodness is all there in us when we are born. We just need help. Our parents and relatives, clan aunts and uncles, animals, plants, gifts from dreams and the spirit world all help us."

Just pitiful. It made me smile.

I asked the other Sisters about this at supper. Yes, they'd heard the Crow creation story. Yes, they knew it did not have an original sin teaching.

"That's right," Dolores said. "That's why they needed the missionaries to teach them the Bible story."

What good did that do? I wondered. Instead I said, "It sort of complicates our emphasis on God sending Jesus as a redeemer to die for our sins. So, why would they be interested in Jesus?"

The conversation ended there. They couldn't dispute a core Catholic teaching and understanding about Jesus.

I puzzled over this for months. Eventually I remembered a class about Franciscan theology I'd had while in the novitiate. Sister Estelle had taught us that essential to Franciscan theology was something from Saint Bonaventure, a learned Franciscan, bishop, and doctor of the church. In 1588 Pope Sixtus V had declared him "the Seraphic Doctor" in recognition of the significance of his theological writings and his emphasis on the passionate love of God for humanity and all creation. It was one of the few details that lodged in my mind from those classes.

Although Bonaventure's theology is complex, Sister Estelle had a gift for teaching very simply and clearly. Until these classes, I had not heard of Saint Bonaventure's teachings. I was puzzled by what we were learning because it seemed to contradict the traditional Catholic teaching that I had embraced all my life. Yet it was beautiful and made sense to me. A pope, after all, had approved of Bonaventure's work.

Sister Estelle explained that Saint Bonaventure had taught that Jesus came to Earth as an outpouring of God's love. God did not need original sin in order to manifest his love for the world, he'd reasoned. Why would we even think that? Bonaventure's insight was more in keeping with God's unconditional love for humanity and all creation. Jesus was born not primarily because of human sin but because of God's love. Due to our human weakness, Jesus is mediator, our teacher and healer, revealing what it means to be fully human, to live in God's love.

Like a helper for pitiful and helpless human beings, I mused, something the Crows seemed to have known long before we'd arrived.

Language. I surprisingly encountered language in Crow country. I grew accustomed to sitting with students and school staff at lunch, just listening, listening to Crow. I absorbed rhythm and cadence. I was awash in the lilting beauty of new sounds.

I wanted to learn to speak it, if only a little, but the other Sisters advised against that, saying it would be very difficult and time-consuming. There were no books or tapes. There was no dictionary or grammar. They knew the Crow word for greeting people—Shodagi!—but only that.

I had studied Latin, Greek, and French, but primarily as grammar and vocabulary to be memorized, not to use to understand a speaker's worldview. One of the priests who was studying Crow and committed to learning to speak it himself told me at a meeting, "Language is the matrix of culture." Matrix, from the Latin for mother. We commonly call people's first language their "mother tongue." Language runs deep, as deep and old and vibrant as DNA, as a mother's gift of life.

7

The Sweat at Big Days'

Praise God, sun and moon, all shining stars,
mountains, wild animals and flying birds.

PSALMS 148: 3, 9, 10

Long before I met Heywood and Mary Lou Big Day, I knew of them through June and Arnold Hart, a VISTA volunteer couple from Missouri who had come to Pryor for a year to teach gardening. They were living in the tiny house that had once been Heywood and Mary Lou's home. We occasionally invited them to meals at our convent. They sometimes stayed with us when electricity and heat went out in their house in winter storms. We had a wood-burning fireplace.

They described Heywood and his family as being very traditional, living by Crow traditions and the wisdom of the old ways. They said Heywood worked hard to support his wife and four sons. They described his rigorous sweat lodge ceremony. They both participated in it as often as possible.

Throughout the year, I would notice a column of smoke rising from the Big Day yard several times a week. Heywood and his sons were "firing up" the sweat, heating stones for the ceremony in a robust bonfire. Seeing the smoke, men would congregate from all over the valley to pray with him and seek healing for whatever ailed them.

All this was enough to accentuate my insecurities over ever speaking to Heywood when I'd see him at the post office or encounter him and Mary Lou at local powwows, traditional Crow dances accompanied by drumming. Powwows were held within hearing distance of the convent in a cement-block hall across Pryor Creek from the school. I'd just smile when I met them, give a nod of respect, and look down. I couldn't think of anything worthy to say to them.

Not so the new pastor, Father Randolph Graczyk. He arrived in Pryor the second year I was there. For over a decade he had been living on the Crow Reservation in the town of Lodge Grass, Montana, almost 130 miles away. Having already met Heywood, he knew how to drive right over to the Big Day home, reintroduce himself, accept a cup of coffee, and then sit down to listen to whatever Heywood had to say. Soon he was observing the same sweat fire smoke through binoculars from his dining room window and driving the mile-long deeply rutted dirt lane to join the prayer and enjoy Mary Lou's meal afterward.

"Mary Lou told me you can come to sweat with her and the other women on Saturday," Randolph told me after Mass one Wednesday. "Why don't you call up Sister Claver and ask her to join you."

Claver lived at St. Xavier Mission School, ninety miles east over the hills. I'd heard her enthusiastically describe being in numerous "sweats." Father Randolph, too. From their stories about sweats I sensed these ceremonies created familiarity and bonds of trust among the participants. It seemed they also promoted healing—of body and soul, heart and mind. Claver and Randolph both spoke of the sweat as an important and revered way to pray, deeply woven into Crow spiritual traditions.

During the year I'd lived in Pryor, I felt enriched by everything I'd learned about Crow culture and traditions. I wanted to learn whatever people wanted to share with me. Because I believed it would make me a better teacher and because somehow it resonated deeply with my own heart and spiritual quest. Although I was somewhat intimidated by a spiritual ceremony unlike anything I had ever experienced, I wanted to share in this way of prayer myself. None of the other Sisters at Pryor had prayed in the sweat. And then there was Claver. I was confident she would like to join me and would be supportive and helpful. I called her that evening.

Claver arrived early Saturday morning with her wrist and forearm in a snow-white plaster cast.

"Of course I can still go in the sweat! I'll just wrap this thing in plastic bags. The sweat will help heal my bones. Marya, it's really a powerful way to pray. Your whole body is the prayer, not just your mind and voice. It's very holy." She pursed her lips, squinted her eyes almost shut, and nodded her head knowingly. She seemed thrilled by memories of praying in sweats.

"We all strip naked right outside the sweat lodge and crawl in. Don't worry; the men will be up in the house eating. And as for the women, no one really looks at anyone. Bodies are nature. Do you have everything you need? A towel, washcloth, hankie? My nose always runs in the sweat."

"Crawl in with a broken wrist?" I asked.

"The other ladies will help me. I'll scoot in on my butt and sit close to the door. You go in ahead of me and sit next to me. I will explain things as we go along."

Several other women had gathered by the time we arrived. We all introduced ourselves. Some were Mary Lou's relatives. I recognized a few from church. We hurriedly undressed and piled our clothes on old couches covered with blankets that gave a feel of homey hospitality to the sweat area. Then we walked quietly to the sweat lodge.

I felt a little shy and uncertain, but not terribly self-conscious. I knew Crow women were very modest. They had high standards for appropriate dress: knees covered at all times, no low-cut blouses. Old women in traditional garb of cotton blouses with long sleeves, long skirts, and an enveloping shawl secured with a huge safety pin were as covered up as nuns.

As I approached the lodge naked and passed the fire, feeling its heat on my skin, I was surprised to feel, well, modest. It was all God's nature: the fire and rocks, bare feet on the cold ground, my body. I stooped to crawl into the dark womb-like lodge.

Claver's seating plan put me almost to the back of the cozy lodge, where, unknown to me, it gets the hottest. The ample old woman who was leading the sweat sat immediately inside the door, to the left as we entered. Then Claver, beside her. They both took up a lot of space. The other women crawled in with us, filling the lodge. We were all sitting in a circle against the sides of the low, dome-shaped, tarp-covered lodge. Woven willow saplings secured with ties formed its structure, somewhat similar to an upside-down basket.

Clean quilts and sheets covered the ground. We sat on the towels we'd brought in with us. To the right of the door was a wide and deep pit, which soon would be filled with glowing, red-hot rocks. A sheet of metal had been propped against the lodge just behind the pit, protecting the tarps and deflecting heat.

Sparks shot skyward as a woman shoved burning logs off the rocks with a pitchfork. She selected a rock and hefted it from the fire to the pit and, using the pitchfork, bounced it on a stump to dislodge any coals, then dropped it with a thud into the pit. It was almost the size of a basketball. One by one, more rocks were added until the pit was almost filled. With each rock the lodge became hotter. Decidedly hotter, and we hadn't even started yet.

"Don't worry," said Claver, "even though there will be lots of steam when she pours water on the rocks, there is always air in here to breathe. If it starts to burn your nose, just hold your wet washcloth over your nose and breathe through it. The sweat lodge is hottest near the top, and along the sides. I'm going to hold my broken wrist up to the heat. It will help it heal."

Burn my nose?

She crooked her knee at an angle and balanced her elbow on it, raising her wrist toward the low roof of the lodge. The plastic bags crackled.

"Be careful, Sister," cautioned Mary Lou. "Marya, help her hold up her arm."

Indeed, the casted arm was heavy, the angle of balance awkward. In the muted light I could barely see what I was doing. The leader signaled the beginning of the ceremony by lifting a dripping dipper of water toward the evening sky, praying.

She splashed water on the rocks. It hissed, exploding into steam. The fire-and-rocks woman dropped heavy tarps over the doorway and we found ourselves in a hot cave of absolute dark.

The other women took turns telling stories about sick relatives, a son in prison again, a spouse who finally went to treatment for alcohol and drug addiction, a baby in the hospital, a daughter desperate for a job. One of the women cried softly. The baby was her first grandchild. Others comforted her, humming low groans. The leader sprinkled more water over the rocks. Mary Lou asked her to pray.

Steam seared my nose and ears. I fumbled around in the sheets, trying to find the washcloth. The prayers and weeping continued.

Then silence. The hardworking fire-and-rocks woman heaved the door open, throwing tarps over the top of the lodge. Cool air rushed in, and the sight of a sparkling night sky. Round one was over. Three more to go.

The women began talking with each other in muffled tones.

"How you doing, Marya?" Claver asked as she carefully lowered her casted wrist to a more comfortable position. "You know, don't you, that four is a sacred number to the Crow. Four is about the whole cycle of life: infancy, childhood, adulthood, and old age. And the four seasons. And the four directions, too, which include everything! Everything is in fours. So, with four rounds of sharing and prayer in the sweat, our ceremony encompasses all life, all space, all time."

"Oh, time," I said. "How long will this last?"

"I have no idea. It depends upon how long everyone prays. Usually, though, about an hour and a half."

I relaxed into the cooler air flowing into the lodge. The fire-rocks woman had tossed more logs on the fire, and it cast a soft glow into the lodge. I noticed I was no longer self-conscious about being naked. There had been no embarrassing banter about anyone's body. The women sat comfortably and talked gently, sometimes empathetically, sometimes playfully, with each other. Just being there with them, I felt accepted. Safe. Natural.

Throughout the second round Claver remained intent on holding her casted wrist into the hottest air near the top of the lodge. I helped her as best I could, but the steam and heat were turning my muscles to rubber. All I wanted to do was sink into this rocking of women's words and enveloping warmth. I heard water murmuring as the old woman ladled still more from the bucket. Steam flooded the lodge, cascaded down my back, and descended into every pore. The universe was suddenly all heat.

More prayers and then the door was again flung open to grateful coolness. A few more hot rocks were added, the door lowered, and again steam and prayers. I prayed silently for everyone I knew, my family and all our Sisters. Our way of prayer seemed very distant here. Claver was my anchor to the familiar.

By the fourth and final round, Claver declared her wrist healed. I collapsed into the sheets. This time the women were talking among themselves in Crow. I prayed to live.

Mary Lou asked, "Sister Marya, are you awake? You haven't said anything."

"Oh, dear." I laughed, embarrassed. And then we were all making chuckling noises and there was nothing sweeter in the world. Claver somehow maneuvered her arm to bestow a sweaty hug.

The door was once again flung open. I was drenched in sweat. I emerged into the cool night air under a sky drenched with stars.

"If you want to, Sister, you can jump into the creek," Mary Lou said. "Heywood and the boys cut steps into the mud. The water's cold but it feels good. Go all the way under, kinda quick. And then come back up."

The other women encouraged me to try the plunge. It scared me. But down the bank of muddy steps I slid and into the icy creek with a gasp. And another. My whole body gasped, tingled alive. I finally had enough breath to shout.

Back up the bank and someone indicated a seat for me on a couch. I wrapped a towel around myself as I saw the other women had done. The fire-rocks woman brought over a bucket of warm water for my feet. And then we all just sat and relaxed. Eventually Claver and I dressed and returned to the convent.

Several times a month Father Randolph told me that Heywood and Mary Lou were having another sweat. This information was an invitation. I went as often as school and other commitments allowed. Once I went with a miserable cold and sinus congestion. The leader rubbed my back in specific places as I knelt, my forehead to the ground, beside her. She prayed for me softly. The next morning I woke with no symptoms.

Mary Lou made a beach towel–sized, bright gold sweat towel for me. She hemmed it with wide tape of red, purple, and orange geometric designs. One of the other women gave me an oversized washcloth made of a light fabric. I kept these handy in a cloth bag, with soap, several more washcloths, and extra handkerchiefs.

I always got home from the sweat after dark, late. The other Sisters always left the convent door unlocked with the porch light on. Their simple thoughtfulness felt like a final blessing of the ceremony.

We Catholics have grown used to being helped with our prayers by gifts from Earth: water, fire, wheat, grapes, smoldering resins, oil pressed from olives, salt mined out of rock, beeswax. But I'd consistently believed God was more responsive to the human effort to pray, our words and songs and silences. I was shocked when it dawned on me——thanks to the sweat and those hours of prayer with fire-seared rocks and creek water——that these gifts from Earth were not mere accessories but actually were *essential* to my prayer. And the sweat flowing from my body became the most fervent outpouring of prayer I'd ever known.

The Big Day sweat lodge sat on the north bank of Pryor Creek. The creek began in snow on the Pryor Mountains, and as it flowed it irrigated hayfields, filled water troughs for cattle, and right here, provided a cold plunge for men and women after a sweat. Forty miles north, it poured Crow country water into the Yellowstone River, then the Missouri and Mississippi. I sometimes thought about our sweat prayers caught in the creek's current, flowing east and south across a continent and through big cities, blessing people, farms, hillsides, and valleys all the way to the Gulf of Mexico.

8

Crow Adoption

In whatever we do,
we enter with our own human brokenness
in communion with others,
and speak a word of hope.

VISION AND JOURNEY #16 , THE RULE AND

CONSTITUTION OF THE SISTERS OF

ST. FRANCIS

You don't need to be afraid of us, Sister," Gwennie said to me. "Just tell us how Fred and Dorcella are doing in school."

Gwennie and Larry Plain Bull were sitting across the table from me, drinking coffee and eating doughnuts after Sunday church. I was evading their question, talking vaguely about how hard their children tried, how well they listened, how much I enjoyed having them in class.

"Okay," I said. "They are blessed to be fluent in their own language, even though this could make learning to read in English more of a challenge than it is for kids who speak English as their first language.

At the same time, being able to understand and speak two languages is an added advantage because they have two ways of understanding the world, two ways to think about something, and many more words to use than those of us who only speak one language. You gave them an advantage when you gave them their language."

I was saying too much. They already knew all this. Gwennie was taking university classes to become certified as a teacher. Perhaps it was helpful to them to know that I knew this and appreciated their language. I got up to bring more coffee and replenished the doughnut plate. Sitting down again, I stumbled on.

"So, as their teacher, I have the responsibility to learn how to teach them, helping them become more confident in using English, as well as breaking it down into smaller parts they can easily learn to read. Last year Sister Wilhelmina and Sister Phyllis introduced a new way to teach reading, designed for children whose first language is not English. I'm excited about the program because I see it helping Fred and Dorcella make progress. It seems to be helping all our Crow speakers. And one more thing, they both understand that marks on a paper are actually words that mean something. That's a big thing! Even English-speaking students I've taught didn't always understand that."

We continue this conversation at every report card conference.

Two years later, when it became clear that Sister Phyllis was losing her battle with cancer, she reluctantly retired at the end of the school year to our health care center at the motherhouse in Oldenburg, Indiana. We grieved her untimely death that summer. The St. Charles Parish Council, which also served as the school board, asked me to consider accepting the position of principal. Our leadership council approved, and I agreed. In late summer, as the new principal, I was thrilled to hire Gwennie to be lead teacher for the intermediate grades. She was the first woman in Pryor to graduate with a teaching certificate.

Within a year, she was proposing many ideas for integrating Crow cultural ways into our school programs. One of them was organizing the powwow for the annual American Indian Day celebration, observed cooperatively by the public school and our school the last Friday of September. I confidently entrusted to her the countless, totally mysterious to me, details of a powwow. This year, unknown to me, she was planning something unexpected.

As usual on American Indian Day, the entire school was a swarm of people: visitors from the surrounding area as well as parents and children dressed traditionally for dancing. Today the hallways echoed with the jingle of dancers' bells and flashed with every color on the planet. Our students had transformed from jeans and T-shirt kids into Native American Pride in beautifully crafted dresses and shawls, leggings, shirts and vests, ornate beadwork jewelry and eagle feather headgear, bustles, and fans. Girls in buckskin dresses walked erect, carrying carefully folded shawls, swinging long fringes. Boys in leggings and vests leapt and strutted to their classroom doors, imitating prairie sage grouse, their porcupine quill headdresses bouncing.

I stood at my office door enjoying the diversity and activity. It looked like chaos to me, but I'd learned that underlying it was an order I couldn't see. When the drum was struck, more than two hundred students from two schools would dance into the gym in precise rhythm and formation, arranged according to their dance style and dress. Every year it happened. Every year I was amazed.

During the run-up to this event, called the Grand Entry, I dealt with a stream of phone calls, welcomed visitors, looked for more safety pins to help with ties or clasps that wouldn't stay exactly in place, and hoped the drum group would arrive on time. Into the hub-bub walked Gwennie. She handed me a bag she was carrying. "Larry and I want to adopt you as a daughter today. It's sort of quick for you to think about, but we wanted to surprise you. Here are your clothes. Let's see if the dress fits you."

"What! Oh, Gwennie." And every frame in the school froze silent for an instant.

Several years before, shortly after he arrived in Pryor, Father Randolph had told me about his adoption by a Crow elder, Gloria Cummins, into her family.

"These adoptions are real, of the heart," he'd told me. "Gloria treats me as a son, part of her family, and I call her Mom."

I'd learned that it wasn't unusual for Crow parents to adopt nieces or nephews, or even cousins' children. Sometimes it's a way that families help each other. Sometimes, someone who's had several children "gives" a newborn to a childless beloved sister to raise. Adoptions deepen the ties of kinship and widen the circle of care and support for struggling young families.

Non-Crows are rarely adopted, although it happens. By adopting a teacher or Health Service doctor, families express their love and gratitude for the service and care an outsider has provided. They want to strengthen the bonds between them. They want to express the familial connections they feel.

These adoptions are not legal in the sense of US law or Crow government. They don't make the person a member of the Crow Nation.

They do mean that the adopted person will always have a place at the family's table, at birthday and graduation parties, and at clan celebrations. The person also learns to show special respect for clan aunts and uncles and in turn prays regularly for children who show respect for her as their clan aunt.

I think I may have had an inkling of these special relationships from within my own family. Mrs. Patrick, our next-door neighbor in Cincinnati, befriended my parents, especially my mom, who was still grieving the loss of her mother two years previous to when she and my father got married. Mrs. Patrick became her support, confidant, and friend. Perhaps even a kind of surrogate mother for Mom. My sisters and I grew up loving our visits with her. She had a wonderful porch swing wide enough for three little girls. She was part of our birthday celebrations, and we called her Auntie Pat. She was part of our family.

The royal blue dress fit perfectly. So did the high-top moccasins, beaded with blue and purple flowers. Gwennie helped me tie them securely with buckskin thongs. Next she helped me secure the wide belt around my waist with buckskin ties. The belt was heavy, solidly beaded with beautiful multicolored geometric designs. Then she handed me a shawl to carry. She showed me how to fold and carry it properly. She stepped back to admire her efforts.

"Oh!" She suddenly remembered something and began rummaging through her big purse. She produced a simple two-strand necklace of red and white beads. Two genuine ivory elk teeth hung in the center. She tied it around my neck. "Your auntie made this. Only women in our clan, Greasy Mouth, can wear this particular style of necklace. Every woman has an elk-tooth necklace, but the colors and patterns vary for each clan."

"This is my shawl," she said. "You won't need it after the ceremony begins."

Ceremony! I'd never been to, much less *in*, an adoption ceremony. I usually tried, impossible as it was, to quietly blend in when I attended Crow "doings." Not this time. I had no idea what to expect.

"Time for you to go in the gym and sit with the teachers," Gwennie told me. I felt a bit self-conscious walking past the bleachers crowded with parents and families. The shawl fringes swayed with each step.

Soon I was sitting with my students on a folding chair at the far end of the gym. There were announcements in Crow. As a circle of drummers struck a huge bass drum, I caught English phrases: "Intertribal. Everybody dance!" Children and adults streamed from chairs and bleachers to the polished gym floor. They spontaneously formed a wheel as they circled the gym. As groups and individuals began to fancy dance, or shawl dance, or grass dance, or solemnly step the stately traditional dances, they all kept the same rhythm and moved in a harmonious flow. Like a galaxy, I thought.

One of our Crow teacher aides urged me to get up and dance. But I was glued to the chair, apprehensive about the approaching adoption ceremony and transfixed by the drumming and dancing. She gave me a knowing nod.

When the drum ended the dance with an emphatic bang, the announcer said something in Crow. Dancers cleared the floor. Then four young men dressed in long beaded loincloths, tights, eagle feather bustles trailing more feathers, porcupine quill headdresses, and carrying eagle feather fans began to circle the gym. Their feet drummed the floor; the many bells tied to their legs rang in rhythm. They leaned forward slightly, shielding their eyes with their fans as if looking for someone. They stopped in front of me, dancing briefly in place, and then moved on, circling the gym. They did this three times. The fourth time I caught a signal that I was to dance with them. I got up and stepped awkwardly to the drum rhythm, following them all around the gym. At long last they found Gwennie and Larry, who had been standing beside the announcer all this while. With them were Father Randolph and a very old man who lived up the valley.

Led by the four warriors, I approached them. I had surprisingly caught the rhythm of the dance and felt poised and happy. I took my place between Randolph and the announcer, facing my new parents.

Gwennie was telling the announcer what to say. He spoke in Crow. The noisy gym dropped into silence; not even a bell jingled. Randolph, who understood Crow, was listening carefully.

"You are being taken as a daughter by Gwennie and Larry because they appreciate all you've done for their children as a teacher and principal," Randolph translated for me.

But why adopt me? I believed all the teachers worked to help the students. Perhaps because I'd hired Gwennie and supported her. I instinctively appreciated her teaching style, which was more Crow and less within the strict procedures of Catholic school guidelines. Perhaps because I looked for opportunities to listen to her and learn from her, relishing quiet conversation in the tiny library with her when I had questions about how to be a principal in a school of Crow students. And perhaps because I invited her to represent our school at regional workshops. However, this wasn't what she told the old man to say. It was because of how I had been a teacher for their children, Fred and Dorcella. In a flash of insight, I realized that adoption was not about deserving or merit. It was about happiness in knowing each other. It was about family and love.

"Gwennie and Larry also want to give you a Crow name," Randolph continued. The announcer stepped to the side and the old man leaned forward on his cane to speak into the microphone.

"He is saying you have always shown respect for Crow traditions and people, and that is why he is giving you this name," Randolph said. He nodded slowly, listened some more. Nodding again, he seemed pleased.

"Woman with a Good Heart," he said to me. "It's a good name." Tears burned my eyes, and then Gwennie was smiling as she wrapped me in a bright multicolored blanket. Larry shook my hand.

I knew something about "good heart." In the three years I'd lived in Crow country I'd learned that when people said someone had a good heart, they meant it as a special compliment: the *person* was good. To say a person had a good heart was a wonderful thing to say. When parents came to me, concerned about their children's progress, they sometimes said, "The teacher doesn't understand our ways or know our language, but we see she has a good heart." I didn't want to excuse the teacher's cultural misstep. At the same time, I learned that having a good heart meant her efforts could still be appreciated. As the old man had said, a good heart meant the person respected people and the culture.

Right then, absorbing what Randolph had just said, I knew better than to try to earn this name I'd been given. I hoped I could be faithful to it. In time, I would discover its faithfulness to me, guiding and comforting me as I tried to follow my good heart into a new spirituality of care for Earth.

"Now you are a member of the Greasy Mouth Clan," Gwennie was saying to me at the meal. We were all sitting together, Gwennie and Larry and my new brothers and sisters: Bert, Lori, Marilyn, Fred, and Dorcella. All family.

Gwennie continued, "Our clan symbol is the sun. Hunters in our clan often had dreams of animals telling them where to look to find them. That way people in our clan always had meat, so that's why they call us Greasy Mouth." She nodded toward the elk-tooth necklace I was wearing. "Our clan necklace." She looked around the gym and pointed out my clan aunts and uncles, indicating people I could call upon for prayers.

People came by to shake my hand and call me by my beautiful Crow name. "Your grandma," Gwennie was saying. "Call her Kaalé. And, look out. That young man over there is in your teasing clan. He can tease you a lot and you can't tease back."

I wore my adoption outfit all afternoon, even as we swept the gym and I attempted to restore some order to my office. Back in my convent bedroom that night I slowly folded the blanket, moccasins, and belt into a drawer and hung the dress in my closet. I sat upright in my bed, staring into darkness for a long time.

I was wide awake to something new, some kind of love I had not imagined possible. It reached across cultural difference and the chasm between two unrelated languages. It stared down past and present injustice and suffering with gratitude for the simple gesture of teaching a son and daughter how to read. In my heart, it bonded respect for Crow people and culture with respect for my birth parents' teachings about beauty, animals and land, and care for people.

This love can never be deserved or won. It is not tentative. It stands beside you in a wide valley, in front of the whole community, and says, "She belongs here, now. She is our daughter. She has a Crow name, a place to sit when clans gather."

Just put on your Crow dress, I whispered to myself in the dark. Fasten the belt and tie your moccasins. Pull your blanket around your shoulders. Dance.

9

Opening the
Sacred Bundle

Lord, teach us to pray.

LUKE 11:1

At the age of eleven, after fasting from food and water for several days in the Crazy Mountains of present-day Montana, the future chief Plenty Coups was given a dream that began with a chickadee coming to him. Then he saw the disappearance of the great herds of bison. This horror was followed by the spread of a vast herd of strange spotted bison that overran the prairie, consuming the familiar bison upon which the people depended for food, clothing, and shelter.

When Plenty Coups returned to camp and his family, elders helped him understand his dream. Chickadees, because they can speak in many tongues, teach people to listen carefully. The strange spotted animal warned about an impending disaster that would overrun Crow life. This dream would eventually help the adult Plenty Coups (Aleek-chea-ahoosh, meaning "Many Achievements") guide the Crow through smallpox epidemics, starvation, and the unimaginable losses of forced reservation life. He recognized the spotted buffalo of his dream when he saw the white man's cattle.

Baptized Catholic in 1917 when he was sixty-nine, Aleek-chea-ahoosh went to Sunday Mass in the little log church of St. Charles Mission until he died in 1932. Out of respect for his Crow spiritual practices like fasting and the sweat lodge, he continued to care for a bundle of wrapped sacred objects. The bundle is now displayed in a case in the Chief Plenty Coups State Park Museum. Behind the bundle signage states that often the fur or feathers of an animal protector of the person are kept in a bundle, along with powerful herbs and other objects significant to the person's spiritual journey or dreams.

The items in Plenty Coups's bundle are unknown. It had not been unwrapped and opened since his death. No one knew how to do that properly.

"I'm going to a bundle-opening ceremony this Sunday over in Lodge Grass," Father Randolph Graczyk told me after the daily church service in early spring 1976. Because I knew he was inviting me, I told him that I'd really like to go with him, but I had to go to a school meeting in Great Falls over the weekend. I hoped there would be other invitations.

"People open their bundles to release and renew the bundles' spiritual powers," Randolph explained to me. "There will be incensing of the room with cedar, singing, tobacco offerings, and long prayers. During the ceremony, people will be healed, or helped to understand things, especially their sufferings, in a new way. The leaders will pray for the whole world. After several hours of songs and prayers, the bundle will be carefully rewrapped. This particular bundle is opened twice a year: when the leaves turn yellow and after the first thunder."

In autumn, rainstorms usually fall silent, just the whispering rain. And only once did I ever hear thunder in winter. "Was that thunder?" we all said to each other in disbelief, looking out into blowing snow. Then it struck again.

Aside from this one time, winter storms were always silent. A foot of snow can fall and we hear only wind. But when mountain streams break free of ice and swell with snowmelt, when thousands of lupines open their purple flowers to the songs of returned meadowlarks, when clouds roll down the valley heavy and gray, rain pours, lightning cracks, and thunder roars. It scares children, makes dogs howl, and throws us into the language of storm.

Don't we all have "first thunders" in our lives, experiences that shake storms through our souls? We ponder them, noticing how they rattle familiar patterns of thinking, and ignite fear, or hope. Eventually we wrap these memories into bundles kept in our minds and hearts. Sometimes we write about them in journals or letters to trusted friends. They subtly shape our lives. On occasion we reread the journal entry or open the bundle of memories. We prayerfully reflect upon and care for their contents in our minds and hearts. They motivate us, nudging personal dreams and even energizing our futures. We want to pass them on to our children.

Listening to Father Randolph, I recalled the thunders that shook my German American traditional Catholic upbringing. They prepared me for Crow celebrations and ceremonies, which, "though differing in many particulars from what the Church puts forth, nevertheless reflect a ray of the Truth which enlightens all men" (Catholic Bishops,

Second Vatican Council, October 1965, Declaration on the Relationship of the Church to Non-Christian Religions, Section 2).

The neighborhood Indian mound, a squirrel's race across my shoulders, and a hillside of wildflowers shook little cracks into the learned religious certitude that encrusted my spirit. Unknown to me the spiritual journey to respect Crow traditions and a growing sensitivity to Earth as also sacred, not just heaven, began early in my life. Even as I attended Catholic school, went to daily Mass, and dutifully memorized the catechism of Catholic theological and moral teachings, I had recognized and cared for the other sacred, other rays of Truth.

"It thundered last week," finished Randolph. Even I had noticed. It signaled the arrival of spring, and after a long winter that thunder excited my spirit.

Monday. The priest will have come back with a story. I walked over to his usual table in the make-do eating area in a corner of the gym and put my tray down with its school lunch spaghetti with tomato sauce, Sylvia's homemade rolls, canned green beans, and yellow Jell-O.

"How'd it go last evening?" I asked. Children and balls were bouncing around the tables.

He leaned back, looked around, and slowly stroked his short-cropped beard.

"The family has had this bundle since the free-roaming days of following the buffalo. It's one of the few that had been successfully hidden from destruction by soldiers, government agents, and missionaries. Luckily there has always been someone in the next generation who wanted to learn how to take care of it and open it properly." He paused. Looked around. Seemed to be thinking.

"The leader burned cedar and unwrapped the contents of the

bundle. So many people came I thought we might be up until sunrise with the prayers, but a few stars were still out when I left Lodge Grass for my two-hour drive home."

That was it. He had nothing else to say, yet his appreciation was tangible.

Once again, I felt as if I'd been privy to glimpsing a sacred moment in the Crow community. In Randolph's simple retelling, a ray of Truth touched my spirit: Truth about an ancient form of prayer, about a family's courage to stand in that Truth and pass on a sacred practice despite danger and persecution. Or maybe it wasn't so much about courage as about respect for the traditional ways of prayer, and gratitude for their healing powers.

"Thank you," I said.

He nodded as if knowing my thoughts.

10

Time for Change

I am quite confident that the One who began
a good work in you will go on completing it.

PHILIPPIANS 1:6

s I absorbed the spiritual traditions and teaching of Crow friends, colleagues, and family, I noticed how they energized and enriched my own spiritual journey. Though I often felt shy and insecure when I approached ceremonies, dances, or family celebrations, I also noticed that once inside, I soon felt peaceful. I had learned from Father Randolph how to sit down and simply be present.

For almost five years I'd observed Father Randolph at Crow spiritual ceremonies, at family celebrations and local powwows and sports events. I saw how he quietly walked into a gathering and greeted people, found a place to sit, and then was present, alert, and engaged, without saying much. He listened and did not ask intrusive questions. I had to learn there even was such a thing as "intrusive questions." I had to learn the difference between learning while simply being with people, letting what they shared influence my thinking and world-view, the chasm of difference between that and actively pursuing and acquiescing information as if it was a commodity I could own and use.

Since my first day in Pryor when the Gros Ventre Fred Gone taught me about weather and throughout the seven years I lived among the Crow, their traditions, wisdom, and courage inspired me, enlivened my faith and personal spiritual practice. I noticed that what I was learning harmonized with my Franciscan tradition. I noticed how the Pryor valley and mountains nurtured my soul in every season. When I realized that I was becoming restless, that I no longer felt called to be a teacher and principal, I felt deeply conflicted.

School year seven began. I was beginning to acknowledge to myself that I no longer wanted to be working as a grade school teacher and principal even in Crow country. I believed I'd done everything I knew how to do. Our little school had become one of the first reservation Catholic schools in our local system to score at or close to the national norm on achievement tests. Parents and guardians were actively engaged in the life of their school. Enrollment was just about at capacity. All this was good enough for me.

In addition, I was painfully aware that I had come to the end of my creativity and stamina as principal of St. Charles Mission School. When some of the junior high girls refused to attend the all-school church services, I couldn't work out a satisfactory solution with them or their teacher. I was impatient with parents whose unsupervised children trashed the bathrooms while their dads played basketball all evening in the school gym. I made hasty unilateral decisions that were unintentionally disrespectful and closed off possibilities of mutually working out solutions.

Above all, I needed other ways to think about God and find meaning in the tragedies that tore through families month after month: an adolescent shot dead by police as he left his graduation party, a son driving a car into a tree at ninety miles an hour, the mysterious inability of promising students to finish college, or high school. I sat with the mothers of the dead young men. I couldn't make peace with how gifted students lost their way in alcohol or drugs. Was there something more we could have done to meet their needs while they were in our school? I asked myself, Am I in over my head? Or is this burnout?

In addition, I was feeling increasing anguish over what I perceived as accelerating destruction of species and Earth, relentless proliferation of nuclear weapons, and increased global poverty. Unexpectedly, in late winter of that year, a letter arrived from Sister Claire Whalen, director of the Office of Ongoing Education for our Franciscan congregation. She was inviting me to consider a master's degree. She had something to suggest that she thought I'd appreciate and enjoy.

At first my heart leapt. But not far or high. I wrote back telling her I didn't feel right about spending the community's money so uselessly when we lived under a shadow of nuclear war and so many people were suffering.

But Claire had other ideas about the future of the world, as well as my future. She wrote back describing a nine-month program in Chicago at Mundelein College, offered through its Religious Education Department. The program had been developed and was directed by Father Matthew Fox. Upon completion of their studies, participants received a degree in Creation Spirituality. Whatever that was, I felt drawn to find out. I studied the brochure she sent me. How could

I possibly turn down a course of study that explored spirituality in nature and built upon biblical teachings that Earth was fundamentally good, revelatory of God?

Intrigued, I studied the detailed program description. Core curriculum: Creation Spirituality, Creation as originally and inherently good, Creation Spirituality as a valid but largely ignored or suppressed tradition in Catholicism. The core curriculum also included studies in scripture, Catholic mystics and theologians, and cosmology. Cosmology?! The artist in residence for the upcoming year would be mathematical physicist Dr. Brian Swimme. I wondered what a scientist was doing as "artist" in a spirituality program. I felt the beginnings of some excitement about this program.

Seated at the little writing desk in my room, I read on late into the night.

I read that every other week the program hosted a prominent lecturer. Each semester, students participated in an art course like dance, watercolor, or pottery. They also were required to volunteer regularly in a local social justice project of their choice. All of this was integrated during weekly meals prepared by students and discussion led by a Jungian psychologist.

I called Claire. She told me that it was time for me to pursue advanced studies, something expected of our Sisters. She said this program was new and that she saw a good fit between it and my gifts and interests. She was leaving the decision up to me.

I read the materials over and over. I talked with the other Sisters and friends about the program. I wasn't sure I wanted to live in Chicago. But I couldn't stop thinking about the program. I liked the fact that I could take classes that would prepare me for pastoral work in parishes. Perhaps even back here in Crow country.

It was late winter, with snow flying, when Claire invited me. Two months later, snow melting and hills greening, I reached for Claire's hand and jumped.

I prepared to tear myself away from Crow country and move to Chicago. I sensed that if there were connections between the traditions, wisdom, and spiritual practices I found so appealing in Crow life and the Catholic, Franciscan tradition of the brotherhood and sisterhood of all beings, much of which I cherished, I would find them in this program. Despite my anguish over a church that forbade the full participation of women, being Catholic and Franciscan was deeply woven into my soul and worldview. Perhaps in this program I might even gain some new insights into my questions about the meaning or necessity of Jesus's life and death.

In April I began going through files and cleaning out my office. As I did this tedious work, I noticed I was feeling glimmers of hopeful anticipation. The office was the easy part.

Mary Frances Flat Lip, a dear friend as well as our indispensable Crow-speaking school secretary, and I planned one last trip together in the old blue van. We decided to picnic on the other side of the Pryor Mountains where mustangs ran. The road into the Wild Horse Range was deeply rutted, rock strewn, and dusty. We bounced slowly across Vermillion Flats and eased down into yellow rock canyons that opened onto wide, rugged landscapes. Sagebrush grew tall there, interspersed with mountain mahogany and rabbitbrush. All the while we scanned the open ground for horses.

We ate lunch in the van. She spent the whole day with me, sharing friendship and a mutual love of the land. She was helping me say good-bye to the mountains and wild horses.

That day we saw no horses. But then we saw the wolf. Or rather, as Mary Frances said, "Look, Sister, there is a wolf showing himself to us." Because the wolf knew of our presence long before we came into view. And stood there in sage to the left of the road, back straight, head up, ears and eyes alert, showing himself. Hitting the brake, I glimpsed his majesty. But by the time the van rumbled to a stop, the wolf had vanished. Months later, I could still see that wolf showing himself across half a continent and into an apartment in Chicago. With a catch in my throat, I'd see Wolf and somehow feel sent, or anointed, or simply blessed.

I changed my language that day, too. I tried never in the presence of wild beings to say, "I see." Instead I adopted Mary Frances's "Look, there's a pair of redtail hawks, showing themselves."

In June, the parish and school hosted a farewell potluck picnic in nearby Chief Plenty Coups State Park. My parents Gwennie and Larry were there with family, Sylvia and Fred Gone, Dorothy Spotted Bear, Chester Turns Plenty, Mary Frances Flat Lip, Bruce Spotted Bear Sr., and so many parents and friends. And former students—Dorcella and Fred, Delia, Bobcat, Darrell, Kim, LaDonna, Alma Rose, Belle. After the meal, the people circled round as Father Randolph and Larry Cunningham, the new principal, presented me with a surprise gift. I opened the black case and pulled out a beautifully crafted, shining Hohner guitar. I held it up for everyone to see.

But there was more. Nested in the case was a hand-tooled leather shoulder strap, painted with red, orange, yellow, and blue geometric designs. Mary Frances stood nearby smiling. Her son had done the exquisite artwork.

"Ahó," I said. Thank you. Fighting tears, I added, "Wherever I play this, I will think of you and pray for you." And then I was crying.

I strummed a C chord and the instrument's resonant tone comforted me. Everyone was clapping.

There is no "good-bye" word in the Crow language. Instead, I'd learned a string of five syllables that translate roughly into "See you."

I truly hoped so.

Part III

The Institute in Creation-Centered Spirituality, Chicago

11

Moccasins in Chicago

And at once the Spirit drove him into the desert.
He was with wild animals.

MARK 1:12–13

In August of that year, 1981, three other Sisters and I moved into a second-floor flat on Thome Avenue on the edge of the Rogers Park and Edgewater neighborhoods in Far North Side Chicago. It was within walking distance of Mundelein College on North Sheridan Road, where the Institute in Creation-Centered Spirituality was part of the Religious Studies Department. The first several months of learning my way through city blocks to class, orientation to the program and professors, and finding the neighborhood grocery store sped by.

One December afternoon, I sat with Sister Darlene, one of the Sisters in our little community, at our kitchen table. One window above the sink faced a brick wall. The enclosed porch behind me looked down on our landlord's small vegetable garden and an alley that arrowed between us and another row of two-story apartment buildings, back porches clinging to each of them. In fact, narrow streets and apartment buildings crowded in from all directions. I felt as though we were floating in a tight boat on a sea of brick, cement, and asphalt.

Although I didn't know them well, the other Sisters I lived with and I formed a haven of familiarity and kindness. Mary used the porch for her room. It was well insulated because it had been used as a playroom by the landlord's numerous grandchildren during the years that three consecutive sets of parents had rented this apartment from their parents. The porch's many windows, however, were little help against the coldest Chicago winter ever recorded.

Darlene and Nancy each had a large room off the spacious dining room, their windows pressed into a thin cut of light that sliced between us and the neighboring apartment building. I miraculously had the smallest room in front, overlooking the street. A bed, a small desk, and a banging radiator filled most of the floor space. I stacked my books on the windowsill, the radiator, and the floor along the wall behind the door. I clicked away whole afternoons and late into the night, typing assignments to the rhythms of Chicago traffic and distant elevated trains. Blessedly, this afterthought bedroom, papered with a pattern of delicate tea roses for a granddaughter, gave me an almost wide view of sky, and more.

The window that began right above my desk spread to a sycamore tree that may have been planted at the same time as the fifty-plus-year-old apartment buildings were built. Its yellow saucer leaves were hardly the vast autumn wheat fields of the Pryor valley, but they held their own against a busy street that was attempting to march right up to the foot of my bed. Thanks to a tree, the city never overpowered my dreams and thoughts.

Sam and Carmela still owned this building and lived in the first-floor apartment. They had immigrated here as a young couple from southern Italy in the 1930s to live next door to Sam's older brother and his family. Carmela tended the garden, growing the tomatoes, peppers, onions, and green beans she needed for the recipes she simmered all day. Homemade sausage and sauces filled our kitchen with delicious aromas that were no match for our hurriedly prepared meals.

Darlene rarely came home this early in the afternoon from her work at Catholic Charities. We were celebrating her time off with a cup of tea. Our conversation drifted from school and her work to community news. Then, sudden as wind out of a bright Crow country sky, there came a rush of memory of everything that couldn't be seen from these apartment windows. Everything that couldn't happen in Chicago: the ceremonies, dances, adventures into the mountains. I could almost smell the hamburgers women fried in the kitchen of the Pryor Community Dance Hall as drummers and dancers at a late-night pow-wow beat away at sleep. They were doing the "coffeepot dance," which signaled it was time to eat. I felt the press of snowdrifts as I pushed through to get into school on a morning so bright that I thought those stories about a new sun every dawn must be true. I found myself in a mountain meadow picking buckets of fragrant purple-blue lupines and yellow arrowleaf balsamroot flowers to the love songs of meadowlarks. I was surrounded by Crow language at lunch and daily contact with grandmas and parents and teachers, and the bus driver's frequent frustration with kids' behavior. I wept.

Darlene was a trained social worker. She listened to my torrent of memories and handed me tissues. When I came up for air, she asked what else I missed.

"My life," I said, "my Crow Indian reservation life. My Pryor life. Prior to this!" She did not even smile. "I want something familiar, for just a day.

"I really do want to be here," I continued, "studying spirituality, theology, and scripture. I wanted to become a priest when I was a little girl. While living in Pryor, I saw how other Sisters were working side by side in parish ministries with priests. I hope these classes will prepare me for that kind of ministry. Maybe even back in Crow country."

Darlene nodded as if she appreciated and supported my hope for future ministry.

I went on, a torrent of dreams released as we talked. "I want to be directly involved in implementing the teachings of the Vatican Council, especially those that encourage the leadership of parish members. In addition, I feel a desire to help foster cultural adaptation of the Church's liturgy and prayers. I want to help Crow Catholics grow in their faith by reflecting deeply on their traditional teachings alongside the words of Jesus."

Our conversation wandered back to life in Chicago and the insights I was gaining from my classes. I told Darlene that I was beginning to see connections between my spiritual-cultural Catholic cradle and these most recent rooms of soul that had opened within me from what I'd learned from Crow friends and family. Suddenly I noticed it was time to pack my books and papers for that day's guest lecture. I stood to go abruptly.

"Thanks," I said. "I feel better now, just talking about all this and having you listen."

It was cold, but I tied on a pair of moccasins Grandma Rose Turnsplenty had given me before pulling on overboots. The walk to school was unexpectedly refreshing. I climbed the wide stairs in the stately mansion that was our classroom building, passing a genuine Tiffany window cloaked with wisteria blooms. Arriving at the classroom, I shyly settled into a student desk, looking at no one, feeling less sad and homesick, even ready.

Our guest lecturer that day, Father Thomas Berry, was already seated in a chair off to the side of the podium. He appeared old. Perhaps in his seventies, I thought. A bit hunched, he sat quietly, his wrinkled face framed by abundant gray hair. His eyes, however, were alert and animated as he scanned the room bustling with students.

Our host introduced him as a cultural historian, Catholic priest, and Earth systems scholar. Hence, he called himself a *geologian*. The word, though new to me, had a familiar, even sacred ring. It seemed Thomas was deliberately evoking *theo*logian: a person who studies religion, and God, and God's relation to the world. I wondered if he wanted us to associate his Earth and world cultures studies with the reverence and appreciation we had for theology. We clapped as he slowly approached the podium. He had no notes.

Thomas Berry began by saying he was basing his remarks on the work and insights of Pierre Teilhard de Chardin. My old buddy from novitiate days. Father Berry now had my total attention. He quickly moved into the essence of his presentation, saying in his gentle, gravelly, slightly asthmatic-sounding voice that there had to be a psychic-spiritual dimension to matter, to the entire universe, from the very first nanosecond of its existence. No question about it.

He can't possibly *mean* that! I thought.

I wasn't sure what a psychic-spiritual dimension meant precisely. Still, I grasped that some version of spirit and even mind was inherent to matter, from the beginning of the universe. And that's when I scrambled to scratch my astounded reaction into my notes. His gently spoken statement sent shock waves through my assumptions about the nature of matter.

I was thrilled by what I thought he meant. I noticed that Dr. Brian Swimme, who had introduced Father Berry, was perched on the edge of his chair, leaning forward over the student desk, gripping the far edge with both hands.

Thomas Berry elaborated his point, Teilhard's point. All matter has been and is pervaded by this psychic-spiritual dimension, he reiterated. Matter has been evolving, becoming more and more complex, from subatomic to atomic and molecular interactions. From the universe's superhot beginning and continuing as it expanded and cooled, this psychic-spiritual dimension continues to evolve today and will into the future.

"Therefore"—I thought I caught a swift twinkle of pleasure—"human consciousness arose out of the evolutionary process of the universe. You see, God created a universe that continues to create itself. In order for human self-aware consciousness to emerge in the universe, there had to have been this complexifying psychic-spiritual dimension all along the way."

I struggled to make sense of this, even as it thrilled me. If he really means this, then what? It seems there would be no need of a sudden infusion of spirit into the human by a deity, either kneeling in the mud of Earth and breathing over the newly formed Adam and Eve, or pronouncing it accomplished from a heavenly divine dwelling. Rather, the entire observable universe, including human beings, human consciousness, and even *soul*, emerged out of the original flaring forth of the universe. Is this really what he is saying?

Wait a minute. I thought it took God to make a human soul.

Thomas stopped for a break. I remained in my desk as some students left and the room filled with chatter. I slowly began to decipher what I'd puzzled over since first reading Teilhard in high school and the novitiate. Thomas had just explained that there had been a gradual evolution over millennia of animal, mammalian, primate, and, finally, human consciousness. Human self-aware consciousness, awestruck consciousness, I am *me* consciousness, unfurled like a rose and ran like fire through time into becoming soul. Human soul flowered forth from the 13.8-billion-year flaring forth of the known universe. The universe always was and continues as one evolutionary process.

"Like from snowmelt to streams to river to sea," I mused.

After the break students returned, and settled back into desks. Thomas returned to the little wooden podium. Voices hushed.

"God made a universe that keeps making itself," Thomas repeated.

Tears of recognition burned in my eyes. The Great Oneness of all that exists, so respected by the Crow, intuited and praised by Saint Francis, is right here within modern physics and the empirical discoveries of my twentieth-century Euro-American culture. Trained paleontologist, scientist, priest, and mystic Teilhard de Chardin worked over many years to wed empirical knowledge with Catholic tradition, doctrine, and meaning. And in this classroom I have heard it at long last from within my present-day spiritual home.

I recalled that scripture I'd discovered in a chant for the feast of Pentecost and frequently relied upon as an anchor in my spiritual life as a young Sister. "The Spirit of the Lord fills the whole world." Over those years I thought of God's Spirit filling the whole world from above and beyond it. A distant God, separate from creation. But Teilhard's insight is different, deeper, and holier even. Through that sacred power, evolution, God's Holy Spirit unfurls and fills from within. God is One-With, Emmanuel, as we sing in the Advent hymns. Close. Spirit suffuses matter, in the manner of light. I began to sense the meaning of energy. Spiritual insight about reality recorded in scripture and empirical knowledge derived from the scientific method flowed for an instant in harmony for me. I hadn't moved an inch in my chair, but I felt as though the whole universe had just shifted within me.

Thomas continued his lecture but I would primarily remember Teilhard's essential insight that matter throbs with spirit and that spirit needs matter's relationships in order to evolve and exist. I began that afternoon in snowy Chicago to understand that universe is the Divine Milieu, as Teilhard called it, filled with spirit, always everywhere in matter, which of course, is matter–spirit/energy in continual exchange and renewal. Perhaps this is resurrection. Matter is never inanimate. By its very nature, matter is matter–spirit/energy relationship in lock-dance. After all, $E = mc^2$.

Those Crow and Northern Cheyenne junior high science students knew this, too!

I was almost afraid to believe it, it felt so freeing, and beyond the constriction of what I'd been taught and believed about God, creation, people, soul. Even heaven and earth.

I walked home after the lecture, buoyed by the happy discovery that I had landed in the right place and program of study that would serve me well in my quest to harmonize Catholic spirituality and teachings with my sense of sacred Earth, sacred nature.

And there would be more to come.

12

The Tie That Binds

A Ceremony in Crow Country and a Lecture in Chicago

He is the image of the unseen God.
All things were created through him.
COLOSSIANS 1:15, 16

Every year in early summer the Catholic Church honors with a special feast the presence of Jesus in the consecrated bread we call the Holy Eucharist. Every day during the Mass the priest prays over bread and a cup of wine, saying the words we believe Jesus said at his last meal with his friends before he was killed: "This is my body. This is my blood." We believe that with these words, the bread and wine actually become the body and blood of Jesus. To share them in communion unites us with Jesus and each other in bonds of love and healing. The community of believers *becomes* the body of Christ. We are united to one another in Jesus Christ and what affects one affects us all. This special feast is called Corpus Christi, Latin for "Body of Christ."

Some rural parishes still celebrate this feast by having an outdoor procession. The priest carries a small wafer of bread, the Body of Christ, placed in the center of a golden metal sunburst on a polished stand. Familiar hymns of praise and thanksgiving are sung during the procession. Sometimes as many as three outdoor altars are set up and decorated with lacy white cloths and bouquets of flowers, most of them cut that morning from families' gardens. The procession stops at each altar for prayers and a blessing. Sometimes Mass is offered at the last altar.

I loved the prayer and pageantry of this feast in Crow country. The five parishes took turns hosting the celebration. It involved elaborate planning and commitment from sponsoring families. Because four is the sacred number of wholeness in Crow tradition, there usually were four outdoor altars, each placed in front of a large white teepee. Brightly colored blankets of geometric designs covered the altars and several more were spread on the ground around them. Each altar was sponsored by a different family of the parish and often family heirloom beadwork, necklaces, and belts were draped like bunting from corner to corner. Sometimes an altar was dedicated as a memorial to a deceased family member, and photos of the loved one were placed among bouquets of wildflowers.

The summer I left Crow country for Chicago, the parish community in Lodge Grass sponsored the celebration and we gathered in a pasture of the Real Bird family ranch. Attending that celebration would be my heart's farewell to the Crow Catholic community. I would gather up memories to carry to Chicago and nourish me there.

Near the ceremonial area several rows of tables had been set with food, stacks of plates, and boxes of utensils. Bowls of salads, baskets and bags of bread, kettles of soup, and platters of desserts had been brought by families of the host parish. Women were grilling meat. One year in Pryor, the men had roasted bison in the ground the entire night before the celebration.

Horses were part of the ceremony. They were outfitted with strikingly beaded or hand-tooled and hand-painted bridles, saddles, and stirrups. Some had feathers or other sacred items tied into their manes and tails. Some of the women riders dressed traditionally in beaded buckskin dresses. Men wore colorful shirts and pants decorated with beadwork or embroidery. Young men and women, clan leaders, and mothers with infants held their horses steady or circled them slowly while they waited in the shade of cottonwood trees for the procession to begin. The horses and riders would lead the procession around the pasture, moving slowly from altar to altar. At each altar they would stand to the side as we prayed, as we listened to long explanations in the Crow language, as we sang songs in English, Crow, and Latin and knelt in the grasses as a priest lifted the bread, the Body of Christ, in blessing over us all.

Kneeling on the edge of the crowd, I noticed the wavering green and yellow of bent pasture grasses in sunlight. I felt deeply peaceful, mesmerized by serene chants and the gentle drone of prayer around me. The grasses seemed alight from within.

I took the hand of my heart and walked into the shining beauty of the world, of nature, and discovered an old place of soul, oddly familiar. I opened the door of my desire to know the holy. A new awareness opened to me: there is no outside, I sensed. Only inside. We are all inside, inside the world of air, inside the skin of Earth. Earth, home of our prayer; Earth, holding all we love; Earth, dwelling at the heart of human longing. I experienced myself and my family, people, plants, all animals in creation's holy communion. In this sweet oneness, I felt God's presence.

With a jolt, I woke to the ringing of the little golden bells. They signaled a blessing moment in this ceremony. I was still kneeling. People were bowing. Some made the sign of the cross. And then it was time to move to the next altar. Beside me, an infant in a stroller slept. She was startled awake as her mother struggled to push the stroller's small wheels through the thick pasture grasses.

Perhaps all the rosaries prayed with neighbors in our living room back in Cincinnati helped prepare me for this moment in the June warmth of Crow country. Perhaps all those rosaries we offered to God for world peace were a subversive introduction to this recognition of the whole communion of life. Maybe learning to pray is quite simple, rooted and growing in this: to *like* the drone of rosaries with family and neighbors, and to *like* the shining of grasses and a blue arc of sky and dust feathers blowing around hooves of horses. As I readied to leave this place to pack off to Chicago, I took with me the certitude that all life holds firm as holy and that nothing, no being, is outside the holy communion of Earth, of the universe.

Since high school I had been intrigued by New Testament scripture passages about the Cosmic Christ whose glory permeates all creation, uniting everything in God's love. As a young Sister attending a lecture in a Carmelite monastery, I learned that Teilhard de Chardin described this glory as a radiance that is inherent in matter everywhere in the universe all the way back to its very beginning. Regardless of how we attempt to name this oneness of the universe in God's love, that Corpus Christi afternoon in Crow country I learned that sometimes we glimpse this splendor.

Although I had only a vague idea of what this experience could mean in my life, for years after I would carry its memory with me into many churches. I would walk into our motherhouse chapel in Indiana, the pillar capitals carved with vines, birds, and flowers, looking for grasses. I would sing with hundreds of other Montana Catholics in the cathedral in Helena, looking for grasses. I would sit quietly in the Basilicas of Saint Francis and Saint Clare in Assisi, in St. Peter's in Rome, waiting for that sea of communion to break through me. I would even find myself seeking it in little churches in Papua New Guinea, buildings whose leaf-woven walls were already porous.

Back in the pasture at this Corpus Christi celebration, everyone was standing. I stood, too. With a subtle shift of weight and a graceful lift to the reins, riders turned their horses to the fourth altar. I joined the procession behind the young mother pushing the stroller. The grasses brushed our legs.

I left Crow country hoping that my studies in Creation-Centered Spirituality would complement what I had already experienced and absorbed of creation's all-embracing sacred community of life, including water, air, soils, sun, moon, and stars. I wanted to discover creation's holy communion shining forth in my Catholic tradition. I hoped to study new scholarly insights into the meaning of the life, teachings, and death-resurrection of Jesus that reached beyond the limits of redemption from original sin. Little did I realize how profoundly my expectations would be fulfilled.

Over that long cold winter in Chicago, I gradually realized my studies had settled in for a permanent stay as, mysteriously, spaces opened in my understanding of the world and spirituality. My heart gradually had eased into being familiar here. New ideas had found niches in my thinking.

An early lecture by Father Matthew Fox challenged me to wake up to my culture's dualistic, divisive thinking, especially regarding the dualisms of matter/spirit, male/female, body/soul, heaven/earth. And he challenged us to realize that these pervasive dualisms created unjust structures of power, control, and racial and economic inequality in society. I struggled to grasp the scope of his thesis. Although it apparently permeated my worldview, "dualistic thinking" was a new concept to me!

In the main, there were only three startling and new insights, but they would summon me to deepen my spiritual journey, eventually pervading the house of my faith like the fragrance of purple irises filling rooms from Mom's bouquets on the dining room table. Those three insights would, surprisingly, come from science. They would shed light on my clouded, culturally determined worldview and have the potential to dismantle my dualistic thinking.

"The urge of science is to tell the story of what's here," mathematical physicist Dr. Brian Swimme said at the start of his class lecture one bright morning in May, the last month of our nine-month program. We were in the large second-floor classroom of the white marble mansion that housed our program. In the mansion's former ballroom, sunlight and views of Lake Michigan flowed in through banks of large windows to my right and behind me.

"Religion focuses on what could be," he continued. "The past, primarily the focus of science, and the future, religion, come together in the present of our lives." Although an interesting way to begin, what does this have to do with anything, I wondered.

Professor Swimme was the artist in residence for the year. He'd become part of student vocabulary. Everyone called him by his first name. I'd never thought of scientists as artists, or as being willing to talk about religion, either. But here he was, and students had been packing his classes and talking him into offering discussion sessions beyond the required hours.

Not me.

Science was not on my personal list of what would prepare me for church ministry. I didn't understand its significance to our program of Creation-Centered Spirituality. By now I knew I would be returning to serve in seven Crow and Northern Cheyenne parishes in Montana. I didn't see much connection between knowledge of the universe and preparing Northern Cheyenne and Crow people for leadership in their church communities, which was what I would be doing. Most of my priest and Sister friends in the institute were attending the scripture and theology courses, and that was where I went, too. I had also meticulously pieced together elective courses that I thought would prepare me to participate in church planning meetings on par with the priests.

All this helped me ignore that I felt terribly inadequate when I was around the other students who seemed to have grasped the significance that science has for spirituality. They were catching connections I couldn't comprehend. They were articulate and motivated. They dove into reflecting on science with an excitement that didn't make sense in my world.

Why would the latest findings in science, details about subatomic particles, and the grand-scale data of the entire universe be of interest or importance to me? Fascinated as I was by the Teilhard books over the years, I didn't want to complicate my spirituality with science.

I'm a Catholic Sister, not a scientist, and my call in life, I told myself, is to help us humans make sense of our lives through religion. Our Sisters who taught the sciences in my undergraduate classes taught them as absolutely separate from our faith in God and how we pray. I really did want to study sacred scripture and liturgy and theology. And science and religion were two profoundly distinct worlds, connected only by the chasm that kept them apart.

Despite my desire to integrate evidence of billions of years of evolution into the biblical creation story, I did not want the power of scientific information and theory to eat away at long-held beliefs about God and the world that were precious to me. More than precious, I revered these beliefs as the bedrock of my life as a Sister. I equated faith with *belief* and found no room in that for ongoing *discovery* of God, for God's sake!, in science, including its mind-bending marvels and high-tech eyes and ears into nature's beauty.

So I did not sign up for any of Dr. Swimme's elective classes. When he lectured in the spirituality courses, the three-times-a-week required core of our program, I took meticulous notes, then skipped over those pages as I wrote my reflection papers and trotted off to a scripture or theology class.

Intent on preparing for work in the Church, I'd carefully shut down any openness to reflecting on the universe as an essential part of my spiritual endeavor. In fact, my faith and I had managed to get through almost an entire year of study unscathed by the sword of scientific inquiry and knowledge. After all, in my mind they were separated by that chasm, regardless of the effort Brian and other professors were making to guide us into the unmarked terrain of science-faith integration, of science enriching faith, faith inspiring science.

I didn't grasp that our culture's antagonism between science and faith was one of its deadliest dualisms. I was learning that faith without science was blind to our dependence on the rest of the natural world, from which we are intrinsically woven. And science without faith or religious sensibility can collapse into a materialistic worldview that supports exploitive economies that are inherently destructive to Earth's systems that support life. In my resistance to learning and integrating science into my faith perspective, I was successfully flunking the most important coursework of the entire program. That is, until that May morning.

Dr. Swimme repeated that the work of science is to try to learn and tell the story of what's here, the whole universe, the stars in the sky and beetles in the garden. Interesting. The universe is a story, he said. He quoted a very famous and important philosopher I'd never heard of, Alfred North Whitehead. Whitehead had written that in a time of cultural collapse or inadequacy it's helpful to look at how the overarching theory of that culture fails to grasp the *interconnected* realities.

"We're here to learn how our culture fails to be coherent with itself and the world. This is my first important point this morning," he said.

Already I was distracted. I'd seen a lot of cultural collapse and inadequacy. I'd lived in the midst of the poverty of Indian reservation towns where basic human services were woefully inadequate. And this, within the borders of the richest nation in the world. In some of our cities, wealthy neighborhoods were located just up the hill from grinding poverty. How is it we can create economic and cultural systems that separate some people from the housing, health, and educational benefits some of us enjoy and believe that's acceptable? How is it we can see the deprivation and suffering of families and not feel committed to changing how we organize the gifts of our culture and nation? I heard my father's voice inside me, a voice that objected to spending money to refurbish a church when, only blocks away, desperate families were living in substandard housing.

Dr. Swimme continued his lecture and to my surprise was actually addressing my questions. I learned that during the past five hundred years Western cultures had created a kind of science that viewed the universe not as *story* but as a collection of separate and distinct objects, held together and functioning much like a *machine* through laws or forces like gravity and electromagnetism.

"We've studied life, the planet, even the universe," he explained, "by taking it apart in our minds and experiments. We then set about examining the *pieces*. Worse, we've done this with the mindset that everything not human is *out there*, separate from us. The laws of nature, too, are imaged as *outside* us humans, even though we are affected by them."

I translated this as science having failed the holy communion of nature, having failed the Body of Christ. I knew I was right not to mix science with faith.

He continued, "Inevitably the inner contradictions of a culture begin to show up: for example, unequal distribution of health care services in a country dedicated to the proposition that all people are created equal. Some people object and try to create more just systems. Many other people, especially those in power and those who are benefiting from the current way of doing things, tend to shift their focus to personal experience and the needs of their families as something separate from everyone else, and everything else. That generally good and thinking people can do this makes sense from a worldview that sees the universe as a machine of separate parts. This thinking influences all our cultural systems, like government, health care, housing, and education. But there's an alternative to that thinking, based in our latest findings about how the universe is actually structured. It is not a machine of separated interacting parts at all."

His eyes widened as he addressed the class. "You're going to like this."

He pulled a book from his bag, held it up, and got very excited. "Guess what! This book is not just here in my hand. As soon as I held it where you could see it, it became part of you. It is now inside each of you, and me, too," he says. "Our eyes are *in* our heads; seeing occurs *within* us. Sight of the book activates our minds and is instantly united with memories and images from the past about books. First of all, we recognize a book. We know it's not a magazine or a radio. Feelings are evoked. Our mothers are reading to us. We remember how heavy the stack of homework books used to be. We recall the smell of a favorite book of fairy tales. These impressions are all put together by the individual. In no way are things like this book simply located in just one place like my hand. The book is in my hand and part of each of us instantaneously. There is no *out there*, separate from us."

I shook my head, trying to shrug off beloved memories of the Corpus Christi revelation: there is no outside, we are all inside and connected in the Body of Christ. That was spiritual. This is rational science and interesting philosophy.

"Relationship *is* the ground of all reality. Are you aware the whole universe walks when you walk?" Brian asked.

Seriously? Of course I'm not aware of that. It never crossed my mind. It turned out to be his second important point.

Suddenly I was in a darkened theater in the visitor center of the Bighorn Canyon National Recreation Area in the heart of Crow country. My friends and I were waiting for the interpretive movie to begin.

The building's foundations are anchored in five hundred feet of layered Ordovician and Cambrian dolomite and limestone. Earth and tiny reef-building creatures of shallow seas began making this gray rock more than 500 million years ago. The canyon is a bulwark of layered ancient stone channeling the summer tumult of the Bighorn River. On nearby Pretty Eagle Point, with its spectacular views of the upper canyon, Crow men and women for centuries have fasted from food and water for as long as four days in searing July heat seeking vision and insight to guide their lives.

I've viewed this interpretive movie many times with visiting family and friends. As it begins, a yellow and black swallowtail butterfly drawing nectar from purple penstemon flowers fills the big screen. The Crow elder narrating the film is saying that the spirits of their ancestors still walk this land and that each creature we meet remains with us as part of our lives. He tells us that the good thoughts we leave behind will enrich the land and touch those who live here or come to visit. These statements and the beauty of the film touched my heart every time I'd viewed it.

Remembering that film while sitting in a Chicago classroom that May, it dawned on me that I'd learned that past, present, and future are drawn together in the Crow vision of the circle of life. I pulled my thoughts back from that movie in Crow country to Dr. Swimme's lecture. I scribbled into my notes that the people I'd come to know and trust did not live in the "simply located" world of my culture, where everything is "separate and out there." They seemed to have grasped the mystery and beauty of a whole universe walking when we walk.

"So," Brian then said, "our job is to create a civilization that goes beyond the dualistic thinking that separates us from the rest of the universe, the Earth, and certain groups of people, too. Another word for this machine universe is *materialism*. Everything we call *thing* is considered to be simply matter. Only humans have spirit and depth. To help us get beyond the inadequacies of this thinking, let's continue our assessment of Western materialism and culture by delving into the deepest, most pervasive interconnectivity of the universe."

I sat there, expecting some profound spiritual insight. "This interconnectivity permeates everything. It is a presence," he said. Sitting in the classroom listening to him, I could almost smell the grasses of that Corpus Christi experience. "We call it the field theory of electromagnetism."

I had no idea what that was.

A few hands went up. "Field theory of electromagnetism?"

"Some background first. I'll get to it, I assure you."

I was trying to keep pace with Brian as he raced across the landscape of subatomic theories and experiments. He was saying the most important understanding we can grasp about evolution is that it is an *emergence over time of real newness in the universe*. He was drawing the four building blocks of DNA protein, represented by the letters G, A, T, and C in square boxes linked by little lines. DNA suddenly looked like a string of railroad cars arranged in some bizarre order.

"Every"—he was so emphatic I underlined the word twice— "living being is made up of these protein elements of DNA." The same proteins that determined my height and unruly hair and directed my growth over the years, these proteins in a different arrangement created the wild horses of the Pryor Mountains. Oh my, the Crows got it right after all when they teach that all creatures, including us humans, are relatives. And Saint Francis of Assisi, too, who reinvented

129

the chivalry of his day by calling every being—worms, crickets, a sow, birds, fish, a wolf—"brother" and "sister." I polished off the line of notes with my own string of exclamation points. We're all related.

Meanwhile, Dr. Swimme was pursuing his own train of thought. When an intricate pattern of proteins in an individual doesn't replicate itself exactly, a new being emerges from this work of the universe. Brian insisted that what we commonly call mutation is really a manifestation of the inborn creativity of life, of the universe itself. For three and a half billion years, life on planet Earth has been shaping and reshaping itself in response to changes in climate, food, water, and the chemical makeup of the atmosphere. This ongoing evolution of life is not simply a mechanical rearrangement of matter. Never. Life is not a machine. Embedded in a planet hooked to a star within one of millions of galaxies, life *is* the universe at work. The universe is never a machine; it is not mechanical. In fact, the universe is truly creative, through time and space relentlessly bringing forth fresh and new beings. Like people, who are creative. Like *God*.

Most of my adult life I have been on the hunt how to possibly give name to this tender, unrelenting love that eventually makes intolerable those unworthy life choices we humans constantly make that are contrary to the gifts we brought into the world. Influenced by the women's movement of the 1960s, I found traditional names for God inadequate and limiting in the way they excluded feminine names and used only masculine pronouns in reference to God. I was put off by names that emphasized might and power, harsh judgment and condemnation.

As a young nun, I began editing prayers and psalms in our prayer books, adding "she" to "he," "mother" to "father," or changing all the male pronouns to "you." That got cumbersome and tiresome. I felt angry that I even had to do that. I felt isolated when I prayed aloud with groups. But I persisted because I felt God's nearness when I prayed. I felt something true and good. Although I worried that I was venturing into uncharted, unorthodox territory, I trusted the Genesis scripture that human beings were created in God's image, men and women, all of us.

When I arrived in Crow country and encountered a language that did not use male and female pronouns, I could barely imagine how liberating that could be: to have no "he" or "she" or even "it" when referring to people and other life-forms. It felt so inclusive and egalitarian. Their word for the ineffable, life-giving Being also did not designate gender. One of the closest English words we can have for Akbaatatdia, the Crow word for God, may be Creator. But we must understand this as not a distant, disengaged, mechanical creator, controlling and determining the universe. Rather a dynamic presence, animating and supporting the universe, Earth, all that exists. From within. And simultaneously, beyond any reality we can possibly imagine.

This felt sublime, simple, and true. I welcomed "Creator, Akbaatatdia" into my soul. I began to pray, "Loving Creator, beautiful and good . . ."

In class that day, I listened to a scientist and unexpectedly met a creating universe. How do I light candles and burn incense and bow to a *Creator* universe? That, I sensed, would be years in the learning. I slowly pulled my attention back to my note-taking, to the field theory of electromagnetism, the third important point.

"And then, contrary to how we think the universe ought to work, we've encountered in our scientific experiments a vast field of interconnectivity at a level we can't see or measure. Look at this," Brian said. I hurried to copy another set of drawings he was scratching on the chalkboard. "The electrons soaring around the nucleus of an atom: they aren't at all like planets orbiting the sun. They are better thought of as a cloud of potentialities, sometimes waves, sometimes particles, that can jump from one position to another without traveling the intervening space. A particular electron can disappear and then re-emerge in a different location without leaving a trail."

Impossible, I thought. How do scientists know that? What connects them? What holds that electron?

"There's more. You can take two particles that form a system; let's say electrons, each with a spin opposite the other. Let them drift apart, even great distances, and then change the direction of the spin of one of them. The spin of its partner particle *instantaneously* changes to the matching opposite spin and at precisely the same speed. Distance in space cannot overcome their interconnectedness. We can't see or feel or smell what actually bonds them. We can only observe their deep relationship."

A wave of bending prairie grasses broke through me right there in a Chicago classroom. A field, a presence, permeates the universe, I realized. In this universe distance does not mean separation from or between beings. Rather distance is more a measure of the reach of influence between beings, how far and varied the touch from one to the other, from each to all. When we pray, we are acknowledging this amazing mystery. Prayer is a willingness to accept and try to live this intimacy that exists throughout the universe, *is* the universe. It so enthralled me that I almost needed the ringing of little bells to bring me back into the classroom. I barely heard Brian say this communion that *is* the universe is called nonlocal causality and that we've named the power that keeps it happening electromagnetism. Somehow, I managed to get all that into my notes.

It was 1982 and though it was still a theory I had every reason to believe that there was plenty of evidence indicating there is indeed this astounding reality dwelling below the radar screen of human sense organs. In 1997 the phenomenon would be conclusively proven by physicist Nicolas Gisin and his team at the University of Geneva. They sent photons seven miles in opposite directions, something like the distance across a whole galaxy to a photon, and showed that interfering with one provoked an instantaneous response in the other. In an attempt to further describe this binding soul of matter, nonlocal causality got another name: *quantum entanglement.*

Meanwhile, my beloved prairie grasses daily turn their sun-driven energy to growing extensive roots at unbelievable depths of six to ten feet below the topsoil. This remarkable achievement enables them to survive years of drought as well as maximize absorption of rain when it does blow across the plains. A single square yard of blue grama and buffalo grass may contain up to five miles of roots so thickly woven that the original prairie sod was almost impossible to plow. The ground literally rang when steel plows broke through and turned over its root entanglement. "A storm of wild music," one wheat farmer's child recalled, many decades later.

The prairie grasses of a Crow country pasture were half a continent distant from my Chicago classroom, but the storm of insight at a Corpus Christi celebration that showed me the interconnectivity of Earth and all life was suddenly ringing with wild scientific music. The partnered spin of particles became a point upon which my sense of God suddenly took a pivotal turn to embrace the whole bonded universe. I didn't dare collapse God and nonlocal causality and quantum entanglement into being the same. Not at all. Yet I knew that I now had an authentic way of imagining the pervasive, inclusive presence of

God, within myself and all that exists, the shimmering Earth and throughout the known universe. And way beyond what we can know. In all this expansiveness, I felt a tender closeness of God. And in God, a closeness with all that is. This was hardly what I expected to experience during a lecture by a scientist, right there in the third row of a second-floor classroom itself caught in the arc of a lake whose blue stretched to meet sky.

Is this a kind of evolution? I asked myself. Is a real newness emerging in how I perceive my world? The universe? Is the DNA of biblical faith replicating into something fresh thanks to a universe story based on scientific information? And not just me personally. Am I one of many people who discover that knowledge of an entangled universe actually enriches and deepens the spiritual insight of a planet's holy communion?

I did not need to frame that page of notes and hang it near my desk in a Chicago apartment along with an icon of Jesus and his friends celebrating the Passover meal, their last supper together. Instead, I drew open the window shade above my desk to a sycamore tree with big leaves and Chicago's brick walls of vibrating atoms. To see anything is to see all and recognize holy everywhere, a faithful communion billions of years old.

13

What the Crow Elder Knows

Lodge Grass

Our prayer rose like incense.

We thought you might not come back to Indian country once you'd lived in a big city like Chicago," one of my friends from Pryor said to me.

"I missed the horses," I said, and she nodded. That is, I missed something wild and muscular beyond the reach of a city's excitement. "Horses" means I missed the mind-bending miles of grasses and spring smell of sagebrush after rain and the possibility of a rattlesnake coiled at the front doorstep. The excited new owner of boxes of theology and science books and a master's degree in religious studies, I still missed the daily song of Crow language, the traditions of Crow culture haunting the edges of my Catholic faith and personal dreams. I missed a whole family, the family of the Pryor community and land, and especially, Gwennie and Larry Plain Bull, my adoptive parents in the Crow way.

And I missed her, Mary Frances Flat Lip, who gave me the wolf "showing itself to us." So I'd come back.

She and I sat down to a school lunch of grilled cheese sandwiches, red Jell-O, and canned pears. We talked about her grandchildren, about the son who hasn't been around in a long time, about how she prays.

I had graduated from the Creation Spirituality program at the end of May but stayed in Chicago throughout the summer for additional courses in theology and scripture. Father Dan Crosby, the director of ministry for all the Crow and Northern Cheyenne parishes, had contacted me in January to invite me to consider creating a new program of lay ministry training for all seven parishes of Crow and Northern Cheyenne country. The pastoral teams of the parishes had determined they needed such a program and encouraged Dan to ask me to take the job. I would also serve the Lame Deer parish, Blessed Sacrament Church, by being on the team and directing the music ministry. By August, I was packed and ready to leave Chicago for my new ministry and home in Lame Deer, in Northern Cheyenne country.

I looked forward to living with Sister Claver Ehren, who had mentored me through my first sweat lodge ceremony years before in Pryor. She was the new director of the parish religious education program for children. She began her new ministry by visiting the parents and recruiting them as teachers. A large woman with a ready laugh and seemingly boundless energy, she made countless home visits, distributing materials and training parents to teach their own children at home. Listening to Claver's lively stories when she came home for the evening meal, I sensed parents believed they could do what they had never dreamed of doing because Sister Claver was convinced they could.

Other than Claver, and the priest and Franciscan Brother, I knew no one else in Lame Deer, Montana. I also knew next to nothing of Northern Cheyenne history. Our pastor, Father Paul Reichling, encouraged me to take a Cheyenne history course being offered that semester at Dull Knife Memorial College. I enrolled. The professor was Northern Cheyenne, Gail Small, a lawyer.

I worked part-time in the Blessed Sacrament parish, helping with the weekly services and singing at the many funerals. In addition, every week I drove a used bright orange Fiesta to six other reservation towns to teach a ministry training course in Crow or Northern Cheyenne Catholic parishes. Every week, almost five hundred miles of grasses and sage and horses skimmed past the Fiesta's windows.

But before I started teaching, I blanketed my desk with pages of course notes and circled my chair with books that I'd collected in Chicago. I created a six-week ministry training course, collaborating with the priests and nuns at each of the parishes. Each session included input about the Catholic Mass and the call from God for laypeople to share in the various liturgical ministries. We would then pray together. The third part of the class would provide practice for each person's chosen ministry: how to approach the altar, read the scriptures, distribute Holy Communion.

Throughout October and November, the pastor of the Lodge Grass parish, Father Jim Antione, had published invitations in the Sunday bulletin, advertising the new course in church ministries and encouraging people to participate. Franciscan Sister Cecily Schroepfer, a pastoral team member of several years, personally invited people she knew had the gifts for ministry. That is how I found myself walking into a classroom in the Lodge Grass Parish Center.

Two couples and several women had signed up for the course and were seated at a U-shaped table. Cecily was obviously pleased with the turnout and began the session by thanking everyone for coming and introducing me. The group sat quietly, almost stiffly. This was something totally new for them. They were used to having the priest do everything at Mass except take up the collection. Occasionally, Father Jim asked an elder to offer a prayer in Crow. An accomplished musician, Sister Cecily and a Crow women's choir led most of the singing. Other than that, Mass was the priest's job. Certainly not theirs.

They had never seen a Crow person, one of their own, perform a ministry during Mass. In their memory and experience such things had never been allowed. When I asked why they had come for the class, most said it was because Sister Cecily had invited them. Some added that they weren't sure they would be accepted by their peers. Others felt unworthy. Some wondered why this was being offered at all.

I reiterated what I knew Sister Cecily had already shared with them individually. I said that when they were baptized, God's Holy Spirit had filled them and blessed them with gifts for service of their families, the community, and the parish. I shared scripture passages that described the gifts the early Christian communities had received and shared. I emphasized that of all the gifts, the greatest gift was love. And surely, they loved their parish community. Many nodded. Now, I finished, that love was needed in a new way.

Cecily smiled. I sensed a shy willingness to give this a try. I suggested we take a break, have some coffee, and then gather in the church to pray together for each other.

Cecily and I arranged chairs in the church into a circle for our prayer. Together we invited everyone to sit down. We had lit some charcoal for burning cedar. It gave off a faint welcome smell. People sat with heads bowed, praying. Waiting.

I asked for a volunteer to help lead our prayer. "We'll start by burning cedar," I said. "Would someone like to carry the bowl of incense around our circle?"

I was unaware that tonight I would soon be learning something that would reshape my prayer for the rest of my life.

The familiar Catholic practice of incensing a congregation with fragrant smoldering resins imported from the Middle East adds solemnity to a service. It's a way of reverencing the people as the quiet incense floats through the air. It blesses everyone. In Crow parishes, the practice is tweaked a bit. Fragrant cedars, previously used for centuries in Crow and Northern Cheyenne spiritual ceremonies like the sweat lodge and Sun Dance, are now used in Catholic churches as well.

When the bowl is carried past people, they draw the cedar smoke to their hearts.

I'm always amazed how this simple ritual quiets a congregation, even children, as people reach toward the smoke, pulling its pungent blessing to their bodies, their foreheads, their hearts. And there's something solid in praying with a fragrance from the place where we live. Just about everyone knows where some of the most fragrant cedar trees grow.

JW, a local Vietnam veteran turned ranch hand, offered to carry the smoking bowl around our circle to begin our prayer. "As you pass by people," I reminded JW, "say a prayer for each person."

That's when Alex LaForge, a tall, bent Crow with a deeply weathered face, slowly got up from his chair and walked over to speak to me. He's a respected leader in the community. I'm almost embarrassed to have him in a class listening to me because he's so learned, a true elder.

"Sister, you've forgotten," he said quietly, leaning close to my ear. I had no idea what he thought I once knew. "When JW walks past each person he doesn't need to say anything. *The burning of the cedar is the prayer.*"

Of course. I asked Alex to share his teaching with the group. JW, stiff and limping and wounded in ways beyond what we see, then silently circled the group, carrying Earth's cedar-fragrant prayer to each of our hearts. I leaned gratefully into the silence, joining a prayer that doesn't need human words.

I learned. Sitting up all night with a sick child *is* the prayer. Desperately hoping month after month that a son will survive prison *is* the prayer. Patiently talking through a misunderstanding with a spouse or friend *is* the prayer. Salmon swimming unknown miles back to the streams of their spawning *is* the prayer. Penguins incubating the one egg in frigid wind *is* the prayer. "All that exists, prays. All the rocks, plants, and animals pray to God," read a poster in our Sisters' chapel in Pryor. I was learning.

When JW finished and sat down, Cecily concluded our prayer by leading us in the chant: "Spirit of the Living God, fall afresh on us."

After a short time of silence, we were ready to start practicing for ministry.

Cecily gathered people interested in Communion ministry around the altar. She handed each a small plate with one bread wafer. I heard her say these breads were straight from the plastic shipping bag. They had not been consecrated by Father during a Mass. They were practice breads. She showed them how to hold the host and lift it in front of the person receiving it.

"Now," she said, "this is the most important part. Look at the person when you say the words, Body of Christ. You must realize that you are not just talking about the bread, you are addressing the person by their true name as a Christian: Body of Christ."

I took my group to the reader's podium, called a lectern. "Of course you're going to study your reading ahead of time. Of course you're going to practice at home. When you stand here and begin to read, remember that the Word of God is a Living Word. It has the power to touch and help the spirits and hearts of those who hear it. It is *your* voice that is carrying the Living Word of God to everyone's hearts. Imagine that. Isn't that wonderful!"

We brought the group back to the circle of chairs.

"Would anyone like to offer a closing prayer?" I asked. Alex nodded and stood. He prayed in his Crow language, naming each person. I felt tears burn.

The four years I did this work in those seven parishes I never once got to talk about the wonders of the universe, of nonlocal causality, of the psychic-spiritual dimension of all matter. I occasionally shared my notes with Claver, often used them for my meditation times. But the universe was never woven into my formal work. At first, I thought I had failed my coursework, that a lot of money could have been saved if I'd merely taken some theology and liturgy courses by correspondence.

But I loved the work and the people I served. I know now that all the magnificent powers of the universe were at work in us as we made new, heartfelt connections with each other and God, as we evolved into new, more adult faith communities of shared gifts. I knew we were communities where the universe prays when we pray. That was enough for me. It didn't matter that no one else heard those words. Love is, after all, the greatest gift.

Part IV

Finding a New Way

14

A Woman Leads the Way

Leadership Conference Regional Meeting
Donaldson, Indiana

*You water the mountains, to bring
forth food from the earth.*

PSALMS 104: 13–14

One way to understand Catholic Sisters is that we live our lives by a desire to follow a call from God. Usually not an audible call, but rather something we hear in our hearts, something like a dream nudging us from within toward the convent. Sometimes a Sister teacher invites a young woman to consider joining the convent, sometimes a friend. Once she gets into the convent, the community itself becomes part of the call. In a mutual process of prayer, observation, conversation, and inner listening, the woman and the community clarify together whether or not this woman has a call to live this life.

Our name for this process is "discernment." It requires honesty, mutual respect, and an openness of heart and mind to unexpected outcomes. It is characterized by inner freedom. Especially freedom from fear and the need to control.

The sense of call continues throughout our lives: a call to a different ministry or to a particular group of people, a call that responds to a newly emerged need in society or the Church, a call to serve in a foreign country. Call is lively and energetic; it morphs with a Sister's age, acquired skill sets, interests. It also runs deep like a river in her soul, changing but constant in its flow.

In late winter of my fourth year in Lame Deer, I received a call from several of our Sisters asking me to consider being open to a leadership position in our community.

This shook me. If elected by the Sisters, I would serve for four years with four other Sisters, responsible for the welfare of the whole congregation. It would mean moving to Oldenburg, Indiana. I didn't really want this type of ministry, but I felt a vague sense of call I couldn't fully understand or ignore.

We were enjoying an early spring that year. Where could I go for silence and solitude to do my inner listening, I wondered. I felt the mountains summoning me, the Pryor Mountains. Most of all, I wanted to go to the remote rugged canyons and mountain ridges of the Pryor Mountain Wild Horse Range. I wanted to sit and ponder in a region where wide vistas would open my soul and where uncaught nature could inform my thinking.

My plan was simple: sleeping bag, a tent, some food, my Bible and journal, pens. I would drive over the Bighorn Mountains from Lame Deer, and head north across open country toward the Pryors. I set off, pleased with my plan. When I arrived in the town of Ranchester at the base of the Bighorns, a blizzard was closing in, the mountains lost in clouds and wind. Not a chance of getting over those mountains safely.

I had no plan B.

Then I remembered a small monastery of Benedictine nuns that had recently been established in a ranch house somewhere in the region. Ranchester had a library. What better place to ask about the location of a monastery. Sure enough, the librarian was able to get a phone number for me. The nuns had a guest room available. I was welcome to come stay several days with them.

First discernment lesson: be willing to change plans to say good-bye to wild horses. The storm stayed in the mountains. I saw them, shrouded in clouds each morning and afternoon, when I took long walks in ranch pastures, careful to avoid cattle. I tried to talk myself into a firm no to this invitation from my Sisters. But when I did, I felt a storm close in around me, shutting out life, beauty, possibility. During our noon meals together, the Benedictines listened as I described my mix of feelings and reluctance to make such a big change. They gently helped me prod open my heart. I finally realized that at the very least, I could agree to participate in discernment with the community.

Back home in Lame Deer several days later, I signed the Leadership Discernment form and submitted my name to the election committee.

I went to Chico Hot Springs with our pastoral team to walk icy trails along streams, cross-country ski in nearby Yellowstone Park, and soak in hot pools morning and evening. I tried to forget about the discernment. "I love being here and doing this work," I said to the pastor, Father Reynold Rynda, over the song of the stream. He nodded, saying the team and parish would miss me if I was elected, but said it was important to stay open to the possibility of God's call to the ministry of leadership. I had hoped he would urge me to withdraw my name, but he was a man sensitive to the inner voice of God's Holy Spirit. Later that spring, while I was scrubbing the oven in my Lame Deer home, the phone rang and Sister Marie Kathleen, our current president, told me I had been elected to the General Council.

The Lame Deer parish had a farewell gathering for me and gave me a handmade elk hide drum with a beautifully beaded drumstick. People in the various parishes gave me beaded necklaces, a blanket, a shawl. Once again, I tearfully packed to leave Indian country.

The last week of June, two Sister friends drove a van from Indiana to collect me and my luggage and boxes of books. Several days later, we arrived in Oldenburg in the late evening. They helped me lug my stuff up to my room in one of the motherhouse buildings.

I felt raw, vulnerable. Rooting through stacks of boxes, I located my sleeping bag and tent tarp. I went outside and spread them on the ground on a hot, humid Indiana night and slept on damp grass under a maple tree behind the motherhouse. The next day when I found a place at a table in the dining room for the noon meal, Sisters I barely knew said to me, "We hear you slept outside last night." I was shocked. My private life seemed ended. On July second, the community celebrated the formal ceremony of installation of the new leadership General Council: Sisters Kate Holohan, Julie Hampel, Carol Ann Sunderman, Joan Laughlin, and me.

The day after our installation, I walked into the spare office to begin my new job. At forty, I was the youngest member of the five-person administrative team of the Sisters of St. Francis. We'd been elected to serve and lead our Sisters. I did not know the specific jobs this would entail.

I began by unpacking my favorite books about scripture and Earth spirituality and because the room had no bookcase, I stacked them in my open steamer trunk. I draped the trunk with a brightly striped Native American blanket pinned with mallard and grouse feathers. In a box among the books, I found the brass figure of a prancing horse Father Reynold had given me and placed it front and center on the desk.

I had no idea what to do next. In half an hour we would gather in the Council room for our first meeting. Kate and Julie had been on the previous Council. I trusted they would mentor the three newbies through the maze of responsibilities.

I sighed and opened a drawer to retrieve a stack of small photo portraits of the almost five hundred Sisters I had been elected to serve. Their names were written on the backs of the photos. Over two hundred Sisters were retired here at Oldenburg. I went through the pictures, one by one, attempting to memorize names. Except for a few former teachers and several Sisters I'd lived or studied with, I didn't know any of the others. I fought back tears of fear and loneliness.

At the Council meeting that day, and those that followed through the summer and fall, I gradually learned what being responsible for the well-being of all these Sisters entailed. We were responsible for the overall budget that provided for their health care, education, professional development, and daily living needs. Approximately three hundred Sisters served in Catholic schools and parishes and in social service agencies in nine US states, as well as in a high school in Kenya, an impoverished barrio of Guaymas, Mexico, and the southern high-lands of Papua New Guinea. Among the five of us, we looked forward to visiting each of them every other year.

By the third Council meeting we had divvied up the various re-sponsibilities. My job description included working with the Office of Life Development, where a director assisted Sisters as they dealt with problems in their ministries or discerned new directions in their work. I also served on our justice and peace committee. In addition, I was assigned to assess and address the unique needs of the Sisters who served overseas and in diverse cultures here in the United States.

As I got to know them, I really enjoyed and grew to love the other four Sisters on the Council. I quickly learned I could trust their knowl-edge of Sisters and the community, as well as their commitment to God and ministry. I gradually adjusted to the routine of office work, the schedule of prayer and meals at the motherhouse, and not having a private life.

Soon after arriving in Indiana I began taking long walks around our congregation's nearby run-down farm. Because it was more eco-nomical to ship in food for the motherhouse community and academy students, we had ceased operating the farm almost thirty years be-fore, in the 1960s. I discovered secluded glens of beech trees where I could not see houses or hear traffic, even rumbling trucks. Up and out early one day, I absorbed the quiet curve of a hillside pasture glowing in sunrise. I wandered our brick barn, the largest brick barn with an unsupported roof in all of Indiana. I saw that the quaint little brick pump house, built over a deep well fed by two alga-choked reservoirs, was stuffed to the ceiling with debris. In addition, I saw we'd been "storing" items among the trees of the farm's several small, wooded areas: broken beds and dishwashers, porcelain sinks and toilets. And just plain trash, sprawling piles of it. It was heartbreaking to see what we do with land; even land we own.

With the support and encouragement of the other four Sisters on our leadership team, I sent out a letter to the entire congregation describing the state of our farm and asking for help in cleaning it up. I asked volunteers for guidance in studying the feasibility of a vision for its possible revitalization.

Good nuns that we were, we formed a committee and started organizing farm cleanup days. By my second year in Indiana, as many as thirty Sisters scoured the land on spring weekends and summer Saturdays, collecting trash to be hauled to a real dump, emptying the pump house, storing salvageable items by category in the large garage. Retired Sisters sat on metal folding chairs in the emptied and swept butcher house rolling baling twine and talking about gardening. At the end of each cleanup day, we gathered in the rustic pump house for prayer and song. We wanted to bless the land anew.

As a leadership team, we had no clear vision for the revitalization of the farm. A major portion had been sold for a housing subdivision as the town expanded. Homes were built on lush pastureland. We were gradually destroying farmland, land we'd bent our hearts and backs to, land that had fed our congregation, students, and orphans for over a century.

And then Sister Miriam MacGillis, Dominican Sister and founder of Genesis Farm, showed up. She was scheduled to be the keynote speaker at an upcoming regional meeting of Sisters in leadership of almost twenty congregations whose headquarters were located in Michigan and Indiana. Sister Joan and I made plans to attend.

I had read about Sister Miriam's work of reenvisioning a mission for an old dairy farm her congregation had inherited in the Delaware

Water Gap region of western New Jersey. She had begun by studying the evolution of the universe and Earth for an entire year with cultural historian and Catholic priest Father Thomas Berry, PhD, and then set about researching community supported agriculture (CSA) as well as organic farming. An art teacher by training, she turned her talents to teaching the art of Earth Literacy, a twelve-week graduate-level course she designed. Genesis Farm was the campus, its farmhouse the living quarters for eight to twelve students, most being Sisters discerning about a ministry change to care for Earth. I was thrilled to have an opportunity to hear her in person.

Her full-time ministry was to oversee the 150-acre Genesis Farm, which fed over a hundred families with weekly harvested vegetables and fruit, all grown with composted natural fertilizer and without pesticides and herbicides. She worked with the farm's five gardeners. She saved heirloom seeds, organized vegetarian cooking classes, and gathered friends for solstice and equinox celebrations. She taught the story of the universe as the most compelling context for discerning humanity's role in Earth's community of life, including how to care for a farm.

Miriam also lectured widely. This afternoon, in a motherhouse in Donaldson, Indiana, in a room full of leaders from congregations in Indiana and Michigan, she began by hanging a well-worn poster from the podium. It was the NASA photo of Earth from space. "This is you," she said.

She was short with silver-gray hair. Talking, she tilted her head as if listening. Pointing to Earth she continued: "This is what we all breathe, eat, and drink. This is where we pray, celebrate children's birthdays, and bury our parents.

"*Here* is where we experience the Divine, thrill to the mystery of life, drop bomb after bomb on each other and on rivers and gardens, on other animals and plants," she said, uncannily echoing the most cherished and well-guarded convictions of my heart. "Earth is home. Earth is primary," she insisted. "Without it, we don't exist.

"However," she continued, "we behave as though what *we* do is primary, and Earth is secondary. We design our governments, laws, and educational systems to enable us to continue to exploit the gifts of Earth. We treat Earth as if it exists to provide resources for us to use in whatever way we want. Not so. Earth is primary," she said, pointing to the poster reverently.

Her melodic voice softened, and she sounded like the holiest spiritual guide you've ever had.

"*Earth* is primary," she repeated, "and our religions, our politics, our economics, our agricultural, educational, and health care systems are in fact all derived from Earth and depend on Earth." Again, she dipped her hand toward the lovely planet glistening within black space.

Of course. At some level, I knew this. We all knew this, but rarely, if ever, acknowledged it, or lived fully what it implies.

"Therefore, everything we do, what we eat, how we heat our homes, the kind of cars we drive, our insurance policies, whom we vote for, *everything* must be judged by whether it harms or enhances the whole Earth community. Because Earth is primary. Caring for our families, teaching in schools, working in parishes, all of it is engaged with *Earth*, and must be judged by how it affects Earth."

Miriam had moved in front of the podium and pointed again to Earth. "So, where to start?" she asked. "Pick one thing, anything. Your water. Learn where it comes from, how it's contaminated and by whom, and what exactly is done to it to make it safe to drink. Or learn about your food supply. Or find out where your trash goes. What are you leaving for the next generation to clean up?

"Reexamine your congregational mission statements, priorities, and goals. And budgets; especially your budgets. Do they reflect the fact that Earth is primary? Are they energized by awe and respect for a sacred planet? What are you as leaders doing to foster a healthy planet for future life, all life?"

When she finished, I did something I never, ever have done. I am always too shy to approach a speaker. This time I hurried to the podium during the applause and waited last in line. When I got my turn, I said, "That was wonderful. We have a run-down farm. Can you help us?"

We walked over to lunch together, planning. She offered to come to Oldenburg, walk our farm with me, and discuss possibilities. She said she would be happy to provide an evening of conversation with the farm committee and any Sisters who wished to come. She recommended hiring Jesuit Father Al Fritsch, a Kentucky farmer and scientist and the founder of the nonprofit Appalachia—Science in the Public Interest, to assess the farm's potential and resources, from buildings to reservoirs to pastures. I was so excited I could barely eat.

Waiting for the afternoon session to begin, I ignored conversation around me. Instead, I mused, staring out the window into a wash of autumn color. If I took what Miriam said seriously, it followed then that Jesus's command to love your neighbor as being your very self is rooted in a *planet*. Earth is neighbor, is self, and is us. To love Earth is to love ourselves, and our children, and the everywhere neighbor as our selves. To poison water, strip the mountains, contaminate bodies of fish with mercury, and savage the climate is to impoverish ourselves and our children, and cruelly burden them. To violate the planet is to violate our very selves, and our children. No one really wants to do that.

But we do. Primarily for money and profit.

I knew by heart the words of Saint John in his first letter to the early Christian communities: how can you claim to love God whom you cannot see if you hurt the brother and sister whom you do see? (1 John 4:20) Here I am, seeing Earth, always seeing Earth. Saint Francis saw Earth as "our sister Mother Earth," our *sister*. It's all one love: Earth, others, self, and God.

Most of that night, I couldn't sleep, didn't want to sleep.

Finally, after twenty-five years as a vowed Sister of St. Francis and serving in inner-city and Crow and Northern Cheyenne schools and parishes, I was able to admit what I'd kept secret, sometimes even from myself. I had sought to give my life and heart to loving God and serving God's beloved, especially people who are economically poor. Yet I was nagged by another love, a love that didn't seem compatible with dedication to God. This. I'd loved Earth first and with my whole heart and soul. I'd loved the body and spirit of a planet.

I wanted to live my vows wholeheartedly. And I was, well, restless. I often wondered what would capture my heart. Could God? I wanted to fall in love, where the bottom falls out from everything and you either fly or die.

My eyes were wide as I stared at a blank ceiling in a guest room in Donaldson. I had to admit this had happened. Not in a vaulted chapel with stained-glass images of Jesus, Mary, and the saints. Not during hypnotic early morning prayer vigils. Not while singing hymns in exquisite harmonies that could break the very heart of God. Not then.

But on a narrow, rock-lined road high in the Beartooth Mountains of Montana, mountains rising to thirteen thousand feet on my left, sky plunging deep into a glacier-carved valley on my right. Round a bend, cushions of brilliant blue alpine forget-me-nots and gem-clear lakes glistening below snowbanks clinging to mica and granite cliffs.

To dedicate myself to anything smaller, less thrilling than *this* seemed impossible. I stood up from kneeling to smell those flowers and said to YES to heart-stopping love for beauty, for Earth.

Finally, bolstered by Sister Miriam's clarity, I could claim it. I love Earth. I love the body and spirit of a planet. I love the air of a winter night, the brassy shine of sun on a mountain stream. I love Earth when weather is dangerous and when wildflowers bloom. I love Earth in the liquid song of a meadowlark, the sting of a bee, the light of the full moon. I love this planet. Unreasonably. I knew right then I wanted to be the kind of Sister that Sister Miriam was.

Familiar self-doubts rose. Alone in the dark, I wrestled with my thoughts and feelings, with myself. This Earth love distracted me from loving God. It seemed abnormal even, its energies and passion illegitimate. I doubted that love for the planet could have an acceptable place in the spiritual life. At best, it could possibly fit with praising God for the gifts of creation. At worst, it could create a divided heart that worshipped God in creation.

I'd learned of the heresy of pantheism, adoring creation as God. I'd accepted that this must be avoided at all times. I had decided to steel myself against this seductive evil and wholeheartedly embrace the teachings, prayers, and spiritual practices that cast the physical Earth as a place of exile and suffering apart from God. Heaven, in its privilege as the dwelling place of God above and beyond Earth, is the true home of the soul.

Still wide awake, my thoughts were darting everywhere. As a

young Sister in Kansas City, I'd struggled to withstand the seemingly spiritual attraction I felt in snowfall, in pigeons wheeling against a blazing sunset, and the sight of cracked asphalt glistening with rain. Walking the few steps from school to convent, I'd stop to bask in whatever caught and refreshed an exhausted teacher. And then hurry on, late again for community prayer.

Back in the sixties and seventies, I was vaguely aware of rising peril to life from industrial pollution and the nuclear arms race. I knew species were going extinct at an accelerating rate and somehow accepted that as a sad normal. I missed entirely the tidal wave of awareness and political resolve unleashed by Rachel Carson's 1962 *Silent Spring*. The historic Clean Air Act (1963), Clean Water Act (1972), Endangered Species Act (1973), and Wilderness Act (1964) passed unnoticed by me, the Sisters I lived with, and my family. I might as well have been living in another country.

And now there's Sister Miriam, who's acutely aware of the increased challenges to Earth's life and dedicating her life to exploring and creating solutions. I toss and turn, sleep evading me. What am I to do?

The next morning during the drive home I was pouring all this out to Joan, the other Council member who had attended this meeting. I was trying to convince myself that to love a planet is all right, maybe even normal. Sister Miriam MacGillis had placed care for Earth front and center on the desk of her life. Could I?

I was so emotional about it all that I was crying, trying to explain things to Joan between sobs and wiping my nose.

"I've never heard anybody preach about it in church, Marya," Joan said, looking at me from the driver's seat, "but I think it's a good thing to love the Earth."

Years later I'd look back on that drive with her and realize that was when my great life shift began. Like an earthquake that starts with the merest crack deep within Earth's crust and radiates upward to shake down mountains, drop the sea floor, unleash a tsunami. This shift in me radiated relentlessly through my heart and soul, calling every cherished belief into question, into the scrutiny of that great question: does this harm or protect and foster Earth's life community? It would mean judging every ministry I chose, every lifestyle decision, every prayer I prayed and hymn I sang in the light of that question. It was exhilarating, depressing, and exhausting. But I sensed I couldn't give it up. Because of that love.

"I think it's a good thing to love the Earth," Joan repeated.

I settled into the seat of the car, stared out the window at Indiana farmland, and let it all sink in. Miriam doesn't separate *anything* from everything else. Caring for the planet is not one more item on every Sister's already overlong "to do" list. Our treatment of the planet is embedded within every item on the list. It *is* the list.

Consequently, the farm committee and I set about convincing a congregation of Franciscan Sisters that it is indeed a "service of God and youth" to reclaim our farm, restore the barn, garden organically, and raise grass-fed, grass-finished cattle. Miriam came as promised and walked the land with us and Paul Wissel, the aging man who had been our last farmer. As we walked, she sprouted ideas. That evening she hung her poster and gave her talk to over two hundred assembled Sisters. In the course of two hours she managed to persuade us to move forward. Even those Sisters who worried about limited finances for our other ministries were willing to give the farm a new try. Many of the elderly Sisters had grown up on farms and they cherished the land, grieving its neglect and loss. Some had enjoyed walks in the cleaned-up woods during their annual retreats. Others had prayed in the quiet pump house turned hermitage. Others wondered how caring for land could be authentic ministry, even a call from God.

In the end, we took a vote. Revitalizing the farm passed. Now to begin the real work.

15

Anniversary Sun Dance

There was the bush blazing,
but the bush was not being burnt up.

EXODUS 3:2–3

I had two reasons for flying to Montana. One of our most serious responsibilities as leaders was to visit the Sisters where they lived and worked. In addition, I was to give attention and support to the unique needs of Sisters serving overseas and in diverse cultures in the United States. So far, I had visited and learned from Sisters in Papua New Guinea, Mexico, and Kenya, as well as Navajo country and, once again, Crow country. Unknown to me, a third reason for my visit to Pryor and the two Sisters serving there would soon present itself.

Shortly after I arrived, Father Randolph told me that his friend Heywood Big Day wanted to meet with me. Something about a special Sun Dance Heywood was planning. I agreed and within a few days Heywood and I were sitting at the oval table that almost filled the floor space of the tiny library of St. Charles Mission School. Heywood still fired up his rocks for a sweat several times a week and was still the language and cultural consultant for Father Randolph, who was learning to speak Crow.

That afternoon Heywood began by saying it was good we could meet because he had been working on a plan to "put up" a Fiftieth Anniversary Crow Indian Sun Dance that summer in Pryor. He wanted to commemorate what his father, William, had done in 1941. I had no idea why he arranged this meeting to tell me this.

"You know about why my father brought the Sun Dance back to us Crows?"

"Father Randolph told me," I said. "But I'd like to hear more from you." Heywood nodded.

He told me how as an infant, he had been sickly for weeks, steadily losing weight. A doctor diagnosed double pneumonia. His desperate father, William, did the traditional prayer for healing. He undressed his tiny son and carried his limp body out into the crisp March mountain air. He held him up to the sky, greeting the rising sun as he prayed to the One Divine Being, "If you let my boy live, I promise to bring the Sun Dance back to my people."

It was a massive vow. The baby grew stronger and now he was sitting at an oval table in the St. Charles School library.

Two years later, in the summer of 1941, William brought the most sacred ceremony of the Plains tribes back to Crow country. Forbidden by the US government and disparaged by Christian missionaries, there had been no Crow Sun Dance since 1875. Even in 1941 US authorities could have intervened. Instead, the Sun Dance proceeded peacefully and since then continued to attract more participants every year.

To my surprise, Heywood pulled the sleeve of his shirt to his elbow and placed his dark forearm next to my pale arm. "Even though our skin is very different, and you are not Crow," he said, "every door in this valley is open to you."

Although startled, I nodded.

"You probably know that on the third and final morning of the Sun Dance, four women bring the dancers the water that ends their fast. They have not had anything to eat or drink for three days and nights. They have been dancing. It will be very hot at that time, the full moon in July. The women who bring in the water must be elders and have respect for Crow traditional ways. I would like you to be one of the women. Mary Lou will help you."

Shocked, I stifled a gasp. This seemed beyond me. I was forty-six. I was hardly an elder. On the other hand, I respect and cherish what I know of Crow traditional ways. I let the invitation shudder through me. I'd hung around the periphery of other Sun Dances, awed by their majesty, the sacrifices of the dancers, the ability of leaders to re- member innumerable details of healing rituals, songs, and restric- tions as well as the overarching flow of a ceremony that heals people and realigns a universe disturbed by human ignorance, negligence, and pillage.

Heywood sat back in his chair, pulled the sleeve down to his wrist, and waited for my reply.

"Of course," I said slowly. "I feel humbled that you are asking me to do this. It's an honor, I know. I will need a lot of help and guidance about what to do and what to not do. I know Mary Lou will be my best teacher for this."

"Thank you, Sister." We shook hands. After he had gone, I sat alone in the library for a while, letting the import of Heywood's re- quest sink in. That evening the Sisters invited Randolph over for dinner. "This is very significant that Heywood asked you to be one of the four women."

"I'm already nervous," I said. "I know you'll help me with this."

When the day came in July, I rose before dawn and put on the royal blue long-sleeved dress cut in traditional Crow style that Gwennie had given me when she and Larry adopted me as their daughter. A wide beaded belt and high white moccasins beaded with flowers and the distinctive necklace of my clan completed the outfit.

I heard a car horn in the driveway. Time to go. Holding the new galvanized water bucket and ladle that Mary Lou had brought to the convent the day before, I soon was sitting stiff and erect in Randolph's car. He turned down the familiar rutted road leading to the Sun Dance lodge, across Pryor Creek from the Big Day home.

"Heywood has been doctoring people almost constantly since things began," Randolph told me. "And a couple hundred more people have shown up for the closing today." He shook his head. "It's a lot of responsibility."

The three other Water Women had already assembled at the entrance to the Big Lodge with Mary Lou. We waited for instructions. Nearby was a pickup loaded with four large brand-new galvanized trash cans.

At a signal from Mary Lou, the three elders and I crowded into the pickup with her. Heywood Jr. was driving. Several other young men jumped into the pickup bed with the trash cans. Junior put the truck in gear and we lurched forward, rumbled across the wooden plank bridge over Pryor Creek, and bounced down the lane to the paved road. From there it was a short drive to Chief Plenty Coups State Park. The cans clanged against each other as the truck drove across a meadow of high, uncut grasses and white wildflowers to Chief Plenty Coups's spring, beside his former home and store.

Out of the pickup, we stood together on wet, slick mud at the edge of a clear pool of water surrounded by tall cottonwood trees. The spring gurgled from under rocks and tree roots. One by one each woman, leaning heavily on Junior, stooped stiffly to fill her dipper with water and pour it into her bucket. I waited until last, careful to imitate how they paused to pray before dipping water from the spring.

The sky, immense and blue, spread over the cottonwoods and spring. The grasses and flowers dipped in a dawn breeze gently. Silence engulfed us, brushed lightly by the leathery whispering of cottonwood leaves.

We stepped back from the spring. Using our buckets, the young men quickly filled the trash cans and hefted them into the bed of the pickup. Mary Lou told Junior to drive slowly.

"Heywood is in no hurry," she said.

Back at the lodge, we lined up and waited barefooted at the entrance. It was still early morning, but the sun was already warm on the back of my neck. Then, at a signal from Mary Lou, we four women walked slowly inside to the center of the lodge.

The sacred privilege of this moment took my breath away.

Most of the 104 men and women were leaning weakly against poles beside their resting mats. Some were lying down. During the fast many of them had been dancing for hours in the heat. They filled the lodge with prayer and suffering. I'd just walked into it, a furnace of supplication that embraced the needs of the Crow, all people, the whole world, the universe.

We lined up behind Heywood. He stood beside the thick tree

trunk center pole that supports the roof rafters of the lodge, which is open to the sky. His arms were outstretched, facing the Big Lodge door, facing east, facing the fiery sun. Eagle feathers hung from his wrists.

Young men hefted and dragged the brimful cans into the lodge. Water splashed. Heywood prayed in Crow, giving thanks for water and for women who give birth with water. Exhausted from the fasting and doctoring he'd done, he nonetheless continued his long and final prayer, faithfully holding back a flood of thirst with words, clearing a path to freedom for his people.

The bright colors of fasters' blankets, skirts, woven belts, and calico dresses began to blur in my sight. There was no breeze here, only heat and Heywood's barely audible prayer filling the lodge. I stared past him, through the smoke of cleansing fires, into full sunlight. It poured across the prairie into the lodge and surrounded me.

Then I saw that I wasn't simply standing in sunlight. Sunlight filled me, drew me back to Sun. I became one with Sun. I then saw the animals and plants, rivers and oceans, mountains, the Pryor valley, all of us, in that light, all one in Sun. Every separation I had ever learned evaporated. The spun web of creation was flowing here, in that radiance, trembling on the rise and fall of Heywood's prayer.

Someone was pulling at my sleeve, pointing to one of the water cans and the quadrant of fasters I was to serve. I knelt before the first man. Shaking, I handed him the ladle, precious water dripping.

I moved slowly. Men down the line leaned forward and urged me to go faster. "We're thirsty, Sister!" I snapped to my work, regretting I had lingered.

Their prayer finished, bodies revived by even just swallows of water, the dancers, one by one, rolled up their bedding and walked like the newly resurrected out of the lodge. I stood aside watching them, arms at my sides, ladle dripping from my hand. Heywood was the last to leave.

The great Big Lodge stood empty, but full and silent.

The sun was high then, a dome of glory over lines of people on either side of long tables laden with platters of cut watermelon, apples, oranges, grapefruit, and whole bananas. Ice cubes and slices of lemon swam in shining glasses of water. The murmur of life rose like water from a deep spring.

I sat down at a table to eat with Heywood, Mary Lou, and their family. As we finished, Randolph caught my eye and signaled he would drive me back to the convent. I didn't know how to return to that world. I didn't know how to speak of what I had seen. Or if I even was permitted to. All I could know then was vivid memory of that timeless quiet in the vibrating lodge, seeing the Great Oneness that flowed across millennia and welcomed me, held me in the circle of life, of Earth.

16

Sister Claire Acts

No one lights a lamp and puts it under a tub;
they put it on the lamp-stand.

LUKE 11:33

She surprised me. "What?" I asked. "You would like to move to Michaela Farm and work there?"

Sister Claire Whalen had served as professor and chair of the Education Department and then academic dean of Marian College, now Marian University, in Indianapolis. She was the director of ongoing education for Sisters of my community. As director, she'd convinced me almost twenty years before to seek an advanced degree during the heat of the Cold War.

She was short, wiry, and energetic, with a full shock of attractive white hair. Her smile could sway a crowd, although that's superfluous to her mind-bending knowledge, logic, and passionate wisdom. She'd just completed a sabbatical and wanted to create a new position at our renamed Michaela Farm. She would call it education program director. Because she was past our retirement age, she would work as a volunteer.

She would live with other Sisters in community and not need a salary or stipend. She also wanted to plant trees, thousands of them.

"And I think I could help organize an internship program," she added. "I didn't grow up on a farm, but I'm from the Victory garden era. Throughout my life, wherever I could have a little garden, I did."

I submitted her proposal to create a position of education program director for Michaela Farm at our next monthly Council meeting. I shared that Claire would apply for that position. We all realized Claire would bring considerable, needed skills to the commitment to revitalizing the farm.

She began her new ministry "in service of our sister Mother Earth," in 1993 and set about accomplishing all she'd envisioned, beginning with educational programs that included assisting the farm's director, Sister Anita Brelage, with the intern program. In 1997 she helped launch a formal internship program. Throughout the following six years twenty-one young women and men were welcomed as interns and instructed by farm and farmer, including Sister Anita Brelage, Sister Donna Graham, and Sister Claire. Interns learned farming and gardening skills, contributed articles to the farm's weekly newsletter, and discovered the inevitable challenges and rewards of community living.

During this time Claire oversaw the planting of twenty-two acres of trees in the farm's unused fields. In a woods severely damaged by wind, young saplings were skirted with tree protectors. Claire initiated a donor tree program. People from all over donated trees and protectors in memory of loved ones. Claire kept maps of where donor trees were located. "You can visit your dad's tree," she told me, "a redbud near the hermitage just beyond the reservoirs."

Claire researched farm soils. True to her background as a geographer, she developed extensive maps of the multiple farm buildings and gardens, soils, woodlots, and farm boundaries, as well as walking trails for enjoyment and meditation. She orchestrated the production of a farm video, guiding viewers through land and animals, teaching at every step.

Recognizing the inherent beauty of Michaela Farm, she worked with farm staff and interns to repaint the sheds and plant flowers and vegetable gardens in farm yards that had been neglected for decades. Throughout the 1990s Michaela Farm grew into a place that provided food for twenty to thirty families and the motherhouse community of over a hundred Sisters. Restored and fruitful beauty served to widen and energize Claire's personal vision and sense of mission.

As Claire learned more about the benefits of local, sustainable agriculture, she became determined to find a way to provide fresh vegetables for those who could not afford that "luxury." In 2001, she approached formal associations of clergy women and men serving in various churches in two neighboring towns, Batesville and Brookville, Indiana, to procure matching funds for a grant she had requested from the Dominican Sisters of Springfield, Illinois. They agreed. With these combined funds she bought fresh produce from Michaela Farm and, within three years, from several other farms. Christened Share the Bounty, the program provided nutritious food during the growing season as well as cooking classes for low-income families in three nearby towns and surrounding areas.

Claire kept detailed paperwork and financial records of the program, tracking produce purchases and distribution. She collaborated with Kathy Cooley, a dietician at nearby Margaret Mary Community Hospital, and with women in Brookville who worked with low-income families through the county extension office. They taught Share the

Bounty cooking classes and assisted with identifying families that qualified for the program.

By 2005 the Share the Bounty farmer and community service networking effort sparked another grassroots group, the Food and Growers Association (FGA). Gathered and encouraged by Claire, this group focused its energies on an enhanced farmers' market in Batesville. FGA also encouraged a CSA program. Claire accepted the leadership of FGA, but soon passed it on to Kathy Cooley.

Encouraged by members of the newly formed Food and Growers Association, Claire organized a multifarm cooperative during the spring of 2006. By June the Laughery Valley Growers Cooperative (LVG) of eight local farmers was packing thirty CSA boxes for local subscribers. The co-op named this direct-market venture FarmFresh CSA.

During this time, I learned some of the benefits of the CSA system. Primarily, it gives individuals and families the opportunity to purchase shares of locally grown produce from growers at the start of the growing season, paying an initial flat rate for their weekly box of produce. Throughout the season shareholders and growers alike absorb the risks of low yields and the happy benefits of bumper crops. Some CSAs arrange a bartering system with shareholders, who exchange hours of work in gardens for a reduction in the cost of their shares. A CSA grows local community.

Claire continued to cultivate the multifarm cooperative, now called Laughery Valley Growers. By 2010 its popular CSA was distributing a hundred boxes of fresh vegetables, salad greens, berries, and fruit each week to customers from Batesville, Indiana, to Cincinnati, Ohio. Claire also continued to secure donations from the Batesville Area Ministerial Association. These funds purchased fresh produce from additional co-op growers to help stock the food pantry operated by local churches. Throughout these years, Michaela Farm was a co-op member and significant supplier for the CSA.

All of these projects demanded hours of bookkeeping, planning, and coordination of growers, packers, distributers, and volunteers. But Claire didn't stop there. She developed recipes for the FarmFresh CSA newsletters that were tucked into shareholders' boxes. Readers also learned about their growers and farms, as well as the nutritional and environmental benefits of eating locally grown food. The newsletter was made available on the co-op's website along with many recipes for making delicious meals with CSA box contents: vegetable casseroles, salads, and salsas. The 2013 FarmFresh CSA had eighty-four subscribers.

"I always have my ears and eyes open for what will benefit our growers," Claire said during a visit with her. "I like to learn and I like to share what I learn." She learned that Christ Hospital in Cincinnati wanted to give its employees the chance to purchase CSA boxes. A deal was struck, beneficial to growers and hospital employees: weekly boxes of produce were delivered to employees at the hospital throughout the growing season.

Watching the miracles Claire had managed to bring about, I sensed that something profound drove her. Could it be human dignity: farmers, growers, people, and families who need to eat? Could it be her attunement to the demands of integrity and justice? Could it be a vision of moral beauty, a genuine Franciscan vision that embraces Earth and people with love? I suspected all three, and as her perennial intern, I continued to learn from her as I finished my leadership ministry and sought to discern how to serve the Earth I loved.

17

Reinventing Myself

Search and you will find.

MATTHEW 7:7

Unknown to Claire, her actions activated my resolve to serve Earth in ministry. Our leadership team would be completing our second term of office on July 1 of that year. What was next for me? Where would God's call and the needs of the world lead me? In the spring of 1994, I began to make my own plans for a sabbatical.

Initially, however, I reverted to an old dream I had to do advanced study in sacred scripture. I even considered that such a degree could lead to more study and eventual ordination in a Christian denomination other than Roman Catholic.

I chose the best school of theology I knew, Catholic Theological Union in Chicago. It had some of the best scripture and theology professors on its faculty, and its program included a semester in Palestine. I submitted my application of material and waited for a reply.

I found the letter in my mailbox outside my office just as I was heading down to the noon meal. I tore open the envelope, my heart pounding. I continued walking slowly down the long corridor of tall windows that opened above a courtyard. I stopped to read the letter. Directly across from me and built into the opposite wall of the courtyard was a shrine with a life-size statue of Saint Francis. It represented a tradition that supported me and my discernment.

My hands trembled as I unfolded the letter and read, "Congratulations. We are pleased to welcome you . . ."

Suddenly frozen, I felt the walls and ceiling closing in. I couldn't breathe. Shock. Disbelief at my reaction. Why wasn't I thrilled? Why wasn't I running to joyfully tell my colleagues? In an instant I knew. This was wrong. It was not my path, not my calling. I sensed that the "church ministry" part of my life was over.

Within a week I wrote to the Theological Union declining its invitation into its program. I received a reply expressing disappointment and assuring me a space if I changed my mind. That month I attended a workshop on global issues sponsored by the UN and Global Education Associates, a nonprofit founded by friends Gerry and Patricia Mische. Many speakers at the conference emphasized concern about the degradation of the environment. Sister Miriam MacGillis was among them. While there, I picked up a brochure about a master's program offered by a school I had never heard of: the California Institute of Integral Studies. I was drawn to the school because it featured science, environmental, and feminist professors whose works had long inspired me. In addition, there were several courses about the history and nature of the universe.

I knew I needed some personal discernment time to settle my soul, to be in a familiar place among friends to think, to ponder the direction of my future. While in leadership, our team had worked with a group of Crow and Northern Cheyenne women who wished to create a safe and quiet place for women to pray, to share their stories and learn from each other, to deepen their experience and knowledge of their traditional ways, to become more confident as parents. A Northern Cheyenne woman, Carolyn Martin, and her daughter, April Martin Chalfont, donated four acres of land on their ranch. The Sisters of St. Francis purchased a seventy-by-fourteen-foot mobile home from another of Carolyn's daughters, Misty, and the women's center—named Prayer Lodge by the founding women—became a reality. Perched on a hillside in a wide valley that sloped to the Rosebud Mountains along the eastern horizon, with the Wolftooth Mountains to the south, it provided a homey place that fulfilled the women's dreams.

What better place for my own discernment? I wrote Sister Mary Ann Stoffregen, the resident director, to ask to come for several months. By the end of July, I was sitting on the south-facing deck, daily praying as the sun rose on cool mornings and at night under a canopy of stars and the Milky Way. By day I visited friends, especially Vonda Limpy and her family, and helped with the household chores.

I gradually discerned my next step. Sensing I wasn't ready for the California Institute program, I contacted the organization that had cosponsored the global issues program with the UN, Global Education Associates (GEA) in New York City. I asked to work as a volunteer intern for the coming calendar year, 1995. Sister Sharon Fritsch, the office manager, wrote to welcome me. I felt excited and could leave Prayer Lodge with a peaceful heart.

In January I moved in with two other Sisters in an apartment in East Harlem. To my surprise, I was energized by life in New York

City. Encouraged by the two Sisters with whom I lived, both native New Yorkers, I took long walks in nearby Central Park in every season, learned the transit and subway system, went to plays with friends from work, and visited the city's many museums.

I was learning new skills as I did research for grant applications for GEA. Many of their programs focused on global environmental issues. My work included following Gerry and Pat around the UN as they attended lectures or participated in panels on the global links between poverty, environmental degradation, and lack of education, especially for girls. Dr. Pat Mische, who was a codirector, became my mentor, helping me formulate convincing responses for numerous grant applications. She was a formidable editor. By spring, I was applying for admittance into the Philosophy, Cosmology, and Consciousness program of the California Institute of Integral Studies. When that letter of acceptance arrived, I was truly thrilled, and happy. And in January 1996, I moved from East Harlem to San Francisco.

Over the next two and a half years in the program, I studied the universe and cosmology, bioregionalism, deep ecology, global economic systems, and feminist spirituality. As graduation time approached, I knew that I could not return to a ministry position within the institutional church. As I prayed, the words "Earth Hope" surfaced within me.

I began to shape plans of what a ministry of Earth Hope could entail: research, teaching, writing, gardening, and a slow, consistent turn toward a lifestyle that uses fewer of Earth's gifts. I would attempt to live an "Earth is primary" way of life. From afar I relied on Sister Miriam Therese MacGillis, Father Thomas Berry, and Sister Claire, learning from what they were teaching and, above all, doing.

I followed my heart and an invitation back to Northern Cheyenne country. In 1998, after completing my sabbatical studies, I was delighted that the women of the Prayer Lodge board asked me to join them in working to realize one of their goals: to live in a good way with Mother Earth. I saw that serving their goal could be part of my Earth Hope calling.

I felt privileged to work with the women of the Prayer Lodge board. Ever attentive to their goal, I did research with them and helped initiate plans and fundraising for wind and solar energy systems, ground-source heating and cooling, the construction of a greenhouse, a water catchment system, and native prairie restoration. Guided by their innate respect for life and Mother Earth, I was finding my way into service of our beloved Sister.

In addition, while living at Prayer Lodge, I gradually developed Earth Hope ministry by offering Earth-care spirituality workshops and retreats nationwide at retreat centers whose directors knew me from my studies or years in leadership. Sister Miriam MacGillis invited me to be on staff annually for eight years during eight weeks of the Earth Literacy master's degree program at Genesis Farm in New Jersey. I worked with spirituality aspects of the program. I facilitated rituals and prayer based on the Universe Story and principles of ecology. I continued to learn from Miriam's lectures about sustainable farming while I enjoyed daily delicious vegetarian meals prepared from Genesis Farm's produce. The cook, Laura Greenspan, was an accomplished artist with vegetables, spices, and herbs. I began to see links between what I had learned on sabbatical and while working in the Earth Literacy program with my responsibilities at Prayer Lodge: to live in a good way with Mother Earth. I felt so lucky to be called to this ministry: Earth Hope.

Part V

Earth's Hope,
to Reinvent the Human

18

A New, True Name

He freed me, set me at large, because he loves me.

PSALMS 18:19

S
o, when are you getting here?" my close friend, Vonda Limpy, asked over the phone. "Francis and I will be coming over to Prayer Lodge to help you move in." I couldn't wait to see her and her husband. I had called her immediately after arriving at Prayer Lodge.

So many long talks together, sometimes sitting on a blanket in tall grass by a stream, sometimes at her kitchen table, sometimes during long afternoons in her living room waiting for grandchildren to roar in from school, and always when cooking together, in her kitchen or in the mountainside camp at Bear Butte while Francis was higher up on the mountain alone, fasting and praying.

"We sure fed lots of people on that mountainside. We shared lots of good thoughts when we cooked together there at Bear Butte. We put our prayer into the cooking and that made the cooking and the food extra good! We did a lot of dishes and cleaning up, too. We had lots of obstacles like wind and rain. Remember how a sudden storm blew your pancakes right off the griddle?! And our son Rocky chased them down, put them on plates with bacon; and people ate in their cars. No matter what, people liked coming for the prayers. And to be together there in that good place. They probably liked our cooking, too." We sat quietly, just remembering.

We were careful to observe spiritual practices while camping during Francis's fast. This included doing every task with slow deliberation. No rushing or running around. When I started to vigorously shake out a tablecloth in the wind, Vonda reminded me, "Gently brush off crumbs while it's still on the table."

Francis had asked Charles Little Old Man, a veteran of many fasts, to guide him. Charles's wife, Marcelline, was camping with us, along with their preschool-age adopted son, Clayton, and a puppy. Clayton and the puppy were a lively combination. One day when they got too rowdy, Marcelline walked over to say to Clayton, "Son, your legs forgot." He looked puzzled as he studied his legs, trying to figure out what they'd forgotten. "Remember," she said, "we don't run here. It stirs up the spirits and makes it harder for Francis to pray and fast." I felt a spirit of wisdom come over me as I learned these things.

In the evenings when the camp chores were finished, Vonda, Marcelline, and I would spread our blankets on the ground facing the mountain and pray for Francis, and for Charles, and for all our family members, and finally for the world.

Those days, we all prayed for the removal of the many intercontinental ballistic missiles that were planted along the highways of Montana and the Dakotas. We pictured them being popped out of the ground, the silos empty. And eventually the government removed them. The sacrifice Francis offered—fasting from food and water—and our prayers on blankets as night lit stars and the long slope of Bear Butte seemed to encompass half the planet, those prayers helped bring more peace to the world.

Now that I was back in Northern Cheyenne country, I looked forward to picking up on those conversations and prayers.

So, one late summer morning, I called her and invited myself over. "I'll bring lunch," I said. I made venison dry-meat soup with potatoes, a cucumber salad using my mom's recipe, and brownies. Vonda likes miniature tangerines, so I picked up a bag from the store.

It's almost twenty miles from Prayer Lodge to Lame Deer, then another several miles out of town into the foothills of the Rosebud Mountains. I turned up their familiar rocky, rutted lane. Their home is nestled in a swath of grass, guarded by tall ponderosa pines. Rose and yellow rock etched the top of the slope. The trees I had helped plant almost fifteen years before, when I first arrived in Lame Deer, had grown noticeably in the several years I'd been gone.

Francis's garden had been harvested: corn stalks down, potatoes dug, beans and tomatoes long gone. A hoe rested against the gate, looking a bit relieved. Beside the garden were logs from fire-killed trees. Soon they would be sawed and split for winter warmth.

I parked just below the house and climbed the steep grade to the cement slab reserved for their vehicles: his green pickup, her gray van. Ducking under an arbor of honeysuckle branches, I climbed cement steps to a sheltered porch.

Here a table was stacked neatly with an assortment of camping gear: a cookstove, a propane tank, two red coolers on wheels, and several big metal pots covered with battered lids. Under the table was a box of waking and wobbly kittens, looking at me as if they'd never seen a human before. And on a bench opposite, a pair of well-worn work gloves, a doll with raven-black hair, and one big rock, perhaps for use in the sweat lodge. A child's pink bike rested against one end of the bench.

A wind chime of wooden bees hung from the edge of the roof above the bench, clanking in the breeze. Everyone called her father "Bee." That little swarm of bees was a way she kept her dad close to her, she often told me. Under the bench stood a pair of boy's cowboy boots among a scatter of balls, a bat, and a coil of lasso rope. A wreath of metal dragonflies hung on the door. Her helpers, the sight of them strengthened her. I knocked.

"It's open," she called. And I walked into that warmth and her hug. "Now sit down."

Francis popped open a hissing can of Pepsi, his favorite drink, and handed it to me. "Or would you like peppermint tea?" I sipped the drink gratefully.

I noticed that this time the TV was in a corner opposite the pellet stove. Two rockers and two modest recliners circled the oak coffee table. Everything in the house was chosen for function and durability—grandchildren were frequently here—except for the graceful candelabra lamp that swung overhead, encased in glass panes etched with flowers. The delicate bulbs were shaped like flames.

"Fix her some hot tea," Vonda said, "she likes it better than your Pepsi. And bring over the honey. Not just yourself! You know what I mean."

Then came the stories about children and grandchildren: who

played basketball last year, which one is set to graduate this year, who loves to read, who doesn't. Trish finished cosmetology school in Billings and now has three children; Justin and Smiley are determined "to rodeo."

"Much as I don't like that, especially that bull riding, I guess they've got some of their Grandpa Bee in them." I felt the dread, too. In the four years I'd led the parish choir in Lame Deer, we sang for a bull rider's funeral almost every year. Gored or crushed under a hoof, a death not worth the occasional thrill of winning. At least that's what we older folks thought.

This easy familiarity, like being sisters. Which we are. Several years ago, when I'd come for a visit from Indiana, she'd asked me, "Will you be back this way this summer?"

I nodded.

"Good. Because I've decided to take you as my sister and I've already asked Beaver to do the ceremony. He'll give you a Cheyenne name. Summer is a good time."

How well I remember the catch in my throat, the sting in my eyes.

We hugged each other.

"It's time to make official what's been real for a long time," she continued. Francis agreed from his recliner. "Remember all those times you'd sit on the couch here, reading storybooks to kids? And all that cooking we did together? And talking. I told Beaver I was doing this because when I lost my younger sister, I got a hurt in my heart. It stayed there all these twenty years since. Then I noticed that as we got close with all that cooking and praying and visiting, that hurt eased. So, you became my sister."

Being her sister and the name I was given, Many Roads Woman, settled easily into my soul. The day of my adoption, I stood on a blanket and beautifully fringed shawl on the brow of the hill outside Prayer Lodge, circled by Vonda's family. Beaver Two Moons stood behind me, his large hands on my shoulders. He sang out that Cheyenne name as we faced east, then south, then west, then north. When he'd finished, he said, "Now the spirits will hear you and know who you are when you pray."

My prayer name was true to me. I had taken many roads: from Cincinnati to Oldenburg, then to Evansville, Kansas City, and at long last, the most desired, to Crow and Northern Cheyenne homelands. That road, replete with newness and cultural difference, was also rich with kindness, patience, and forgiveness as I stumbled awkwardly into ceremonies, teachings, and relationships. Sometimes boldly. Often shyly.

I eventually learned to slow my thinking, to listen more, to suspend judgment, and to wait for fresh insights to unfold. I'd learned to ask about protocol at the tobacco ceremony, powwows, giveaways, birthday parties, even hand games: what to wear, where to sit, when to get food. Among the Crow and Northern Cheyenne, my inner road home to Earth became more acceptable, even exhilarating.

"Hurry along the path of prudent happiness, your footsteps stirring up no dust, toward your calling from God," is how Saint Clare of Assisi described the journey into becoming the truer self, beyond and within self. For her it was a headlong rush into owning nothing and living in a cloistered community without material security, because of joy. She experienced joy in her single-hearted imitation of Jesus Christ.

I found it in Earth, right here. Earth and people, nestled in the universe.

From my studies, I'd gradually learned that all life's roads spiral round in a universe at one with itself. It all fits: galaxies, planets, living beings all interrelated. No being stands alone and isolated. All kin.

Beaver, chief of the Kit Fox Society, who chose the name, and my new sister who approved it, blessed all those roads, declaring them ME. Many Roads Woman. An old name. Beaver's mother-in-law's name. And, with his wife Ernestine's approval, now mine, too.

As I sat with Vonda and Francis, as her sister, these several years later, I knew our road together would lead home to Earth, home to our many kin. I knew we would always help and pray for each other. That's what sisters do.

"Tomorrow, let's go chokecherry picking," she was saying. Little did I realize that another learning about the depth of our kinship with all life awaited me. My unexpected teacher in this: an obscure woman who lived in another time and culture. Grandma Nellie Robinson lived a century ago, raised her children, quietly died. As it turned out, she would reach across time to teach through her granddaughter, Vonda.

"I'll bring bologna sandwiches and oranges," I said.

"I'll bring Pepsi," said Francis.

19

Grandma Nellie
and Birds

Blessed are the gentle.

MATTHEW 5:4

All species may be our relatives. We can be thunderstruck by their beauty. We are unequivocally dependent upon the entire web of life for our personal and species existence. I knew that all life was included in the Prayer Lodge goal of "living in a good way with Mother Earth." Yet what good was that knowledge if we don't feel it within us? And how do we learn or experience a *felt* kinship with all other life? How would that shape our behavior?

Late summer in Northern Cheyenne homelands, and the sweet wild plums were ripe. Beaver and Ernestine, Vonda, Francis, and I crowded into the pickup. I looked forward to picking the juicy plums. But I soon learned we didn't *pick* plums! Sharp spines on the branches made picking dangerous and painful. Instead, I helped spread tarps on the ground under the bushes. Beaver and Francis promptly began shaking them. A sudden shower of plums bounced onto the tarps; some even hit us on the head. It was wild and fun.

Shortly after, *finally*, chokecherries, ripening along streams, in roadway ditches, in draws and hollows on hillsides, wherever contours of land catch and hold moisture. A quiet migration began.

This migration is always quiet because almost nothing is as well guarded as the locations of beloved berry patches where the rewards are reliably juicy and abundant. At berry-picking time private owner-ship of land surrenders to the knowledge of sites passed from mother to daughter, remembered in detail by grandmothers whose faces today are maps of wrinkles. Except for bushes growing near homes, berries belong to the whole community.

The previous day, when we'd made our plans to go picking, Vonda had said, "Making chokecherry syrup or puddings on cold and early nights in winter will comfort my old bones." She'd made a shiver sound. I laughed.

Soon I was picking along with her daughter Brenda and several grandchildren. As I reached for the blue-purple chokecherries, the fa-miliar movements evoked memories of helping Dad pick raspberries in our Cincinnati backyard.

"Don't miss any of them," he'd say, and thinking of Mom's jam, or raspberries on cornflakes with milk, I didn't. I scrutinized every branch, grasped every single one. Here in Northern Cheyenne coun-try, I followed behind the children, stripping branches bare. We were eating our share, too. I have no liking, however, for the pungent, mouth-puckering berries and I stopped sampling after that first foray. Any comparison with raspberries had just ended.

Suddenly Vonda was picking beside us. "Is everybody remembering what Grandma Nellie taught me?" she asked. Three children and two adults with purple lips all turned to her.

As a young girl, Vonda Robinson Limpy loved spending summers up in the Muddy Creek valley, on the Robinson ranch with her grandma Nellie. No matter what tasks they did together—hanging out wash, cooking, swatting dust with a broom from a rug hung on a fence—it just felt good to be with her, to learn from her. Sitting together under a cottonwood tree at an old table, Grandma Nellie talked about canning berry syrup as they picked out stems and leaves from berries spread evenly across the table. Being with and learning from Grandma Nellie had been peaceful and fun, and adult Vonda wanted to provide that kind of Grandma Nellie time for her grandchildren.

"When I went berry picking with Grandma Nellie, she always told us to leave some of the best berries for the birds. And if you forgot to put your first big berries on the ground as an offering and thank-you to Mother Earth and the rain, you can still do that, too."

We all stopped and formed a very quiet circle among the bushes. Sifting through our buckets, we chose large berries and placed them on the ground. "Hahó," we said. "Thank you." Vonda smiled with a quick nod.

I turned back to the chokecherries. Grandma Nellie's sense of family somehow included birds. She and her rancher husband worked desperately to coax a dry, cold place in the mountains to feed their family. Despite that, or maybe because of it, in her mind and heart she lived within a communion of life that included respect for the needs of birds, something she probably learned from her grandmother. Right here among chokecherries swinging in clusters from leafy branches in the twenty-first century, I found myself in a circle of five generations of Northern Cheyenne women and girls. From within this circle, I clearly saw how my world defined everything that exists as resources for people only, and for development and profit. In the industrial world I grew up in, no wild creature was considered family. We never deliberately left the best, or any, raspberries for birds.

Today, the majority of biologists and scientists agree we are in the middle of an extinction event. Largely unnoticed and definitely underreported, this extinction event means that between fifty and one hundred species are vanishing every day, a hundred or more times faster than natural extinction rates; faster than at any time in the last 65 million years. Back then, the culprit was an asteroid that slammed into the Yucatán Peninsula. Today, the likely culprit is industrialized, climate-changing, and habitat-destroying humanity. Us.

The renowned biologist Edward O. Wilson describes the current extinction rate as "catastrophically high" and adds that at the current rate of deforestation and other forms of environmental destruction, "it is safe to say that at least a fifth of the species of plants and animals would be gone or committed to extinction by 2030 and half by the end of the century."

The magnitude of this loss of life is hard for me to grasp.

But I can reflect on that world, on our making *threadbare* the tapestry of life. In the now heavily logged eastern forests, the tiny cerulean warbler, a blue and white songbird, has declined in population by approximately 70 percent. Its song may fall silent forever within my lifetime. Will I notice?

We can try to absorb these facts or quietly tuck them away as distant tragedies. Perhaps with reflection, we can sense how our powers of imagination, creativity, and love are diminished by other species' diminishment and disappearance. Can we feel how lonely we're becoming without them, our relatives?

Rachel Carson called this loneliness a "silent spring." And hearing her, my heart felt the chill. We can imagine that silence now. No raptors lifting on thermals over my home. No prairie grass seeds flung against an autumn full moon. Could we have imagined flight on a planet without birds? What is lost in the soul of a child who never sees a meadow of wildflowers?

When Grandma Nellie was picking berries with her grandmother, she didn't know that all Earth's species emerged in an immense, slow dance from common ancestors that lived in the seas more than 3 billion years ago. Over time, Earth's climates and continental movements and predator-prey relationships endowed seeds with power to survive drought and ice, built jaws and teeth, shaped swift bodies that could swim and fly, and cherished consciousness that kept wolf pups fed.

Thanks to modern science, we have empirical evidence for what indigenous peoples, and most religions, have always known: that we are all kin, related and interdependent. In my Christian tradition, plants and animals are a sacred communion. Every year during the celebration of Pentecost we pray the words from the book of Wisdom that reverberated through my soul as a young nun: "The Spirit of the Lord fills the whole world."

Earth spins, circling a star within a galaxy of about 200 billion other stars. Pouring across the night sky with creamy beauty, the Milky Way is our familiar galactic home. Grandma Nellie's people called it Sky Road, a passage for spirit when people died. Within just the last century have we learned that the Milky Way is one of 100 billion galaxies, all streaming away from each other in a cosmic dance driven by primordial energy we call expansion. In all this grandeur we have yet to find another cerulean warbler or ancient forest or monarch butterfly or polar bear.

The warbler's song began in the middle of a star whose fierce heat forged complex chemical elements from simpler elements forged in yet an earlier star. When the second-generation star exploded as a supernova, those elements were blown into neighboring space, where another power, gravity, gathered them up over millennia into a planet. That planet would eventually bring forth from those elements the bones, muscles, and lungs of a gorgeous bird fiercely intent upon finding a mate. These same elements also formed the tuna salad you had for lunch, leaves yellowing and falling in aspen groves, fingers typing this paper, and the eyes and mind reading it. Our kinship line goes back, according to our most recent estimate, 13.8 billion years. The whole universe is one body.

Walt Whitman intuited this when he said, "A leaf of grass is no less than the journey-work of the stars." Northern Cheyenne grandmothers forged their intuition of this long and profound communion into a moral ethic. Leave some of the best berries for your other relatives.

In the Cheyenne language there is no "it." There is no "he" or "she," either. Third-person singular is instead words that specify, that speak of all others respectfully as "thou." These words translate roughly into something like "this one, that one." I try to imagine living within this language. No it. Always I-thou; *never* I-it. No inanimate or soulless beings.

The poet Mary Oliver pondered this I-thou reality. "Why should I have soul and not the camel?" she asks. "Come to think of it, what about the maple trees? What about the blue iris? What about all the little stones, sitting alone in the moonlight? What about roses, and lemons, and their shining leaves? What about the grass?" Grass!

What could awakening to self, to all ensouled beings, mean for us?

Because of the reach of human powers into all the planetary and life systems, our decisions today determine which habitats and species will make it into the next century. In *this* century, through our global economic systems that exploit the natural world, destroy forests and fisheries through overharvesting, and dangerously pollute air, water, and soil, we have become a planetary power comparable to climate, continental shift, and the predator-prey relationship. This planetary power, which we have never before had to this extent, demands of us a planet-sized soul, a planetary spirituality, something very new and challenging and promising for industrialized societies. We have mentors. Walt and Mary and Grandma Nellie. Jesus who counted sparrows. Francis of Assisi who experienced and praised God for *all* the others as humanity's brothers and sisters.

Humans, I am convinced, are born from this planet hungry, not only for milk and comfort, but also for songs: songs of warblers, the alpha female wolf, water splashing clean over stones. My dad comforted me as an infant on his shoulder, humming the chant of the Volga boatmen and holding me near the singing canaries Mom raised along with four daughters. Perhaps the universe is one great song, humming along in elements that bind us all, sounding haunting melodies that flow as ancient origin stories through grass and stones and bone.

Picking chokecherries in a late summer sun, I was simply grateful for all those berries, for a nearby flock of robins, for this summer day. Thanks to Grandma Nellie, I was leaving some of the best berries for birds, hoping that five generations from now there will still be songs in the nearby trees. And maybe even, in the continent's eastern forests, nesting cerulean warblers.

20

First Do No Harm

Prayer Lodge
Northern Cheyenne Homelands

We must join together to bring forth
a sustainable global community founded upon
respect for nature, economic justice, and a culture of peace.
THE EARTH CHARTER: VALUES AND PRINCIPLES

FOR A SUSTAINABLE FUTURE: PREAMBLE

E stablished in 1992, Prayer Lodge had become the realized dream of savvy determined women, ambitious volunteers, and generous donors. A unique setting, it provided a safe and quiet place where women of all races, cultures, and spiritual beliefs were welcomed, inspired, and empowered. It hosted cultural and art events, including learning traditional Crow and Northern Cheyenne dances, beading, moccasin making, and recipes like frybread and berry puddings. Women gathered informally to share stories, pray, cry, and laugh. It provided computer access and massage/bodywork space. It showed respect for Mother Earth through a detailed recycling system, composting table and kitchen scraps, and installing efficient, airtight windows and doors. Both Crow and Northern Cheyenne traditions teach that we are all related and at Prayer Lodge that teaching was modeled in the extended community it fostered and in the respectful ways shown toward nature.

The last Saturday of every month the board held a retreat day and women filled the tiny living room. In addition, they offered quilting classes. As the living and dining rooms became overcrowded, women sat in bedrooms to sew and visit. I taught vegetarian and low-fat cooking classes to groups of women in the cramped, galley-sized kitchen. Men of the Northern Cheyenne traditional Kit Fox Society built a sweat lodge. Society members Charles Little Old Man, Beaver Two Moons, Francis Limpy, and Tom Rockroads took turns doing the work of heating rocks and leading sweat ceremonies for all who gathered for this healing ceremony. Afterward, we served meals for the participants, as many as thirty people. Sometimes the men brought their drums and sang as we round-danced in the living room, threading our way through furniture and the coffee table. Being overcrowded was the reason I was part of a group that was meeting there one night: in six years, the activities and gatherings had outgrown this little lodge of prayer.

Appointed by the board, we were the Prayer Lodge expansion and grant committee. We sat around the dining room table: three grandmas, a mom with a one-year-old, and two nuns. As Vonda's sister, I counted as one of the grandmas.

That night we began to plan seriously for a second building. In previous meetings we had established our priorities: adequate gathering space, a room for sewing and other arts, a state-certified kitchen so women could sell what they cooked there, additional guest rooms, and an office. We had almost no money for all this, of course. After all, we were a circle of Indians and nuns. The Sisters of St. Francis sent a monthly check from our main office that helped pay the bills. The congregational leadership council was happy that we needed more space for our ministry. They promised to help with a portion of the funding. I agreed to help with grant writing.

After an opening prayer, and some lively conversation about the size and type of building we needed, I introduced the idea of adhering to our goal "to live in a good way with Mother Earth." We soon were discussing the merits of creating a wind and solar system to generate electricity for the new building. Despite the added cost, we decided this would become part of our plans.

"How about a greenhouse attachment along the south-facing wall of the new building to provide passive solar warmth, as well as a place to grow vegetables and flowers?" I asked. "And a ground-source heating and cooling system for the original building would eventually become cost-effective, as well as lower our use of fossil fuel."

I expected objections. To my surprise, the women embraced these ideas. A few began nodding. After numerous questions, we agreed to include these additional projects in the plans.

We had no idea how to figure out how much wind and solar we needed. We didn't know how to calculate how many solar panels or what size wind generator we'd need in order to produce the electricity we required. We knew nothing about safety standards and requirements.

A friend of Prayer Lodge, Rita Forner Schulte, came to visit and upon hearing our plans told us about an electrician, Dan O'Neil, she had read about in her local paper. He had begun a business installing wind and solar energy for homes, starting with his own. He and his wife, Diane, lived near Columbus, Montana, almost three hours from Prayer Lodge. Rita gave me his contact information and we got in touch with him. Dan proved to be very interested in our project. He and Diane agreed to come to our next meeting.

Dan helped us analyze our electrical needs and the equipment we'd need to meet them. He researched the costs for us based on our usage history and sent them to us. I added the estimates to our proposed budget. I wrote our alternative energy plan into a grant application I'd gotten from Sister Loretta, one of our board members. At a recent board meeting she had told us that her community, the Religious Sisters of Mercy, had a foundation to help fund projects that benefited economically poor women and children.

"I'm sure we'll qualify for this," she said. The Mercy Sisters had only one other requirement: one of their members must be involved in our work. I wrote our renewable energy electrical system into the section about how we planned to sustain the operation after the initial funding. With Loretta's encouragement, we asked for the maximum amount the grant allowed: $50,000.

One afternoon as I was working on yet another grant, Loretta called.

"Better sit down," she said. "Are you ready? We got what we applied for—all of it!"

I whooped and screamed and danced around my desk with the phone to my ear. This, along with a substantial gift from my cousin Marilyn Woolley and the contribution from my community, would guarantee Prayer Lodge another building and renewable power.

Loretta then told me how the Sisters of Mercy had acquired so much money to give away. She related how they originally had a large motherhouse, the headquarters for their nine Sisters of Mercy provinces in the US, in Silver Spring, Maryland. It also served as a residence for the many Sisters attending nearby Catholic University. However, by the late 1960s Sisters were pursuing social service and theology degrees in other schools. The order began to question the need for such a large building.

Meanwhile, the area had become very affluent. Sisters coming to the motherhouse from poverty-stricken places where the order ministered were uncomfortable with their headquarters. After months of discussion they put the place up for sale and the US Postal Service bought it. The Sisters relocated to a smaller place.

Then the question became what to do with all the money their order had gotten for their property. It was clear to them that, although they were not rich as a community by any standard, they could not pocket the money for their own use. Assisted by the leadership of Sister Rosemary Ronk, they decided they would use it to help fulfill their mission of serving the poor. They used the principal to make socially responsible investments based on stringent social justice requirements and then set up a granting system throughout their nine Sisters of Mercy provinces. They soon had a million dollars and more in interest to give away annually to their ministries serving poor and minority women and children. Every year for almost thirty years.

They started Mercy Housing in several cities, buying and renovating government housing projects. Low-income families could earn sweat equity as part of their effort to provide new homes for themselves. Apartment residents also participated in family enhancement programs and other educational opportunities. And now, miraculously, they'd become the biggest donor for a second building at Prayer Lodge. Thanks to their grant, our new building was assured. They saw our building plan as a wise investment of their funding for the future.

"We're going to do it!" I was still shouting into the phone to Loretta.

"I have the check in my hand," she said.

At our next meeting, April Chalfont arrived with information about mobile units. We decided on a double-wide unit, seventy by twenty-five feet.

We pored over floor plans and figured out ways to get a large gathering room and adjacent kitchen. Of the four bedrooms, one would become an office, another the sewing and arts room. We had fun picking out wall coverings and flooring. We asked for the highest R-value insulation possible, double-paned windows, and airtight doors.

The spring day our building was scheduled to arrive, the board, the whole committee, and husbands gathered on our hilltop. Charlotte Rockroads was the first to spot the two long units hauled by massive semis. She let out an excited shout and pointed. A thrill ran through us as we hugged each other and shouted. As the two drivers negotiated the tight turn up our narrow dirt and stone lane, we clapped. Several women wiped tears. When the drivers brought the two halves together, we could only look at each other and smile with pride.

We'd done it. We had our new building, which we'd named Learning and Spirit Lodge. Covered with cream vinyl siding, it looked plain, simple. To us, it was magnificent.

Company construction workers came within days to secure the building and seal the halves together. Water and electricity were installed and a septic system dug. We contacted Dan O'Neil and he completed the solar and wind system for both buildings. That night I turned on a lamp and sun energy stored in our batteries lit the room.

About thirty miles from Prayer Lodge is a massive coal-fired power plant. Many Northern Cheyenne work there, supporting their families as coal haulers, electricians, foremen, supervisors, and maintenance and personnel officers. On their vehicles I sometimes see this bumper sticker: "Behind every light switch is a coal mine."

Behind every light switch indeed is a coal mine or a nuclear power plant or a dam that is disrupting some river and its surrounding forest or grassland communities as well as the lives of fish. Our buildings and budget certainly benefited from our wind and solar system. We were generating up to 70 percent of our own electricity. We doubled the size of our original building and put in a system that cut our utility bills almost in half. Except for the onetime energy expenditure required to make our equipment, the power required for this system comes from wind and sun.

Dan's system proved a perfect fit for our hillside and our needs. We enjoyed almost daily sun and bright moonlight. We usually get plenty of wind, especially when it's cloudy.

I'd learned to read all the gauges that monitored incoming power. I checked the inverter screen to learn how much electricity we had stored in the battery bank. I planned household tasks like ironing and vacuuming and running the dishwasher when the system was generating a lot of electricity and the batteries were adequately filled.

It felt good, of course, to pay very low electric bills. It felt really good to turn on lights or use the microwave and know I wasn't harming anything, not the air, not a river, not land or forests. Not the future.

All this is true. But there's far more.

Our wind and solar systems became a source of joy in my soul. I discovered that it was deeply and mysteriously *satisfying* to be so connected to the sun. Everything on Earth depends on our local star, the sun, to power photosynthesis and produce food. Along with that, however, to know directly that this star's energy was coursing through the wires in my home, lighting lamps at night, grinding my coffee in the morning, playing music, powering my computer, gave me a *feel* for how I belonged in the wider universe. It became a kind of intimacy with our star, an experience of how its powers are coursing through me all the time. And that sense of belonging spiraled out beyond sun and solar system to include heightened awareness of how this universe at work for more than 13 billion years had assembled and faithfully sustains me.

Belonging wraps us round and assures us we have a valued place in the communion. It comforts us through fear and feeds hope in the future. Sitting at our dining room table with the rest of the construction committee, I never dreamed solar panels could become an occasion of such grace.

We named our windmill Ha-esha-iv, which in Cheyenne means "It's a windy day." Its almost constant whirring whispered like the sound of wind through a thousand cottonwood leaves. I'd close my eyes to the prairie hillside and imagine I lived in an ancient forest.

At night I could see the light on the windmill's tower. It told me the generator was working, gathering power in the absence of sun and pouring it into our battery bank. When I returned home late at night that little yellow light beckoned me. It shone beneath a canopy of stars. It reassured me during our dark winters. Air moving across land and down the slopes of mountains became light to read by in the living room.

We had to get rid of all the "bleeders," such as electric clocks that use electricity by displaying red numbers even when we don't need them. Dan and Diane went through both Prayer Lodge and our new building and helped us locate them. They were the timing devices on the microwave and coffeemaker. They were the TV and VCR that are always warm and ready to spring into action as soon as I turned them on. Bleeders cost the consumer only pennies a day, the advertisements claim, but Dan told me that if we Americans eliminated the bleeders from our homes we could shut down as many as ten power plants in this country. I thought about how I managed fine a few years ago without all my "convenient" bleeders. In our Prayer Lodge energy system, they were a constant drain on our batteries. They had to go.

So we put our appliances on strip outlets that we could turn off when we weren't using them and on when we were. We found windup clocks on back shelves in our closets. We also used battery-powered clocks and recycled the batteries. The only bleeder we couldn't figure out how to eliminate was the answering machine on the telephone.

And we did one more thing. Our electric company provided all rural homes with high-powered security and safety lights on an electric pole that illuminated yards, parking areas, and building entrances. They automatically came on at dusk and shut off at dawn. We decided to give our dusk-to-dawn light back to the electric company and then used the savings to purchase solar-powered motion-sensitive lights for our entrances and parking areas. We got three solar-powered mushroom-shaped lamps to light the walkway between our buildings with their soft, persistent glow. Otherwise it's very dark on our hill at night and the Milky Way is beauty or solace, depending how I feel when I step out on the deck to give thanks for the day before going to bed. I thank Grandma Nellie and the women of Prayer Lodge who reverence the communion of Mother Earth's life. I thank my parents who shared with me their reverence for and delight in nature. I thank

Saint Francis who praised God with all creation. I thank the God of the scriptures for ancient words that speak of the goodness of all beings since the beginning of light and time.

My absolute, hands-down favorite solar and wind device was my clothesline. A clothesline is low maintenance, has no moving parts, and offers the constant allure of regular outdoor exercise, even in winter. I became hopelessly addicted to it. I pretended not to have a dryer. I did laundry at night and hung it in the sun before work the next morning. Bend and stretch, bend and stretch in the newborn light. I took down the laundry before dark, because according to Cheyenne teaching clothing left outside overnight has to be washed again. I carried clouds of fragrance into the house, and then folded and packed the clean laundry into drawers and spread it across beds. I bought fragrance-free laundry soap because I did not want anything to interfere with the clean smell of sky and sun that I could tuck away in Prayer Lodge. Clothesline laundry is a dance, an art.

We needed to replace the wooden deck on the Prayer Lodge building. It was a large deck where a group could gather. The wood was rotting and warping due to harsh winter weather and extreme summer sunlight. What was an alternative?

Since 1600 America has cut down 95 percent of its ancient forests. Worldwide we're still losing approximately an acre of trees a second, most of this acreage clear-cut for home building or paper or agriculture. It's normal now for me a half century after planting numerous trees with Dad to think about how to minimize our use of wood. I brought up my concern at our building committee meeting.

April did more research and found a deck plank product made from recycled plastic bottles and sawdust. If we used this material, not only would we be protecting trees, we'd be keeping plastic out of landfills. We were pleased to introduce a wood alternative to the men who built the deck and later to all the people who came to sit and eat and visit and pray and dance on it.

Even though we had moved into the new building and were enjoying the added space it provided, we continued to meet as a building committee. We had more problems to solve and new ideas to share.

"When are we going to start constructing a greenhouse as part of the new building?" I asked. No one I knew had a greenhouse. As far as I knew only wealthy people, florists, and colleges did.

"We could build it along the south-facing wall and design it as a passive solar heat collector. It would help keep the building warm when the sun is low on the horizon in winter. In summer when the sun swings north and higher it would help shade and cool the building. We could grow greens and herbs during the winter and start things for our raised-bed gardens. It could become a classroom for gardeners and 4-H groups. And it would be beautiful."

Everyone was nodding. Why not? Mary Ann wrote our desire for a greenhouse into the minutes. I translated the minutes into a grant narrative and budget. Again, we got the funding, this time from a friend whose family had a foundation.

A year after we put in the new building, Brother Conrad Heinen, a Capuchin who had recently retired from years of parish ministry and carpentry work on the neighboring Crow Reservation, came for the summer. We had contacted him about our greenhouse plans and he had researched greenhouse designs suitable for our climate. Tom Rockroads, encouraged by his wife, Charlotte, used his vacation days that summer to help Brother Conrad with the construction. Francis

Limpy joined the crew, providing an electrician's skills as well as carpentry. From the ground up, they built a ten-by-thirty-foot greenhouse.

Vonda Limpy brought the next suggestion to our committee. She told us that Francis had been researching geothermal energy for their home because it's so cost-effective. She explained it's a system that draws heat from the ground, which in our area at a depth of six to eight feet is usually about fifty-five degrees all year round. Using a heat exchanger, the furnace heats the house starting from fifty-five degrees rather than from the much colder surrounding air. When the thermostat is set at sixty-eight the furnace only needs to raise the heat thirteen degrees. Therefore, the savings can be dramatic. In summer, it cools the house by blowing the fifty-five-degree air through the ducts—at the cost of running a fan.

Francis gave Vonda many articles and brochures for the committee to study. Soon we were driving to Helena, Montana, to visit a couple who'd integrated geothermal into the plans for their new home. Francis and Vonda both came. The results were very convincing. Using geothermal energy, the couple had cut their annual utility bill to almost one-fourth of what it had been.

The challenge was how to get that fifty-five-degree air into the furnace or house. The solution was to dig four trenches eight feet deep and bury in them coils of black rubber hosing filled with water. Then, the four trenches converge at a pump. By the time the water has been pumped through the hoses it is also fifty-five degrees, having picked up heat from the ground. This water is then pumped to the furnace, where air is heated or cooled to fifty-five degrees from the water.

Our grant money would make it possible for us to install the system in only one of our two buildings. We chose the older trailer because the original electric, forced-air heating system was so costly, despite our excellent insulation and new windows and doors. We ordered our geothermal system and hired a Northern Cheyenne man, Clayton Small, and his backhoe to do the necessary digging.

Clayton carved four trenches down our hillside, each of them eight feet deep and a hundred feet long. Other workers then laid the coils of black hosing in the trenches and filled the closed system with water. Clayton and his backhoe replaced the soil so carefully he could have been filling porcelain teacups. He didn't crack one hose.

An underground pump was installed where the trenches converged near Prayer Lodge that pushed the water through the buried hoses. By the time the water got down the hill and back to the pump, the Earth had warmed it to fifty-five degrees. Then the water was pumped into a heat exchanger that was part of our new furnace. In the summer when our outside temperatures soared to above one hundred, I flipped a switch on the thermostat and the system blew that blessed fifty-five-degree air into every room in the house, using far less energy than an air conditioner. It's a gently cool air, too, almost sweet, not at all like the shock of air-conditioning. Thank you, Francis and Vonda Limpy.

The company guarantees that a geothermal system delivers monthly heating and cooling bills one-third those of a conventional system. However, for most people, including us, the bills generally turn out to be as low as one-fourth of what we'd been paying. We appreciate, of course, the lowered utility bills. The women and friends served by Prayer Lodge smile to know we are using that much less fossil fuel or that much less power from a dam. How precious it is to have Earth's own consistent warmth and grateful coolness in my home, flowing around children and providing comfort and security against any weather.

Now what to do about the disturbed and scarred hillside? If we did nothing, seeds of the invasive Russian thistle would blow in and grow, something no one wanted. Instead, we looked to prairie grasses.

Vast areas of Earth grow the quantum entanglement of grasses. Of the fifteen crops that stand between humanity and starvation, ten are grasses. Our surrounding prairie grassland is a delicate though sturdy ecosystem. Whatever grows here needs to know how to take advantage of or at least endure searing heat, long dry spells, wind, and subzero temperatures. So, we visited a local greenhouse to buy bags of prairie grass seeds.

All afternoon before the first predicted snow of the year, Francis lightly tilled and then sowed the hillside with seeds that promised prairie. He was doing what we humans have done for over ten thousand years, only this time not for human food. This time, the sowing was to restore wild grasses for their own sake. The prairie mixture for our soils was a litany of holy communion, a poetry of names: thickspike wheatgrass, Indian ricegrass, bluebunch wheatgrass, slender wheatgrass, big bluegrass, prairie Junegrass, fringed sage, and white yarrow. Within a week in a drench of falling snow three nuns were spreading straw and hope over those seeds, bedding them down and praying they would survive the winter. They did.

Months later, after a long winter, there was a strange sound in the house. I noticed it especially at the corners. It sounded like dripping. Was a pipe broken somewhere? And then I knew.

It was the long-forgotten sound of spring and the end of the grip of cold. It was the sound of ice and snow surrendering into water. I ran to watch it. First, I heard a quickening thrum, then exuberant streaming: water pouring off the roof and down the gutters and down-spouts and splashing into our barrels. Water reckless and chasing, having survived winter's long confinement. Spring thaw must be ec-stasy for water.

One of our simpler Earth-care projects was a water catchment system. It took almost a year to learn how to care for this system, those green sixty-gallon barrels positioned and attentive at every cor-ner of the building fed by downspouts from the gutters. Living in a place with unpredictable rain, we needed to catch every drop we could and then in the height of summer drought carefully share our rainwater with the gardens and berry bushes, the wild plum under my window, the mountain ash trees. We tried to do this between storms, not knowing, of course, when the next one would be. Sometimes in the blast furnace of July I was weak and poured buckets of rain around the roots of all the plants in our care. It's gourmet nourishment com-pared to our well water. Someday I may wash my hair in this luxury of rainwater but so far I haven't been able to force myself to steal from plants.

As we lived our way into the goal of caring for Mother Earth, I began to see many little behaviors that diminish Earth's life. They may be small and inconsequential in themselves, but collectively their stress is damaging. Behaviors like driving at a speed that uses more gas, leav-ing lights on when I go to another room, buying products without investigating how they're made, ignoring habitat loss for a species I know nothing about, using disposable products, giving up on protect-ing the Arctic from drilling. Just as Grandma Nellie taught us to put our first sweet berries down on the ground in humble gratitude, I want to learn how to put down my Earth-costly conveniences in hum-ble gratitude for life.

Last Christmas when I was at my sister's house in Cincinnati and went through the rooms turning out lights, my other sister noted that it wasn't my light bill. No, but it's my planet, our planet. And she nodded.

Living well on less energy, protecting trees and wood, eating locally grown food when I can, breathing the morning air, thanking water as I shower: all small things. All ways of protecting Earth's diversity, vitality, and beauty, and of nourishing soul. I read recently that if every vehicle in the United States averaged thirty-six miles to the gallon we could end our dependence on foreign oil right now. Homeland security depends more on fuel-efficient cars than bombs and the efforts of our sons and daughters risking their lives in war. Small actions connect to life or death.

I seem to have learned, along with many other people, that grandmothers in particular are keepers and nurturers of soul. They are the faithful link between mothers and ancestors, between the long labor of the universe and tomorrow's children. Their voices carry far into the future, shaping its powers. Also, I absorbed an understanding that fathers in particular show us how to polish soul. I experienced this in my own father. True fathers protect the future. Grandmothers and fathers are warriors on the side of life, refusing to damage or destroy it. Those of us who are not fathers or grandmothers yet are learners, from them and from the futures they dreamed into the present now.

In July we are standing in line at the Northern Cheyenne Sun Dance. We are holding chokecherry branches to which we've tied brightly colored prayer cloths. It's our souls we're holding there in the starlight.

We walk past the line of fasters and stop in front of the sacred woman, primal grandmother. She is seated and has wrapped herself in a white sheet. Her face is painted with white clay. In her eyes shine galaxies and the faces of the next seven generations. I always have the same prayers: may we dismantle all our bombs and learn to live in good ways with Mother Earth. Bending, I lay my branch with its red and yellow cloths beside her. I lay my prayers down in an evolving cosmos, at home in countless sacred relationships, finding my way into God.

21

The Earth Literacy Professor's Bow to the Universe

Genesis Farm, New Jersey

*Blessed are those who hunger
and thirst for uprightness.*

MATTHEW 5:5

The eleven students were seated in a semicircle on metal folding chairs in a chicken house converted into a rustic but pleasant library. The south wall was a bank of high, wide windows opening to hills that sloped into the intimate valley that nested this farm. Forest swelled in startling waves of gold, orange, red, dark brown, and yellow that surged into an azure sky.

But I ignored the vista. Instead, I took notes. Perched on the unforgiving chairs, we students bent over our pages with all the intent of scholars in a university setting. In fact, this twelve-week Earth Literacy course at Genesis Farm in the Delaware Water Gap of western

New Jersey was part of a master's degree program. Larry Edwards, PhD, stood relaxed at the podium.

I was here in Blairstown, New Jersey, because Miriam had invited me to be on staff at Genesis Farm to provide Earth prayer and spirituality sessions as part of the program. This vegetable farm with its academic program was vastly different in geography and culture from Prayer Lodge in Northern Cheyenne country. However, today, I was about to discover spiritual and thought-provoking links between what was taught on this farm and what I lived at my faraway home.

My nightly work here was the alchemy of turning the gold of the day's lectures into prayer and reflection for the next morning when the group gathered around a smoky fire in the program's teepee. I also had to learn to adjust the teepee's ingenious draw and draft system to the prevailing breezes of each morning. Morning after cold morning, I gradually discovered how to warm the teepee and expel the offending smoke.

After seventeen years of government service Larry, realizing the depth of the environmental crisis, had left the National Science Foundation to live and teach at Genesis Farm. This afternoon his topic was titled "The Universe as Self-Emerging."

He introduced his material by saying that he hoped to show how the four primal, fundamental forces or interactions of the universe manifest this self-emerging process and *spirit*. He always taught carefully, choosing each word deliberately. By the time he said "spirit" he was almost whispering, not looking at us directly. Was this due to reverence, I wondered, or because scientists don't usually talk about spirit?

"What do I mean by *self-emerging?*" Larry continued. "The first question always is: how did everything get here? Why is there something, including us, instead of nothing?"

Years of Catholic religion classes supplied me with a ready and solid answer. God. Science isn't satisfied with that.

Nor were the educators who shaped much of modern Catholic education. The curricula of the Catholic high school and college I had attended included science classes as well as theology and Catholic religious teachings. As students, we'd searched the findings and theories of science intent on learning the workings of the universe and life on Earth. Taught by Sisters and priests, all faithfully Catholic, our science classes and lab research were rigorously academic. Parents, other faculty, and the Church officials who accredited the schools supported our study of the theory of evolution as part of their academic responsibilities. Science was taught as a way to learn about and respect God's world.

Discoveries in science, including evolution, were presented as significant to our understanding of the world, not as contradictory to the Bible creation story. That contradiction, if it exists at all, was never addressed. How could God the creator of the universe and God the inspirer of the Bible contradict himself? Instead, my Catholic science teachers seemed energized by the mind-bending insights of Einstein and the thrilling achievements of the American space program. In addition, theology and scripture classes were bursting with new information from archeological and ancient Middle Eastern language discoveries, illuminating and altering old interpretations of the Bible. The 1970s had been an exciting time to be a student in a Catholic college.

However, ours was a typical college with departments that separated our fields of study, like theology and the sciences, with equal rigor. I don't recall any integrative seminars.

Surprised by Larry's use of the word "spirit," I listened intently. Larry generally lectured using evidence derived from extensive experiments, grounded in the scientific method. Unexpectedly, the shadow of a hawk flowed through a pool of sunlight on the floor, but no one looked up to try to glimpse it working the valley thermals, not even me.

"Self-emerging is the capacity of an entity to change in time, to create novel structures out of its own resources, its own dynamics, its own configuration of matter." He was reading directly from his notes, although he'd delivered this lecture in at least ten annual Earth Literacy courses here at the farm and in Indiana, Colorado, and California.

I was enthralled. He was describing the universe as wholeness, acting from within itself. What I ordinarily pictured as objects flying around in space whooshed into an image of cohesive creativity and beauty.

"The four forces which I'll describe in detail shortly, and the myriad other relationships derived from them, are apparently fine-tuned so that the spectacular self-emerging process resulted in what we are and experience now: life, love, beauty, consciousness. I see these relationships as spirits."

He paused and took a slow look around the circle of Catholics, all Sisters and one priest. All of us were well acquainted with the spiritual world.

"In my approach, I essentially am equating God to the sum of all these spirits, these relationships, including the four fundamental forces. In other words, the self-emerging universe is God in action. It's what God does." He paused again.

No one objected. In one way, what he had said sounded very familiar. It reminded me of what I knew from scripture that God's Holy Spirit fills the whole world. I felt beauty in the phrase: the self-emerging universe is what God does. But the part about equating God to the sum of all the relationships of the universe, well, that puzzled me.

"An extreme definition would be that, as far as we can ascertain today, *only* the universe is totally self-emergent. Thomas Berry put it this way: the universe as we know it is the only text without a context, a context with no other context! He's right."

Low-key, steady-speaking Larry was obviously pleased, even delighted.

What a way to understand the universe, I thought.

"The universe does not communicate with anything outside itself. The universe is coming out of its own interior resources.

"Through immensities of time, it differentiates as subjectivities, i.e., galaxies, stars, planets, moons, and on Earth, as the amazing web of life, subjectivities all in profound communion!"

Another triumph. I filled my line of notes with exclamation points.

"Now, I want to address self-emergence in the context of non-duality and inter-being. All being, especially what we think of as separate, like spirit and matter, is *inter-being*. All being is inter-being. I credit Thích Nhất Hạnh for that word." More underlines and exclamation points on my part.

"Spirit can best be understood as an aspect of the universe that is not matter and that makes a difference, is efficacious." He reminded us that mass and energy are equivalent. As energy cools it condenses into mass. Of course, Einstein and $E = mc^2$, I thought.

I raised my hand. "Despite all the science and cosmology classes I've had, this is really mysterious to me. Mass, matter, energy, spirit . . ." My voice trailed off.

"It is all mysterious," Larry said, "but we know a bit of it.

"The universe started out as hot, pure energy. As it expanded it cooled. Something like the gas in your refrigerator. In a millionth of a millionth of a second the temperature dropped enough that the first particles, maybe quarks, could exist. In a few seconds the temperature had dropped enough that helium nuclei, two protons and two neutrons held together by the strong force, could exist. Hot, pure energy of the universe condensed into matter like hot steam here on Earth, when cooled, condenses into water and water, when cooled, condenses into ice. Think of it this way: matter is the child of energy.

"Matter," he continued, not noticing that I was lost in the beauty of that phrase, "is energy in a particular form, a form that occupies space. For example, if you have a box with nothing inside, no atoms, no molecules, no air, no energy, no photon of light, no radio waves, and then you start stuffing photons of light in the box, you will never fill up the box. Photons are not matter. They do not occupy space. If instead, you stuff neutrons in the box, you will eventually fill up the box even though they don't repel each other, and eventually you won't be able to stuff any more neutrons in the box. Neutrons are a form of matter. Mass is different from matter. Mass is concentrated energy. Photons are massive. So are neutrons. Einstein's equation is about the equivalence of mass, not matter, and energy.

"I repeat, it is all mysterious. But we know a little bit of it.

"Energy," he reminded us, "is actually *physical*. Energy has mass, momentum. It can knock you down or push a satellite through space. Since matter is a form of energy, energy has to be physical.

"The relationships that exist, that *are* the universe, are called into existence by the matter-energy configuration," Larry continued, and I scribbled notes as quickly and accurately as I could. I knew from my previous studies this was important. Also hard for me to grasp. I labored to catch every word as Larry read from his notes.

"Now, think about the four fundamental forces we've been studying. The four fundamental forces, evident throughout the observable universe, are special relationships. A person could think of spirit as these relationships."

Larry gave us a five-minute break. I regretted the break to his stream of reflection, but I also appreciated the time to assimilate what he'd said. Most students headed out into the sunshine. I approached Larry and asked to compare my notes with his. We made corrections.

Satisfied, back in my chair, I turned back to previous notes about the four forces. Larry had talked about them in an earlier class. The four fundamental forces or interactions of the universe: *gravity*, which orbits planets around the sun and anchors us and our precious atmosphere to Earth; *the electromagnetic interaction*, which is the force of attraction and repulsion between like and unlike electrical charges as well as unlike and like poles of a magnet; *the strong nuclear force*, which overshadows all other interactions among protons and neutrons in the nucleus, holding nuclei and therefore matter everywhere intact; and finally *the weak nuclear force*, which shows itself as radioactive decay. Except for gravity, I barely comprehended them.

So, I started with gravity and pictured our solar system. Suddenly, like when the optometrist makes the needed correction in an eye examination, I grasped that the gravitational attraction between our sun star and the planets is *not* mechanical clockwork but a *relationship*, as beautiful and real as genuine friendship. Gravity as relationship has effects we can indeed observe and measure. And, I mused, is a manifestation of spirit abiding in matter. I turned to the windows and imagined myself embraced within the Sun-Earth gravitational relationship, my soul alive within this God presence of spirit.

We reassembled, the chairs creaking and scraping the floor. With all this talk of spirit, I recalled hours of singing in the convent choir as a young Sister. I was inspired then by an ancient Catholic hymn that praises the Holy Spirit. "Come thou Holy Spirit, come." We sang the lyrical chant in high clear voices. "Come, heal our wounds, our strength renew, on our dryness pour thy dew . . . Where thou art not, we have naught, nothing good in deed or thought."

Could it be that Dr. Edwards was teaching about the very spirit we praised in the hymn? I knew he had no intention of illuminating anything in Catholic theology. Still, I sensed a connection. Could it be that the spirits that self-emerge as the forces of the universe in fact manifest the Holy Spirit of Catholic teaching? Without the spirits of the relationships called into existence by that holy matter-energy configuration, without the special relationships of the four fundamental forces, there is naught. Nothing good, in deed or thought!

I dragged myself back from the hymn. Since the beginning of the universe 13.8 billion years ago, Edwards said, *matter*, condensing from energy, and *spirit* co-arise dependently, co-dependently arise. He said that the Buddhists have noted this for over two thousand years. I heard respect and awe in his voice.

"Remember, nothing is separate; there can be no dualisms in a self-emerging universe. Matter calls spirit into existence and spirit creates matter. *At the same time.* Neither came first. As matter-energy became more complex through life on Earth, so did spirit, eventually emerging as human spirit."

What could be more sacred than this great emergence?

"Matter and spirit, though co-arising, are not the same and not separate, ever. The great matter-energy orchestration voices music, spirit. Matter as congealed energy manifests spirit's presence through the four primal relationships, the four fundamental forces. These dynamics and forces are spirit!"

Dr. Edwards explained that the four fundamental forces, the Natural Laws—think Isaac Newton, and the quantum equations discovered by Einstein and others—can best be understood as *relationships*, as manifestations of the self-emerging spirits of the universe. These relationships are all-powerful, persistent, and present everywhere throughout the space and time of the known universe.

Again I stopped my notes to reflect. Images of my friends, Crow and Northern Cheyenne elders, crowded my imagination. They know this. Mystics of every spiritual tradition realize it, too. Matter vibrates with spirit. And matter–spirit/energy connects every being in the universe with every other being, living and nonliving. This universe *is* relationship.

Throughout the universe all matter exerts a persistent pull, attracting all other matter. This attraction is as mysterious as awe in a child entranced by a bug, passion in researchers for their subjects, and a farmer drawn to soils and animals. Nor is awe something that suddenly appears in human beings thanks to our big brains and self-aware consciousness. Rather, Dr. Edwards insists, human awe has its origin in omnipresent gravity that emerged in the early universe.

Why is this so important to me?

I can't bear to have been duped into a lifetime of pursuing spiritual meaning and joy in nature by a child's imagination about the powers of an Indian mound, by the beauty of snow and a squirrel's brush of feet and tail on my arm's skin. And I have been plagued by a lifelong desire to ground theological teaching in matter and Earth, which I find irresistible and lovable. I am inspired by the logic, intuition, and mysticism of the theologians, biblical scholars, and ascetics I've studied. But I am more inspired by nature and the universe, the discoveries of science, and the Earth-respecting practices of indigenous elders. I want a spirituality firmly grounded in the real.

I love that science can track the continuity of attraction from particle to particle in the early universe. Hydrogen and helium soar into existence because of electromagnetic attraction, and then swirl in gravitationally self-attracting clouds that eventually ignite, self-emerge, as galaxies of stars. When a star goes supernova, the nuclei and electrons are blown into space and they team up to become atoms due to electromagnetic attractions. Later, as the atoms cool and get together they form molecules.

Planets accrete through attraction among these molecules and eventually become huge. Out of Earth, living cells and organisms emerge, and then bodies, brains, and human beings self-awakening into awe and a sense of destiny. Destiny so powerful and mysterious and holy that we Catholics insist it is from beyond us, from the Holy Spirit of God. We call this destiny God's Call. In fact, it rises from within us, surging out of matter—spirit/energy of bodies.

Dr. Edwards looked around the room. "Therefore," he concluded, "you could say that universe and God emerged together, as One, co-dependently."

I took these words to mean that the *human* experience and understanding of God can best be understood as the universe and God co-emerging, as perceived by our senses and delicate precise instruments. In the deep revelations coming from our growing knowledge of how the universe works, we get deeper, more comprehensive glimpses of God.

I love this.

I already knew God's presence in Earth. I recalled the surprise of love rising in waves from the rock of Manhattan, filling the Metro bus, flooding my heart. And the wonder of love felt in the springtime breath of a river in Vermont, love flowing through me again as I carried out the trash to a smelly dumpster beyond the condo. Caught off guard, I welcomed the tenderness. I look for guidance in my tradition, and discover in the Gospels numerous accounts of Jesus going off to pray in a wild place, in the desert, by the seashore. Was he mesmerized by felt recognition of his God in creation, too?

Now, as I pondered the universe, I found myself again in a flow of divine love.

In grade school and high school religion classes I learned Catholic teaching about God. "God is all-powerful, all-present, all-good, all-loving," we had recited faithfully. These were also the words Saint Francis of Assisi used to address and praise God, the Divine Mystery and Power that so captivated him. Alongside sacred scripture, God is manifest equally through God's creation, the universe: God's self-disclosure, self-expression. I experience in the universe how *real* is this holy everywhere presence of God.

A Carmelite contemplative nun I know, Jean Alice McGoff, faithful to prayer and contemplation for more than sixty years, listened carefully as I described all this to her as we visited the following summer. "Every morning when I kneel to pray I ask to be where God is, to be within the heart of God. Where is that? It's where the creativity of the universe is happening, where the new is emerging," she said slowly and with conviction. "I place myself there in my imagination, and try to be ready and receptive."

As I allowed knowledge and understanding of the universe to dawn in me, I discovered a fuller, richer understanding of God. God, not in words only, but in deeds, and in the interactions of matter and the laws of the universe. I bowed and walked into the space where granite cracks open and light pours through.

The lecture was over. People gathered their things, and some left for dinner. I hurried to thank Larry and tell him it was the most soul-satisfying lecture I'd ever heard.

"I've worked a long time researching evidence for the conclusions I present in that lecture," he said, collecting his papers and books. "It's all real, verifiable."

The next morning as I climbed the hill to the teepee, shivering in the early chill despite my coat and scarf, I smelled smoke. How nice! Someone had lit a fire and adjusted the draft. The white teepee was positioned against a grove of autumn-yellow trees where the slope leveled. I lifted the door flap and thanked Maria, warming herself, for coming early.

The students and staff gradually straggled in until we were all seated quietly in a circle around the fire.

"Our theme for our prayer today is Honoring What's Real," I began. "Please repeat this simple chant after me. The words are from the Preamble of the Earth Charter."

They quickly memorized the words. Then we sang them, using a melody based on a Gregorian chant I knew: "The protection of Earth's vitality, diversity, and beauty is a sacred trust." Silence, as we savored the robust fire and the words.

"Let's recall yesterday's class with Larry," I said. "Those who wish, please share a phrase or sentence or idea that comes to mind. This isn't a pop quiz, just an opportunity to notice what lodged in your heart."

One by one they spoke: the fundamental forces are relationships; the universe is what God does; inter-being; the relationships are spirits; the spirits are everywhere; all that exists is included.

After more silence, I read a quote from Thomas Merton: "It is good and praiseworthy to look at some created being and feel and appreciate its reality. Just let the reality of what is real sink into you . . . for through real things we can reach Ultimate Mystery who is infinitely real."

We sang the chant.

"As you walk down to the library for class," I said, "take notice of one being that catches your attention: a tree, a rock, a dried flower. Pause and absorb its reality. You may wish to give a reverent bow to the Ultimate Mystery in whose presence you stand."

Everyone quietly left. Maria put out the fire, covering embers with sand from a bucket. She left, leaving the door flap open for me. Sunlight replaced fire.

I lingered, pondering spirits of sand. Then I bowed and walked out into the bright morning.

22

Michaela Farm and the Sisters of St. Francis

A Heart-Haunting Relationship

*Michaela Farm, embodying the Franciscan spirit,
nurtures sustainable relationships among land,
plants, animals, and humans.*

FARM MISSION STATEMENT

How then do we live as contributing members of the Earth communion, feeding, clothing, and sheltering ourselves and caring for those in need? That is a question that haunted me.

"You need a writing sabbatical," a friend and associate had said to me. "Where can you go for a month? A place that will give you ample solitude and time."

Hearing her suggestion, I felt a rush of relief and happiness. I knew immediately where I wanted to go. I called the manager of the Sisters of St. Francis farm in Oldenburg, Indiana, and learned that our retreat cottage, tucked in trees at the far end of the reservoirs, was available. I reserved it, packed my car with books, files of chapter drafts, and my laptop, and headed east.

It's a long drive from Montana, across South Dakota, Iowa, and Illinois, but the wide prairie vistas and open road helped clear my mind. Arriving in Oldenburg, I stopped at the local grocery to buy provisions for the recipes I'd brought. I picked up the cottage key at the farm office, drove down the rutted lane past the barnyard and pastures, and soon stood at the cottage door, glad to be home there. I unpacked, put a chicken casserole in the oven, and lit a wood fire in the fireplace. I ate dinner in front of the fire.

The next day at dawn, I stood in the doorway, wrapped in a quilt.

It was righteously cold, this late winter morning in southeastern Indiana. Dark puddles stood in the rutted gravel road, round rims iced white. No long seductive birdsong yet, only bedraggled chirps from leafless trees along the reservoirs, themselves still frozen solid. The cattle, like Yellowstone bison in winter, still hibernating in caves of *slow*, trailed out to winter-ravaged pastures. Moon down, dawn a dull gray light.

Rhythmic thud of wood against metal, the farmer and gardeners were stoking fire in the outdoor furnace that heats the farm offices and greenhouse. I shivered, leaning against the doorframe of my cottage. Someone was shattering ice in the cattle watering tub, which meant its heater had shorted out once again. Clang of barnyard gates and thrum of tub cover as thirsty cattle bumped it open to drink. The tractor engine growled, died, growled, sputtered, throbbed.

I walked to the steamy warm greenhouse, where hundreds of started-from-seed tomatoes, peppers, and brassica such as broccoli, kale, and cabbage plants were ready to be transplanted into larger containers, a tedious job the gardener will do again a second time before outdoor soil is warm enough for the plants' liking. In the chicken house, eggs waited to be collected from protective hens, then washed by hand, weighed, and packaged. All this in a time of massive, mechanized factory farms and global food production systems. Why would anyone get up every morning to work like this on a small farm in modern America? What's the point?

Perhaps like me these insanely hardworking people here on our motherhouse farm are entranced by Earth's morning stillness, by the daily sight of stars winking out in the west and occasionally, a newborn calf dizzy for milk. Perhaps it is the grace of snow-draped pastures beyond the barn, or the promise in a billion raspberry buds or the hungry memory of vine-ripened homegrown tomatoes, warm, juicy, eaten in the garden. Perhaps they relish the confidence and intimacy of knowing the origin story of everything they're eating. Perhaps they're energized by a spirit of independence and self-reliance.

Perhaps it is rock-solid pragmatism: we all must eat. A farm feeds people. Even a small farm. Especially a small family farm.

Numerous studies document the efficiency yields per acre of small farms compared to industrialized agribusinesses. The first eight years of a 1999 UC Davis study showed that organic and low-chemical-input systems had yields comparable to the conventional high-chemical systems, and in some cases, higher yields. The study demonstrated that organic and low-input systems actually increased the organic carbon content of soil and resulted in larger pools of stored nutrients. This is important in maintaining long-term fertility.

Well-cared-for soils are life-giving and enduring. A farm is a renewable gift from our sister Mother Earth who, as Saint Francis of Assisi taught us, "sustains and governs" us. A small farm like ours, using natural methods of soil enrichment and refraining from chemical fertilizers, herbicides, and pesticides, requires hours of labor and knowledgeable input and planning; it gives back nourishment for body and soul year after year, generation after generation, without harming the ecosystem within which it is cradled, without poisoning water downstream or contributing to vast "dead zones" in oceans and the Gulf of Mexico.

Then again, perhaps it is love: some unfathomable allurement, older than our own souls, that drives these small family farmers to participate in the land's potential, to personally dig into fragrant ground and be reminded of an earthy, sacred human origin.

Finally, perhaps it is hope—in photosynthesis, in living soils, in the pregnant seed; hope that your own labor will eventually be fruitful. Given all the vagaries of weather and economics the *sense* of farming is barely comprehensible to us, something like prayer and belief in God. People farm and pray anyway, with no assurance it will all end happily.

I scheduled an interview with Chris Merkel, Michaela Farm's lead farmer and manager, who carries all the farm's relationships in his mind and heart. He weighs the expense of reservoir improvement for irrigation against city water costs. He conscientiously practices the natural farming methods the Sister-owners espouse, forgoing chemical farming methods that might more easily turn a profit. He's learned how to raise truly pastured chickens in concert with the rotational grazing of cattle, while providing just the right mix of natural feed supplements that enhance yolk color and nutrition for chickens and the people who enjoy their eggs.

And things I never think about when I eat: state certification to sell eggs, how to fix the hydraulics of a tractor, what cattle like to eat and digest, barnyard odor and fly diminishment tricks, maintaining fencing and ponds, knowing the fish stock specific for this bioregion, poison ivy control, and daily solicitude for wildlife habitat. Why would anyone *want* to do all this, even be happy to do this?

I asked him.

We were meeting in the farm office. He leaned against a desk covered with orderly stacks of papers. I noticed a cell phone on his belt, pens and pencils arranged by category in his shirt pocket. He adjusted the cap that advertised a fuel co-op and shrugged as he thought about my question.

"I'll tell you what it is, Sister, the reason why I farm and what keeps me farming. Farming is something you're born with; it's in your blood. You just have it, the desire, really, the *need* to farm.

"By the time I was three or four years old I knew I wanted to be a farmer. I did not like school at all because I was not learning about farming. I tried to skip school. My mom told me that if I didn't go to school, I would get sent to reform school. I said that was exactly what I wanted. I thought she had said re-*farm* school! She set me straight and I stayed in school.

"When you have this desire in you, all through school you keep wondering how what you're learning will help you farm. You graduate and find a job so you can pay the bills, and then in the evenings you go out to plant and harvest sweet corn on your dad's thirty acres." His eyes were animated. "People come from all over the Ohio valley just to buy my sweet corn. Honest."

He cleared his throat, bowed his head. "You know what?" His voice hovered just above a whisper. "I'll even say it's a call from God; I farm because of this calling I feel to work with God and the Earth's ability to grow things. I know people who want to farm, have the 'know-how' and try to do it, but can't. They just don't seem to have the calling. And then there are people who could farm but don't have the money to make a go of it.

"You *love* it, Sister, this working with God and nature." He was whispering. "Even on the cold days, even when the calf dies and hail shreds the garden, even late evenings when the chicken watering system breaks down. You leave home, come to fix it, and drive back exhausted but feeling strangely happy and satisfied."

He paused, almost as though surprised by the mystery of this love in his life.

"Even when the weather is all wrong for what you planned to do or for what's got to get done real soon. No matter what the weather, you learn how to work with it. When you farm, you are part of creation's holy work and every day you know it and you get up wanting to do it and ready to do it. Like I said, it's a call from God."

He seemed shy about it, this calling of his. He'd worked at the motherhouse of the Sisters of St. Francis for twenty years. He'd read our mission statements and congregational commitments. He knows we sometimes speak as if we imagine Sisters are the only ones in the whole world having a genuine, certified call from God.

Michaela Farm was begun in 1854 when the local parish priest, Father Francis Joseph Rudolph, purchased forty acres of forested, hilly land from Martin Gloueka. He soon deeded the land to the fledgling community of thirteen German immigrant Franciscan Sisters. In exchange, the Sisters agreed to care for eleven area children recently orphaned by a cholera epidemic. And do the farming that would feed the children and the Sisters.

Sister Michaela Lindemann, was put in charge of clearing, preparing, and planting the land. To feed the Sisters she had been managing gardens around the tiny hand-hewed log convent. Now she turned her labor and heart toward also feeding the orphans. She would manage the farm for eighteen years. According to our convent chronicles, she soon earned the respect of local villagers "as one who knew and could practice the art of working with nature to provide God's gifts in the fruits of the Earth."

But the valley had been cultivated long before Sister Michaela took up her duties. Archeological evidence indicates that people had built homes and small villages, hunted and farmed in the region for at least twelve thousand years. The most recent inhabitants, the Miami Nation, were gardeners of corn, beans, and squash, as well as being hunters and gatherers.

The French claimed the area in 1671, primarily for trade routes, and forced Miami bands to leave their ancestral land and resettle farther west. In 1763, after the French and Indian War, the victorious British gained control of the territory. The new governors forbade settlement by whites in the region, which today are Ohio and Indiana.

However, between 1774 and 1782, in Ohio a Shawnee village was attacked numerous times by Kentucky militia and later by George Rogers Clark, presumably on behalf of European settler-farmers who wanted the land. Terrified and seeking safety, the Shawnee moved their village five times. Among the refugees was a couple with a young son, Tecumseh.

After the Revolutionary War, the new US government effectively forced land cession "agreements" from Miami groups still living in the Ohio-Indiana area, among them the Piankeshaw, Kickapoo, and Wea. Because the government offered large subsidies to the half-starved tribes and their chiefs, some historians compare the cessions to bribery. Tecumseh, by then a recognized orator, warrior, and leader, organized a large confederacy opposing these questionable treaties.

In August 1810 Tecumseh, leading four hundred armed warriors, confronted William Henry Harrison, the newly appointed governor of the Indiana Territory, at his home in Vincennes on the Wabash River. Tecumseh told him: "No tribe has the right to sell, even to each other, much less to strangers. Sell a country! Why not sell the air, the great sea, as well as the earth? Did not the Great Spirit make them all for the use of his children? How can we have confidence in the white people? Will not the bones of our dead be plowed up, and their graves turned into plowed fields?"

Harrison refused to nullify any treaties.

In 1811 Harrison defeated Tecumseh's warriors in the Battle of Tippecanoe and burned their village, Prophetstown. Consequently, all the tribes and bands were forced to leave their homelands for Illinois or Oklahoma. Indiana was opened for settlement by American farmers and European immigrants, who purchased land from the US government. Revenues helped the young country pay for the War of 1812.

On December 11, 1816, Indiana became the nineteenth state to join the union. In 1817 farmers rafted down the Ohio from Pennsylvania, literally cut a path through thick forest from Cincinnati, stopped in this little valley, carved out clearings, and began farming. Waves of German immigrants soon entered the area and the town of Oldenburg was platted in 1837.

In 1841, Harrison campaigned for president on the slogan "Tippecanoe and Tyler, too." He was elected the ninth president of the United States. He contracted pneumonia at his March inauguration and died thirty-two days later. He never governed.

Tecumseh had been killed in battle. His people secretly buried his body. It was never found by the Americans.

Approximately sixteen thousand years before the Shawnee and

Miami the land was overshadowed by a mile-high glacier that, as it advanced south, bulldozed rock and soil from land to the north. Then as the planet warmed and the ice slowly melted, all the rock the glacial conveyor belt had been carrying was dropped, creating the Ohio River valley and watershed. Under Michaela Farm's rolling pastures and gardens, ancient glacial deposits still determine their shape and where the water flows. Newly arrived Pennsylvanian and German immigrant farmers studied the contours carefully, probably not realizing that a long-disappeared glacier was influencing how Indiana family farms were being designed.

Today, I pondered how Michaela Farm is haunted by its long history. The land Father Rudolph purchased to feed orphaned children remains forever a legacy from glacial activity. It remains forever Miami lands seized by force, in effect, stolen. Miami home sites, gardens, and graves of people were indeed plowed. What then is a just and responsible relationship with the farm today? What economic plans, what farming practices will honor its history and provide for the future in the complexities of these times?

Early summer: tomatoes ripening; peas, rhubarb, and asparagus harvested and sold; pepper plants glistening with dew. Reservoirs are green with algae. A wood duck plies the scum, faithfully followed by her one remaining duckling. Hungry turtles also raising young lurk beneath them. Cattle are up to their bellies in pasture grasses, carefully choosing their favorite foods. The morning air is a rippling lacework of arias: wren, thrush, and robin accompanied by flicker and woodpecker percussion from the nearby woods.

The cottage where I've returned to write is tucked in folds of the glacial hills, grassy slopes now flecked with white yarrow and daisies, purple clover and alfalfa. Air is a perfume of honeysuckle, honey locust, and wild roses, also blooming white. An eastern kingbird is incubating eggs in an impossible nest balanced—barely—on the porch light.

I never sit at her end of the porch. Instead, at the other end, is a paper wasps' nest above my Adirondack chair made from planks of recycled plastic.

Faithful to writing all day, I dedicated evenings to helping the gardeners. Planting more than five hundred scallions, one by one, was my first project. Sister Marie Nett, the head gardener, had taken the temperature of the soil and determined it was just right for the tender scallion, which would be sold in the farm store and distributed to the farm's subscribers in their biweekly baskets of garden produce.

Marie and I carried trays of the plants from the greenhouse. She showed me how to lay them out along the furrow that had been plowed for us by one of the other gardeners. I learned just how deeply to plant them. We each worked a row as the evening deepened, fragrant with soil black under our fingernails. Next, in a breezy drizzle of rain and using last year's leaves harvested from beneath trees on the nearby convent lawns, we mulched what I decided was surely the world's longest row of new strawberry plants.

Every evening the second week I was building fence, pulling orange baling twine and stretching it taut around rusted metal stakes, to help hold up towering sprays of feathery asparagus, weeding as I went. Two rows finished; six to go. Meanwhile, the scallions had tripled in height, thickening, compliments of a thunderstorm of rain, complete with plentiful, ragged lightning. Every morning, sixty-four-year-old muscles ached. My fingers blistered and bled.

Still, all day I looked forward to getting back into the gardens.

> Did you proclaim the rules that govern the heavens,
>
> Or determine the laws of nature on Earth? . . .
>
> Do you hunt her prey for the lioness
>
> and satisfy the hunger of young?
>
> Who provides the raven with its quarry
>
> when its fledglings croak for lack of food?
>
> Do you know when the mountain goats are born
>
> or attend the wild doe when she is in labor? . . .
>
> Did you instruct the vulture to fly high? . . .
>
> Can you pull the whale with a gaff
>
> or can you slip a noose round its tongue?
>
> JOB 38:33–39:27

These verses from the Hebrew scriptures are the worrying focus of my morning meditation time. In the words, I discern an unusual job description for God, the responsible Creator. Here, too, word from a God who loves the wild ones, who intended them wild. Here, words describing a Creator who cares about and looks after whales, lions, ravens, and deer. Here, I read about God exulting in the power of wild and untamed creation. Here, I discover an edge, almost *impatience*, in the divine voice, toward human presumption of ownership and arrogant power over nature. Here, Job's God challenges us to respond with respect, awe, and joy to creation, and to trust our human capacity to meet God in wild nature.

David Toolan, a Jesuit theologian, has written that this scripture passage "reminds us that God's universe is not created to fit the scale of our minds." He suggests that God calls us to respond with humility to the wonders of the universe and Earth. He states that these wonders do not exist merely to fulfill human desires and designs.

Scientists put it this way: The universe is not anthropocentric. Humans are not at its center and are not the reason for its existence. Instead, we are brought forth by the creativity of the universe and Earth, as members of this entire splendor and within the web of life, privileged to participate in it.

Saint Bonaventure, the thirteenth-century Franciscan philosopher and theologian, similarly suggests that we are not to "offend the dignity of creation" by acting as if creation exists primarily to serve humanity, to be bought, sold, controlled, and used as we wish. He did not view the material world of rocks, trees, and stars as "brute matter," lifeless and inert. Rather, because the material world is created by God, it follows that it would reflect the nature of God, who is generously creative and relates lovingly with creation.

For Bonaventure, God is a vibrant communion of Father, Son, and Holy Spirit. Creation flows from the love among these three, the Holy Trinity. Because it flows from God's Word and is filled with God's Holy Spirit, all creation is relational, interconnected, interdependent. Like God.

"We are all kin," I'd learned from Dr. Brian Swimme, "not just with all humans, but with all beings. From microbes to galaxies. All kin."

Had I responded to a wildflower, a squirrel, and an Indian mound, experiencing their God-like capacity to *relate*? Is this what farmers and gardeners do? Is this the responsibility that follows when people "own" a farm?

Integral to our being human is that we can experience an ineffable *presence* within matter, within creation. Awe swells our souls, and immersed in nature, we can experience the pulsing heart of divine mystery. For Job and Bonaventure, for Christians and many others, that heart is holy and named God, Allah, Ma'heo'o, the Tao, or Holy Spirit.

Summoned to the Michaela Farm gardens each evening by a holy call, I joined the ancient and endless labor of farmers and gardeners. One can be forgiven the temptation to exchange homegrown food for products shipped from distant farms in other countries, the tiring work borne by unknown people. This evening in the huge asparagus patch, I straightened up from weeding to stretch. Sweat smeared my glasses. Any more mosquito bites and I'd need a blood transfusion. My legs ached and muscles burned. As the sun set, a breeze rippled through the lacy asparagus, providing immediate relief. Wiping my dripping face with the dusty end of my T-shirt, I gazed into the sky, magenta and orange in the west, paling into a pearly pink overhead and east. Perhaps next year a family or some of our Sisters will enjoy asparagus from this garden on a cool spring evening after their own day's work. The thought gave me renewed energy. I bent to yank again at deeply rooted weeds.

Like most family farms in the United States, Michaela Farm struggles to be financially viable. The farm manager's salary is paid out of the limited resources of the Sisters of St. Francis, not from farm income, which has been inadequate to the task. Volunteers provide much of the necessary daily labor in the gardens. Donations from friends who share with the Sisters a commitment to Michaela Farm bought the new tractor.

We Oldenburg Franciscan Sisters struggle to clarify our commitment to the land we call ours. Is it economically feasible to provide continued and caring investment? Why not sell it to "developers" and invest the money elsewhere to provide for an uncertain future? Isn't it more economical to buy factory-farmed or foreign-grown food than to try to raise our own?

Sometimes I feel this way. Sisters who question the financial wisdom of continuing to subsidize the farm make a valid point. In many respects, they're right. Much as it pains me to acknowledge that. We're aging as a group, diminishing in numbers. Fewer and fewer Sisters earn salaries. Health care costs continue to rise.

Then I remember that Michaela Farm is in our hands for a relatively short time. It's an inheritance from long-ago Sisters, our ancestors in faith. Saint Francis of Assisi, whose life inspires our existence as a congregation, insisted that everything we possess, including our bodies and our talents, is a freely given gift from a loving and generous God. In Francis's way of thinking, we can literally lay claim to nothing; we can only respectfully care for our lives, share what we have with others, and use what we need as undeserved gifts from God.

Along with the Franciscan tradition, we study the Bible and discover teachings that Earth and all it contains is ultimately God's. We humans are primarily caretakers sharing in God's own loving care of creation, in God's own solicitude for wildflowers and each sparrow, for young lions, whale, raven, and deer. As farmers and shepherds, the Israelites were commanded to observe a weekly day of rest, the Sabbath, when even animals were not to be used for work and the land was to be allowed to lie undisturbed. Modeled on the Sabbath, the Christian Sunday observance of rest becomes the regular reminder that land is a gift to us, not to be worked relentlessly for our disposal, use, and source of income.

In addition in the biblical tradition, inherent to land being sheer gift, its bounty is to be shared with those in need: the poor, the stranger, the foreigner, the widow and orphan. They are our brothers and sisters. Land is the context for the sacred covenant with the Divine. Land is the ground of our communion with Ultimate Mystery and Love, and all the fierce responsibilities of simply existing. These traditions teach us that land, like people, cannot be owned and controlled, bought and sold for gain. True security instead is founded on the *relationship* with divine love in our care for land and by sharing its gifts.

Michaela Farm, in all its fertility and beauty, its demanding work and teeming diversity, is now in our hands. Like the whole of the United States of America, it sits on the edges of our consciences, spirit-filled and sacred, full of promise and affronting our long-held belief that land is resource for our consumer-driven economy, not spirit-filled gift from an ancient universe, from divine love and creativity.

Earth, North America, Michaela Farm: collection of resources or communion of spirit-filled subjects, our relatives in the interconnecting web of life? How then do we live as contributing members of the communion, feeding, clothing, and sheltering ourselves and caring for those in need?

"We have to be practical," Sisters say to each other as we discern our commitment to Michaela Farm. "Our farm is costing us more than what we get from it. Every year it costs more. This can't continue."

Everyone knows a small family farm is expensive to operate. Our economy is one of scale. Government subsidies are weighted heavily toward massive factory farms. I listen to conversations among the Sisters. The resolve to sustain the farm is wavering.

As Sister Marie and I mulched the strawberry patch on that summer evening, she'd told me about the Volunteer Day the farm staff had hosted the previous fall at the end of the growing season. Sisters had gathered from Cincinnati, Indianapolis, Evansville, and the motherhouse to help. Everyone was over fifty years old. Some sat in wheelchairs in the barn, carefully balling the orange baling twine salvaged from the asparagus fencing, preparing it for easy reuse the next year.

Others were cleaning gardens, bedding them for winter. Fencing staves are hauled to the barn and stacked. Sister Marie, a master gardener, and others cleaned trays in the greenhouse and stored them for when she would start all over again with seeds in mid-January under grow lights.

As they worked, Marie responded to questions from city-dwelling Sisters.

"I actually like the excitement of gearing up for the next season, and the delight of the first new seedlings coming up in the greenhouse, the hardening off of transplants, the setting out into the garden— each little graduation in these plants' lives," she admitted to her volunteer crew. "The thank-you they give back as food is humbling. It is a process filled with awe and gratitude and I get to be part of it."

No one envied her work-filled weekends, the twelve-hour workdays in the height of growing season, the backbreaking labor. She told them of Sister Carol Ann Angermeier, eighty-eight, who helped with the packing of the fifty boxes for the farm's CSA subscribers.

"Those are the fifty families and individuals who buy shares into the gardens," she told her volunteers. "Our subscribers are integral to the financial viability of the farm. We hope to increase their numbers every year."

As I write this, I realize the future and security of our Franciscan community is unknown. It dwells, as it always has, in the loving hands of God and our faith. It is threatened by diminishing investments and fewer, aging members. On one hand, it doesn't seem economically practical for the community to try to maintain a family farm. It breaks my heart just to write those words. On the other hand, perhaps Michaela Farm could become the setting for a better-financed, education-based endeavor that continues to embody our values.

Our current farm director, Sister Peg Maher, writes illustrated reports that chronicle progress on the farm's innovative, Earth-friendly, and labor-saving methods. She shows how these methods result in increased productivity and help edge the farm closer to financial viability. So perhaps we might shift our commitment to the farm toward finding alternative ways to bequeath a thriving, small farm to the future. Perhaps something other than our owning and working it. Perhaps a community of farming families, I muse as I write, who share our vision and respect for the land, who also want to do small-scale farming in harmony with nature's ways, without chemical inputs.

Ten years ago, when I was helping Marie mulch the strawberry patch, she told me that at the end of Volunteer Day, the Sisters and other volunteers stood in a pasture to pray. They sang a blessing over the land. They pondered in silence our heritage and cherished traditions. Perhaps they felt the land stir beneath them, alive and sacred, activating their imaginations, haunting their hearts.

On July 7, 2021, Michaela Farm was sold to the nonprofit Greenacres Foundation. Greenacres will continue sustainable, regenerative agriculture, the CSA program, and the farm store, providing healthy food for the geographic area and the food pantry. It will partner with local public and Catholic schools to enhance environmental education and care for regional natural ecosystems. The farm is called Greenacres at Michaela Farm.

Farm director Sister Peg Maher wrote, "It is apparent that the missions of both the Sisters and Greenacres are very much aligned, and that Greenacres could bring the Sisters' vision for Michaela Farm to fruition. We Sisters have held this place as gift from a generous God for 167 years and now we pass on the gift to Greenacres so that they can tend it for future generations."

23

Discovering Jesus as Nature Mystic

One Litany and Two Parables

"But you," Jesus said, "who do you say I am?"

MATTHEW 16:15

s I stepped further and further away from my past life of full-time church ministry and turned to service of Earth community, I continually asked myself: do the gospel stories and teachings of Jesus have anything to offer me? At times, this questioning was painful and lonely. What if I found nothing?

Although I loved reading and reflecting on the Bible as a young adult, I'm no trained scripture scholar. I'm the usual Catholic Sister student of the Bible: undergraduate and graduate courses about the first five books of the Hebrew scriptures, the Major and Minor Prophets, the psalms and wisdom literature, Gospels, Acts of the Apostles, and the letters of Saint Paul. In their documents, the bishops of Vatican II encouraged Catholics to study the scriptures. I did biblical research enough for occasional homilies and graduate papers, and most important, research enough to feed my daily meditation and prayer. As a novice, I had hoped to someday get a master's degree in sacred scripture.

In scripture courses during my early convent training and graduate education, I learned, above all, *methods* of Bible study, not dogmatic interpretation. I learned to delve into the historical times during which a book of the Bible was written, an effort to understand the circumstances, questions, and struggles that occasioned the writing. I learned that stories were often written years after they happened, emerging from communal memory as well as the creative genius of authors inspired by their experiences of God and Jesus. Their intent was not necessarily to record history in journalistic fashion but to help the community deal with current problems, drawing from lessons of the past.

I learned to distinguish between various genres in the Bible: hymns and prayers, allegory, wisdom teachings and exhortations, parables and aphorisms, and narrative. I learned that prophetic writings may not have been necessarily intended to foretell future events but rather to critique current political and social realities in ways that energized people to act more lovingly and justly in the present. I studied rudimentary Greek, in an evening course at the Yellowstone Baptist Bible College in Billings, memorizing the alphabet and pages of vocabulary, conjugations, and declensions. I learned to decipher Greek grammar and structure. Classes began with a hymn and scripture verse, which put me at ease. Greek is the original language of the Gospels and I wanted to appreciate better the nuanced meanings of words, meanings English may not have been able to delicately translate. In addition, I was intensely interested in new insights that scripture scholars were gaining from archeological discoveries and the recovery of ancient "lost" texts. Translations of the Gospels of Thomas, Philip, and Mary Magdalene shed new light on the gospels declared authentic by the Church.

During my Creation Spirituality studies in Chicago, I took advantage of every opportunity I could to take courses in the Gospels, the times and teachings of Jesus, and theology. I was especially interested in liberation theology, a new and exciting reinterpretation of Church teaching ignited by the extreme suffering of poor people in Latin America. Liberation theology boldly asserts that systemic poverty and the exploitation of people are not God's will. That seems obvious, but gospel phrases like "the poor you will always have with you" were often quoted to justify economic inequality.

In contrast, the transformation of oppressive structures for the benefit of everyone is more in keeping with the Beatitudes and other teachings of Jesus, especially the enigmatic parables that if taken seriously would upturn many social and economic structures. In class, we were encouraged to focus less on the passion and death of Jesus and the subsequent doctrine of redemptive suffering, and more on Jesus's life of hope-filled healing and liberating teaching. Liberation theology, although articulated by priests, Sisters, and theologians, primarily arose from poor people themselves as they reflected upon their circumstances in light of the teachings of Jesus and stories in the Gospels.

We had been encouraged to do research on whatever interested us and integrate our learnings with Creation Spirituality. The Gospel of Saint Luke intrigued me because of the many stories about women in it. I decided to read it straight through as story, rather than focus on distinct parcels for specific instruction, as we often did and heard in church. I was surprised by what I discovered.

In Luke, Jesus moved from meal to meal to meal. It seemed he was constantly eating, either with his friends, teachers of the law and religious leaders, tax collectors, or public sinners. I noted that he was roundly criticized for his willingness to eat with all sorts of people. He was even accused of being a glutton.

He taught in between, of course. But he also did a lot of eating. What could be the meaning of this?

I began to realize that Jesus most often ate with people who were outcasts and outsiders in his society. He was remarkably—and disturbingly—inclusive. It reminded me of how Crow and Northern Cheyenne families welcomed me, the outsider, to birthday, graduation, and ceremonial meals. Someone always helped me with protocols of when to get in line, where to sit, how to defer to elders. I remembered how heartwarming their inclusivity was for me, the shy newcomer, how relieved I'd felt when an auntie explained the "doings," sometimes saying, "There are no English words for what I want to tell you."

I wondered that they wouldn't shun me. I wondered if I was more aware than they were of my being a member of the people who'd massacred their villages, stole their children and lands. Hardly. They knew all that better than I ever could. I wondered what enabled them to suffer through all that history and still meet me as a person.

How did the Crows and Northern Cheyenne I knew come to be inclusive as Jesus had been?

"You are teaching our children," I often heard. "Gerri can read now!" And, "You respect our ways." They love their children. They cherish their traditional ways. Their teachings somehow enabled them to love the enemy, sometimes dissolving enmity into personal friendship. The loved enemy is no longer an enemy.

In Crow and Northern Cheyenne homes and celebrations it became clear to me that sharing food and meals connected us in bonds of quiet acceptance, perhaps even trust. Family stories were told. Plans for the next birthday were made. Fervent prayers were said in whispered languages, heads bowed, children silent without being told. I was invited back.

I had been sitting down to the Jesus meals of Luke's Gospel those many years among the Crow and Northern Cheyenne. In Chicago, I could expand my belief about what makes a meal sacred. The bread and wine we share during the Catholic Mass remained central to my life. Even so, I gradually awakened to knowing that those Crow and Northern Cheyenne meals shared something just as sacred, and perhaps more significant. In those meals I experienced the sacredness of the here and now, the everyday gathering, and sharing stories and feelings with each other.

Was there anything else in the Gospels more specific to my new Earth ministry? I remembered that while studying in California I had done a research paper on Jesus's nature references.

"Learn from me," a gospel writer had attributed to Jesus. I had decided to take Jesus at his word. What was Jesus's relationship with nature? What could I learn from observing his interactions with nature? I wanted to know if there was anything in the Jesus story that could be relevant to my concern about environmental destruction. Did Jesus care about creation? Does creation matter to God? Could the liberation theology insights and breakthroughs apply to Earth and species as well?

I remembered that I had probed the Jesus stories for connections with nature, rather than theological or creedal content. I had decided to read straight through all four Gospels, as well as the Gospel of

Thomas. I had a book, *The Five Gospels: What Did Jesus Really Say?* Once again, I read the Gospels as I would read a book, following the story.

In my little office in Prayer Lodge, I put aside my work and dug through my files, looking for that paper: "Jesus and Nature." I sat down to read.

I was immediately struck by rediscovering *where* Jesus prayed. He prayed in the synagogue on the Sabbath, of course. And, also in the tradition of his people, he went off to secluded, wild, and desolate places away from the crowds and towns. It seemed Jesus did this frequently.

I put down the paper and stared at the rolling Rosebud Valley and distant mountains. I could identify with this spiritual practice of Jesus. My long solitary walks across Pryor Creek into the nearby hills as well as across the undulating grasslands at Prayer Lodge brought a sense of quiet to my soul, opened me to the everywhere presence of God. What was Jesus gaining from hours, even days, spent in solitude in nature? How did this time shape his thinking, his experience of God? I could imagine Jesus doing the things most people do in nature: notice beauty, pick up rocks, thrill to the song of birds, bend to the fragrance of wildflowers, get hot, sweaty, and thirsty.

My attention back on my research paper, I read pages of the nature references Jesus had made. Once again, I felt surprise and satisfaction in reading so many examples of Jesus pointing to nature as a source of insight and wisdom about right relationships among humans, with God and with the rest of nature. I learned that in this way Jesus was following in the teaching tradition of the prophets of the Hebrew scriptures.

In many gospel stories Jesus is portrayed as attuned to and respectful of God's word in creation. "Truth springs out of the ground," says Psalm 85:11. It is a psalm I suspect he would have prayed and obeyed.

As I read, I lingered over a renewed awareness that Jesus spent most of his public life out of doors. He lived on the road, literally (Matthew 8:20). He was on ground and under sky most of the day and night. He woke to the morning songs of birds. The Milky Way glistened across his soul. Dust caught in his throat; rain splattered him. Was the ground hard and rocky beneath his sleep? Did Earth shape his dreaming?

Likewise, the crowds that gathered to listen to Jesus spent most of their days out of doors. They were mostly poor peasants, subsistence farmers, and landless day laborers. At the time, a crushing 35 percent of the annual crop was taxed. Approximately 20 percent was expected as tithe to the temple, as commanded by the Torah. The Romans exacted an additional 15 percent, which could be increased by tax collectors, since that was their form of payment. Rome enforced its tax by seizing land if unpaid. The average life expectancy of Jewish males was twenty-nine years. One percent of the population owned over half the land in the Middle East. It's not hard to imagine the grinding poverty that was the daily experience of the people.

In addition, life was dominated by the brutality of Roman occupation under the rule of Pontius Pilate. He didn't hesitate to call in troops to suppress any hint of uprising. He showed little regard for Jewish religious traditions and sensibilities.

A peasant himself, Jesus understood the grief, anxiety, and terror of his listeners. His father had become a carpenter most likely because his family had lost their land. In this context, Jesus would hardly offer simple "trust in God" exhortations that would insult people's suffering. Rather, he encouraged them to observe how birds live, without toiling or paying taxes. What would an impoverished farmer think, hearing this? Was the teacher saying that nature's abundance is intended by God to be available to people, *all* people, and that it *ought* to be? Was he challenging the taxation system that disproportionally burdened poor people?

This was not sweet nature imagery accompanied by blithe, pious commands to trust in God as simple birds do. These were teachings that subverted the economic and political systems of his day. Jesus's teachings, based in compassion for suffering he understood, encouraged his listeners and eventual readers to observe nature and Earth's functioning very closely and then fashion personal and public life accordingly. I suspect he was clearly saying that social systems are to follow the same imperative. If only.

Most of the rabbis and other teachers of conventional wisdom in Jesus's time taught directly from their sacred scriptures, the Law and the Prophets. They were "Torah Sages." Jesus was not. Marcus Borg, former Hundere Distinguished Professor of Religion and Culture at Oregon State University, said that although Jesus did on occasion refer to the Law and the Prophets, even rather casual reading of the gospels reveals that Jesus referred frequently to the natural world familiar to his listeners. He grounds his teachings in the wisdom he observes in nature.

I was surprised by how once again I was energized as I was inundated with references by Jesus to the rest of nature, as well as the human body. A teacher I could love listening to!

I could readily see that Jesus was indeed attuned to the natural world, about and within him. He observed wildflowers blowing in the south wind, noticed the differences in soils and their effects on plants, knew from experience the solitude and demands of the wilderness. I, who camped on the ground beside a stream in the Pryor Mountain Wild Horse Range, helped my dad mulch his garden, and memorized names of wildflowers, could love this Jesus.

He observed foxes in their dens, followed weather patterns, enjoyed the shade of trees on scorching hot days. He referred to the human body and its functions. He was awed by the flash of lightning and fascinated by the similarity between snakes and the eel-like fish of the Sea of Galilee. He understood how yeast works in bread dough and the effect new wine would have on old, valued wineskins. An artisan probably, he was familiar with timbers and slivers.

I relished that Jesus made vivid and skillful use of his nature experience and observation in many of his sayings, parables, and aphorisms. To what end? Often to set up stories that challenged conventional wisdom and overturned the operating assumptions of social systems.

Scripture scholars assert that central to Jesus's understanding of his life purpose was to address human suffering by healing and teaching, and to announce by word and deed the presence of God's Reign of compassion, nonviolence, and justice among people. But what exactly does that entail? And how do we recognize it? What are we to do? Precisely the questions of his followers.

As a metaphor for this spectacular Reign of God, Jesus turns their attention not to the expected metaphor of the majestic cedar of Lebanon but to the lowly mustard plant. The Reign of God is like a mustard seed, the teacher begins. Surprise holds their interest. Perhaps a few laugh out loud. Why would Jesus choose the smallest of seeds and say it's the one destined to become the largest of all shrubs? And anyway, why is the Reign of God like a shrub?

Mustard tends to rapidly take over cultivated land and grows where it is not wanted. Its seeds germinate quickly, and it grows quickly.

Even when sown on purpose, it's hard to control. It's a dangerous take-over plant, small and unseen until it's too late. Furthermore, birds are attracted to the shrub for shade and nesting. For subsistence farmers, birds can be a problem because they eat newly sown seeds.

Everything about this metaphor is wrong. Which is precisely Jesus's point. He has a big vision for his small group of unseen and insignificant friends. You are a takeover plant. You can grow quickly, and become a force in society for good, for healing, for nonviolence and just economic systems. You will do this not with might and power but through small loving actions by many of you. You will welcome everyone to the meal of my love and joy. Behold the Reign of God.

I find it comforting. Mustard grows wild in Montana, a breezy yellow along roadsides. I think about the parable as I work with the small Prayer Lodge board to create a building that fulfills their commitment to live in tune with Mother Earth. I think about it as I work with students at Genesis Farm, as I lead small retreat groups in experiencing God's commandments embedded in nature, in the lifeways of creation.

I think about that parable as I read the work of the author and environmentalist Paul Hawken. In *Blessed Unrest* he tells the story of what is going right in a world of global wrongs. He writes of how people use imagination, conviction, and resilience to organize to safeguard nature and ensure justice. "These organizations fly under the radar of most media. They are not centrally organized. They are a great work enterprise, Earth's immune system kicking into action. They are well over *two million organizations worldwide* united by the conviction that the world must be reconstituted to ensure its and our own survival."

He quotes Adrienne Rich: "My heart is moved by all I cannot save. So much has been destroyed I have to cast my lot with those who, age after age, perversely, with no extraordinary power, reconstitute the world."

Hawken calls all this the largest movement in the world. I see a global takeover by mustard plants.

The second parable? A very short piece about a fig tree (Luke 13:6–9). Can this brief snatch of wisdom inspire a new human-Earth harmony? If nothing else, it gave me encouragement.

"A man who had a fig tree planted in a vineyard came looking for fruit on it." Figs were valuable; dried, they could nourish a person on a desert journey. But the tree is unproductive, and the savvy vineyard owner instructs his gardener to cut it down. It's wasting the soil and gulping scarce water.

"Wait," says the gardener. And Jesus's tenant farmer listeners may have gulped in shock.

Sister Miriam MacGillis, in her lectures in the Genesis Farm program, has said many times that the first action step toward a flourishing Earth community is to stand up and stop the destruction.

I've learned this is not easy. It requires steady, long-haul nonviolent resistance to violence against Earth. It means practical solidarity with people who live near toxic waste dumps or vast oil and gas fracking sites, with families living downstream from the chemical run-off of factory farms or the horror of oil "spills." It means speaking an inconvenient truth about our ruinous addiction to burning fossil fuels and the emissions that cause climate change. And it demands providing positive, Earth-healing alternatives. Jesus, the parable teller, did just that.

"Let me dig around the fig tree," suggests the gardener, "water it, apply some manure."

I consider this a vital second step: learn how Earth works and follow that. Apply Earth's methods to how we heat and cool our homes, grow food, do health care. Design vehicles that glide through air like fish through water, running on solar-powered cells. Create buildings that generate more electricity than they use, and that recycle the wastes they generate. Plant seasonal gardens. Compost.

"Sir, let it alone for one more year," bargains the gardener.

Step three: don't be in a rush. Embrace the pace at which Earth does things.

I keep learning this gracious instruction for how to give the fig tree of Earth, and my efforts on behalf of Earth, time to heal, grow, and regenerate.

"If your tree bears fruit next year," says the gardener, "well and good."

Jesus's listeners, familiar with the kings and prophets of Israel, see a crowd of images and teachings around a fig tree as they hear the parable. In 1 Kings, the peace and security of Judah and Israel is described as each family enjoying their vine and fig tree. In Zechariah, the people are told to invite each other to "come under your vine and fig tree." Inherent to this idyllic imagery is a scrupulous economic system of just distribution of land, goods, and labor, as well as adequate food for all, shared. Jesus is boldly calling for the realization of these values. Equitable economic systems are rich soils for a flourishing Earth and for peace among all peoples. Step four: work toward this vision.

I've found in Jesus's teachings just what I've needed. I've even unearthed what I've come to call "God's Four-Step Action Plan for a Flourishing Earth Community." I've discovered hope in the rapid spread of a diminutive plant. I've been given a beautiful Nature Litany in Jesus's abundant use of his intimate relationships with the world around and within him. Through service of Earth community, I sense I've stepped closer and closer to the heart of Jesus's life and teaching.

Gospel References

Wildflowers: Luke 12:27–28

Different soils and plant productivity: Mark 4:4–8

Solitude and demands of the wilderness: Luke 7:24–25

Foxes in dens: Thomas logion 86:1–2

Weather-pattern knowledge: Matthew 5:45–46

Shade of trees on hot days: Mark 4:32

Human body and its functions: Thomas logions 14:5 and 69:2, and Matthew 10:30

Lightning: Luke 10:18

Snakes and fish: Matthew 7:10

Yeast in dough: Luke 13:20–21

New wine in old skins: Matthew 2:22

Woodworking and splinters: Matthew 7:3–5

Cedar of Lebanon: Ezekiel 17:22–23

24

This Universe Speaks
as Beauty

Let the beauty we love be what we do.

*There are hundreds of ways to kneel
and kiss the ground.*

JELALUDDIN RUMI

Saint Augustine addressed God as "O Thou Beauty, ever ancient, ever new." Did he really mean it? I have been in the habit of glossing over this name for God, as if he wrote it in some offhanded way in the middle of the night when he had to finish a sermon and wanted to get to bed.

Then I discovered other intimations of God as Beauty. Medieval theologians and followers of Saint Francis, Saint Bonaventure, and Blessed John Duns Scotus taught that God rushes toward, upwells in the beauty that captivates human beings.

Dr. Mary Beth Ingham, Sister of St. Joseph, provides in her book *Rejoicing in the Works of the Lord* a summary of the role of beauty in the Franciscan tradition. Now that captivated me.

Don't we all try to make some sense of our seminal spiritual experiences? Those unforgettable moments when we're entranced by holding our newborn daughter for the first time or when we've lost all track of time in a walk along the seashore. It can be easy to downplay their significance to us as we engage with daily work. However, like Rilke, we keep circling God, that primordial tower, as we ask ourselves a haunting question: am I a falcon, or a storm or a great song? Less likely, the great song.

Clare of Assisi, having experienced a liberating joy in the commitment of her life to God, had to engage with Church authorities in Rome throughout her entire life to gain their approval for her way of life. Ultimately, they conceded to her unusual Rule of Life and the unheard-of commitment to owning no property for security. Saint Francis's imitation of Jesus inspired her, helped her make sense of her own spiritual experiences and convictions.

Plenty Coups, a Crow youth in the late eighteenth century, was beset by visions and messages during his lengthy fast in the Crazy Mountains of present-day Montana. He returned home to a circle of elders. They drew from their tradition to help him understand the meaning of his experience.

Sister Miriam Therese MacGillis and Dr. Brian Swimme were nourished by their long association with Thomas Berry, who studied the works of his mentor, Pierre Teilhard de Chardin. Inspired by the work of Teilhard, they published books and taught courses to energize people to create human communities that meet our needs for food, clothing, and shelter within the limits of the Earth community, respecting Earth's sustaining governance.

I unexpectedly encountered guidance for my Earth Hope ministry from my own tradition. It was during a course of study at the

Franciscan Chiara Center in Springfield, Illinois. Dr. Mary Beth Ingham, our seminar leader, put it clearly: "The awareness that God is encountered in human experiences of Earth and beauty is so pervasive to the Franciscan spiritual tradition it is easy to miss." I was immediately plunged into aching recognition, almost to tears.

Where have I been all these years that I didn't see this, wasn't told this, or simply couldn't hear this? That for so long, I doubted and minimized my earthly God experiences, questioning their validity? That I had to root around in old prayers and scripture translations, hoping for solace? That I had to struggle and work so hard to accept and appreciate my God-Earth calling and spirituality? That I felt so lonely doing this? Mary Beth probably said more that afternoon, but here was precisely where a life trajectory set in motion by a squirrel, wildflowers, the full moon, and Franciscan living at long last made sense, adult sense. Sadly, throughout those years of training to be a Franciscan, I'd indeed missed its full import.

Dr. Ingham explained that in the Franciscan tradition, the human journey is an intellectual-spiritual journey founded upon the recognition and experience of beauty. This experience is to be taken seriously. Beauty guides life decisions that are unique to each person. Francis himself insisted that others were not to try to imitate him, but instead to follow their own unique calling from God. "The Lord showed me what to do," he said, "now, may he show you." More like: now may you notice your own life invitation.

Early Franciscan texts of theology and philosophy from Celano, Clare, and Bonaventure are filled with references to beauty. "We find an approach that is organized around beauty," says Dr. Ingham. "It is the encounter with beauty in this world that guides the spiritual journey toward the fullest experience of divine love."

Right. I then wondered about how to understand the ugly, the mean and despicable? What about violence? What about all the horror in the world: trafficking children into prostitution, forcing boys into armies that slaughter and rape, and bullying schoolchildren for being who they are? What's the Franciscan perspective on that?

Dr. Ingham was actually responding to my unspoken concerns, saying that the Franciscan response to the world's suffering is framed in terms of transformation, drawn from the life and death of Jesus. Jesus, the innocent one who accepted an excruciating execution not as a victim but as one refusing to collude with destructive and unjust authority. He embraced the deprivation and suffering incumbent upon engaging with the world and refused to pass it on to others. In a story about his final meal with his friends, he models how they—and we?—are to live. He washes their feet: humble service. And he shares bread with them, declaring, "You are now my body, given for the world." This encounter with beauty, with breathtaking goodness, changed the people around him, who, with the exception of Judas, then turned to heal and transform the world. It seems to me that the encounter with beauty is, for Christians, to live as Jesus did.

Beauty, as I learned from my parents, summons contemplation. What exactly is that? During my first year of training to become a Sister, Sister Estelle taught us that contemplative prayer was an excelling form of union with divine love. At the time I decided it was something out of range for me, achieved by only a select few of very holy people.

Now, decades later, I am convinced that contemplation is inherent to being human. It resides as potential, a seed of hope in the heart of our humanity. It demands the deep dive, the longest stride of soul. It's why many twenty-first-century people are so bored with our shallow, money-motivated culture, a culture that is grossly unworthy of humanity's gifts and destiny. It's the hungry drive of the true self that, undirected or unfulfilled, can lead to destructive behaviors. The medieval mystic Hildegard of Bingen called it the "seed of God within us that grows into God."

Contemplation is not thinking or reflecting, it is not meditating. It is not a trance. It is the experience over time of becoming the Love and Goodness we seek, the Communion we glimpse within our longings, and the mysterious unknown destiny that summons us. It is not some thing or person we discover. Rather contemplation awakens us into the universe, or Ultimate Communion, or God. We encounter our truer self. We merge with the current of our fulfillment and joy.

I think it is akin to learning that we are not merely *within* the universe. Rather we are part of the universe. We *are* the universe expressing universe-self as a human, here, now. We are not just within an embrace of Love, of God. We *are* that Love, here, now.

Is there any Beauty greater than this? Than being the universe we admire? Than being the Love we seek? Than realizing that the ever-ancient, ever-new Beauty is seeded as each human being, as well as the community of all creation? Deprived of access to this love, human beings can indeed become depraved, contradicting their own joyful evolutionary nature through acts of cruelty and violence.

I think of my dad's response to beauty: you are capable of experiencing it within yourself, he told me. I think of my mom's response to the beauty of the full moon, her desire to share it with me and to give me instructions I could follow throughout my life: wake up, get up, and stand there in the beauty.

How does this play out in real life? Does it have anything to do with raising children, finding a job, and staying alive and well? Can beauty provide instructions and guidance for daily living? Yes, I would discover. Of all places, in jails.

> I asked the earth, the sea and the deeps, heaven, the sun, the moon and the stars . . .
> My questioning of them was my contemplation,
> and their answer was their beauty . . .
> they do not change their voice, that is their beauty, if one person is there to see and another to see and to question . . .
> Beauty appears to all in the same way, but is silent to one and speaks to the other . . .
> They understand it who compare the voice received on the outside
> with the truth that lies within.

> —SAINT AUGUSTINE,
> *Confessions*

25

Speak a Word of Hope

Cosmology Course in Jails

He has sent me to proclaim liberty to captives,
to let the oppressed go free.

LUKE 4:18

The woman called to say she wanted to join a young women's summer camping retreat I was leading. It was designed to develop and dedicate people's leadership energies toward care of Earth. She was not young.

Sister Helen Prejean, my friend of twenty years, had helped plan and would facilitate the retreat. She would certainly enliven it with her humor. Helen had just spent several nights with this woman, named Cece Gannon, while on a speaking tour in northern California. She'd invited Cece to join the retreat. Other than Helen's recommendation, I knew nothing about her.

Intuitively aware of this, Cece told me she'd raised a daughter and a son, both adults now. She was a psychologist and a former elementary school teacher. She had been volunteering in the Santa Rosa County Jail in California for more than twenty years, teaching anger management and reentry skills.

"I'm not pushy," she said. "I want to learn the cosmology Helen says you will be teaching as part of the retreat. She calls what you teach *the Universe Story*. I've never heard of it. Perhaps I can help with retreat logistics in some way. I'll come a few days early. I'll rent a car and bring food. I'm Italian. I cook."

I liked her immediately. It was April. The retreat was in July. I sent Cece a registration form.

In mid-July 2007, fourteen high school seniors and their teachers gathered at San Benito Monastery in Dayton, Wyoming, for an adventure of prayer and service: Camp Earth Hope. They pitched tents under trees. They enjoyed delicious home-cooked meals. Guided by Helen and their teachers, they explored the many connections between gospel teachings, social justice, women's leadership, and Earth spirituality. Each day began with a holy hour of silent meditation, sung psalms, and scripture reflection led by the resident Benedictine nuns.

Sister Helen peppered her daily discussions with personal stories related to her work to end the death penalty. She brought condemned prisoners into the middle of our retreat circle. Eyes and hearts widened. She also was conductor of the soon-to-be-famous Camp Orchestra Chorus.

Benedictine Sisters Hope and Sarah helped retreatants delve into the meaning of the Bible's nature psalms, prayer, and God's guiding presence in their lives. One of the teachers, Noelani Scheckler-Smith, provided art-as-meditation experiences in the nearby spectacular

Tongue River Canyon. I led the geological journey up the Bighorn Mountains and back into time, from the Triassic-Permian to the Precambrian. Dorie Green, a retired literature teacher and friend, talked about Henry David Thoreau, engendering lively discussion on his relevance for our current ecological crisis. Dorie and I also facilitated sessions that linked the story of the universe with questions about what it means to be human and our role in the great pageant of life on Earth.

Youth participants volunteered service hours, assisting Sister Josetta with candle making and Sister Hope with crafting natural insect repellent and gardening. They mastered the muscle of artisan yeast bread. Their final reflective artwork presentations inspired all.

Almost a year after the retreat, Cece called again. She had begun teaching the story of the universe in the jail. She wanted me to help her write the syllabus and lesson plans for the course.

"The guys love this class. Because the jail limits the number of students we can have, I have a waiting list. We're on stars and galaxies and I don't know where to go next," she said. She got clearance for me to go into the Santa Rosa, California, county jail with her. Although unnerved by the clanging and locking doors we passed through, I looked forward to her class. The men filed into the classroom quietly and sat down in a circle of chairs. Cece introduced me as the Earth Hope director who'd inspired her to start this class. Then she reminded everyone about the appropriate behaviors for the class: respect for each other and strict confidentiality. Everything shared in class stayed in the class. Then, as usual, she began by playing a CD of energetic and evocative music.

"Can anybody identify the home country of the artist?" Cece asked as the song ended with a clap of drums.

"It's Latin, but not Caribbean," one of the men said.

"South America somewhere. Brazil. Sounds like Brazil to me," said another.

"Rio de Janeiro, 1980s." Nailed it.

The men opened their Earth Hope class folders, pulled out a map of the world, and located Brazil.

"Cece, isn't Brazil where that big jungle is?" one of the men asked.

"Not jungle, rain forest. And it's being destroyed. Right?"

Cece nodded.

"How much is gone? How much is left?" someone else asked.

"I don't know. A lot is destroyed every day," she said. "I'll Google it and let you know next week."

"Can we hear the song again?"

As the music ended, Cece asked her class of fifteen men to close or lower their eyes. Most did. It was the guided imagery segment of the class.

"Picture someplace outside in nature that is peaceful, safe, and beautiful. Now see yourself there. Notice everything: what you see, hear, smell, and feel. Sit down. Relax." As Cece read very slowly, her voice clear and soothing, I watched shoulders around the room ease down. "Someone you love very much is coming to you, carrying a gift. It is something you need. You open it." Long pause.

"Now, thank that person for the gift and slowly let the scene fade as you come back to this room. Gently open your eyes."

A tall, hefty young man wiped a tear. "Grandma came. She's been passed for years! And there she was, coming over the hill to me."

"And?" Cece said.

"She gave me a wooden box all painted. Inside was a message. It said: believe in yourself. I was sitting on a hill and there were lots of other hills, like around here. My hill was covered with green grass and white flowers and birds were flying around. Grandma came over to me, walking slow and smiling."

"Which self do you want to believe in?" Cece asked.

He ducked his head, as though confused or embarrassed.

"That's the mystery, the adventure," Cece encouraged him gently. "What have we been learning in this class so that we can make better choices, and get to the self worth believing in?"

"We're all connected."

Cece smiled. It was her mantra. "Yes, one with each other, all people, the whole universe. Everything is connected. We're all one. That's the lesson of the Big Bang, the Flaring Forth. Next, what do galaxies teach us? A difficult lesson: when things cool down enough, gravity pulls them together and stars are born, light up! What about us? We have to cool down, too, get sober, and *stay* clean and sober. Clean and sober, we learn to *feel* again. Then *caring* can pull us together, help you pull yourself together, lighting up your true self, the self of inner goodness and right behaviors. Don't you think this could be what 'believe in yourself' means?"

They were riveted. A few nodded slowly. The man who saw his grandmother squinted his eyes and I saw another tear. Cece then said that today we were going to find out more about our inner stars. She then showed a video about the evolution of stars. It was beautiful and informative. When it finished and they had shared their reactions and questions, she invited them to the two long art tables. On each table were crayons and colored pencils, watercolor paints, glue, tape, various colored tissue papers, and construction paper. Cece had one pair of blunt scissors they could share. She placed a large piece of white poster board on each table.

"Before you begin, think about how you would like to depict the story of a star. Remember that many of the elements forged in stars are now in your body. How would you show that you began in a star? A long, long time ago."

After a brief pause, she continued, "Now talk with each other about what you would like to contribute to the star poster. And when you're ready, choose your art supplies and begin."

Two hours later, she and I left the jail and stopped for dinner at her favorite Thai restaurant. She ordered coconut pumpkin soup for two. As the waitress ladled the steaming, fragrant soup into bowls, Cece said, "Tomorrow while I cook, you'll write out the rest of the lessons for me. How many in all?"

"Probably thirteen," I said.

"Okay"—she savored the soup—"that's ten more."

Within two years Sister Mary Nerney was teaching the Earth Hope cosmology program in the intensive therapy unit of the Rikers Island women's jail in New York City. While I was interning in 1995 at Global Education Associates in New York City, Mary and I had been part of a small community of Sisters in East Harlem. I became reacquainted with her when she participated in a weekend retreat I led at Springbank Eco-Spirituality Retreat in South Carolina. Recently retired from a lifetime of family services and jail ministry, she was looking to redirect her energies. Teaching the cosmology program excited her.

Mary and Cece trained other jail volunteers to teach the program in St. Louis, Missouri. Earth Hope provided all the materials and covered their travel expenses, thanks to two small grants from our religious communities. As part of the training, Mary shared her experience with the program. "Once the women, all abused, some abusers themselves, learn they are made of stardust, they change. Their self-image changes. Self-esteem begins to flower. They light up. With hope."

Ten years after she inaugurated the cosmology course, Cece continued to teach it in the Santa Rosa County Jail. She wrote that students attended regularly, and week by week shed bits of their tough personas. They shed tears as they met the truer essence of who they were.

Requirements included writing up five of the reflective questions, creating an exit plan that included a sobriety commitment, a résumé of marketable skills, and job search and housing possibilities. They participated in discussions and presentations. Five were awarded a week off their sentence. In the end, they thanked each other for witnessing their stories and for the safety they maintained in the class. They wept over loss and gain in their lives.

For Cece, it was humbling and rewarding to facilitate men who took such risks.

Cece's students, not unlike Saint Augustine, had been able to understand the beauty of the universe, to compare its "voice received on the outside with the truth that lies within." Through the Universe Story they encountered something so vast, they had to change their view of themselves to accommodate it. Having experienced awe through exploration of their inner and outer worlds, they were better prepared to return to society as contributing citizens.

26

Ancestors and Destiny

Reflections on Deep Time in
the Bighorn Mountains

*Truth shall spring out of the earth, and
justice will look down from heaven.*

PSALMS 85:11

PEOPLE'S COMPANION TO THE BREVIARY:

VOLUME 1

S an Benito Benedictine Monastery was inseparable from the
Bighorn Mountains that overshadowed it. The Little Tongue
River made rippling conversation through the thirty-eight
acres of monastery grounds. Its waters began in snowmelt ten thousand feet above the chapel where nuns chanted psalms to God daily,
within sight and earshot of the river. Their horse pasture, just outside
the back door of the mobile home I rented from them, sloped up into
foothills.

We experienced the Bighorns' weather: early winter and late
spring snowstorms, exaggerated blizzards, drenching rain, winds that

cull the cottonwoods of dead branches, swells of intense heat that updraft to lift hawks, turkey vultures, and, rarely, a bald eagle.

The Bighorns' inhabitants visited us: once a young black bear at my open bedroom window, an occasional moose or fox, and regularly whitetail and mule deer. The mountains' spring-summer procession of wildflowers began just beyond the pasture: crowds of blue lupine scattered with golden arrowleaf balsamroot, and higher, feathery pale purple pasqueflower, patches of white phlox, fuchsia shooting stars whose Crow name means that color and "bird's beak," their shape. Higher still, lemon-yellow dogtooth violets cluster around shallow pools that rim melting snowbanks. I was in the habit of looking first in early April for orange-yellow fritillary, shaped like tulips, hung like bells, smaller than thimbles. When they're in bloom, juncos have returned to pine forests, meadowlarks are lacing sagebrush with mating songs, and Canada geese are laying eggs.

All this life, including grasses, birds, and human beings, was merely a very recent community in the long pageant told by the rock layers of the mountains themselves. I gradually came to think of these layers as a kind of sacred scripture. Each tells life's story and remarkable achievements, each a page of the holiest of texts: Earth. All that is needed is to know how to read the archive of rocks.

The Wyoming highway department did a marvelous, albeit unintentional, job of uncovering the pages as they cut and widened State Highway 14. In 1985, a local geologist and paleontologist, Professor Michael Flynn from nearby Sheridan College, secured a grant to engage students in studying the distinguished rocks, determining their approximate ages. He, and Patricia Hamilton, author of *Rocks in My Head: Or a Windshield Guide to Bighorn Mountain Geology*, led students in a hunt for distinctive, identifiable layers.

Students learned that Goose Egg Formation rock feels like oatmeal, the Chugwater rock like sand. Pine trees prefer acidic soils, indicating the presence of sandstone. They were learning a kind of rock literacy. Today, thanks to the work of Mike and his students, travelers up the mountain get to read *words*. The grant also paid for large brown signs, each announcing the geologic period as well as rock type. To climb the mountain is dizzying, in landscape and time spiral.

"Today we're going up the mountain," I said to the circle of Camp Earth Hope participants. "We will visit ancient rocks, learn some geology, and reflect on some of life's major accomplishments. Similar to stopping to read historic markers when traveling, we will stop at historic geologic sites as we drive up the mountain. I will share with you meditations based on science, based on information from geology and the evolution of life. You've learned some of this information in your biology and chemistry classes. Today, instead of reading books, we're going to read the rocks themselves. And at each stop we will ask: what was life doing when this rock was being formed?"

I repeated the question.

"Our final destination is the Medicine Wheel. It is an old and mysterious stone wheel of twenty-eight spokes. Visiting the Wheel is the most significant part of our mountain pilgrimage. We don't know who created it. We don't know why they built it or what it meant to them. We don't know the proper way to approach the Wheel. We don't know what protocol to observe while there. As we walk the last mile to the Wheel, we will focus on having a pure intention and being respectful. I will invite you to ponder what you can give of yourself to the life community. In the presence of the Wheel, it is especially important to be thankful. It is a place to be instructed. It seems to me to be a sensitive area, sensitive to our presence and what we do and say there. We'll have more time to talk about the Medicine Wheel as we approach the area.

"For now, some practical things. Even though it's warm down here, by the time we're above ten thousand feet, the air will be much cooler. It is often very windy up top where we'll be praying around the Medicine Wheel. That wind could remind you of the wind of the Holy Spirit on the first Pentecost, or of the breath of the Spirit hovering over the beginnings of creation in the Genesis account. Be sure to bring a warm jacket. Also, don't forget your water bottles and your snacks."

They nodded. Some made moves to head for their tents. I signaled to stay put.

"A few more things to keep in mind. The Bighorn Mountains are unique in how the rock is layered with oldest rock now near the top and younger layers below. On most mountains, it is the other way around as newly formed rock accumulates on top of what is already there, covering it. However, in the Bighorns, rock layers were subjected to intense pressure and consequently compressed, fractured or faulted, and uplifted. That means, what?" Blank stares. "It means that as we climb the mountain we will be traveling back in time, in a sense. The higher we go, the older the rock. And the more ancient the life-form.

"My friend Professor Mike Flynn and his students did most of the work to identify the rock layers. We will stop at each pullout by the signs to study the rock and talk about what life was accomplishing when that rock was being formed. You may pick up a small rock near the road to label and place in a bag. You can take these home to help you remember the beauty and significance of some of the achievements of life. Your rocks could become something like the beads of a rosary for you, helping you recall the sacred mysteries that led to our being part of a magnificently diverse community of life. They will help us all remember that we come from a lineage of ancestors that stretches back millions and even billions of years. Here on the table are little cloth bags, one for each of you, and black felt-tipped pens. Help yourself. And then we'll meet at the vehicles in about fifteen minutes."

The road ascended gradually from the river valley past homes and ranches, and then open meadows. Soon we were in pine forest. Our first stop was at a bright red-orange gash in the mountainside, sandstone and shale from Triassic-Permian times, which ran from 299 to 199 million years ago. We paused to gaze from a lookout to the Tongue River valley far below, our attention caught by spaciousness and stillness.

"My sister Regina, who trained in geology, taught me how to label," I said. "I'm not trained; I've just read John McPhee, David Love, and Patricia Hamilton, and consulted with Mike Flynn. Dr. Brian Swimme taught me how to think in geologic terms during the two and a half years I studied cosmology."

I continued, "Recently, I've put together some ideas about the pageant of life, as it is remembered here in rock. These ideas are like a meditation or reflective commentary, based on the story of life's evolution. Each reflection has been drawn from the rock layer pages of Bighorn Mountain geology. Mike told me that he was continually refining the dates displayed on the signage, as new data came in from the field. He warned me not to latch onto the numbers on the signs as exact. In a similar vein, I paint my ideas in broad strokes with a thick brush, based on the dates we have available to us now. I've been inspired in my work by the late Tairyu Furukawa, an accomplished and innovative Japanese calligrapher/artist. He was a Buddhist monk, husband,

271

and father who spent his life trying to save two innocent men from execution. His daughter, Sayuri, is a friend of mine. She once took me, reverently, into her father's studio. It was dominated by brushes, some hung from the walls, others arranged by size on tables. She told me her father often used the largest one, almost as tall as he was. That brush was four feet, four inches long and weighed about four and a half pounds. That's the brush I use for my Bighorn reflections. A professionally trained geologist would give you far more precise detail. I am aiming for something different.

"Mike Flynn said the highway department didn't have the budget to change the signage every time he got more precise about the ages of rocks. I suppose Wyoming DOT and I have something in common here. We work for truthful approximations; the DOT for economic reasons and me, to enliven and stretch the imagination. I can only hope that what I write is at least minimally worthy of Tairyu's brush."

I directed their attention to the red-orange rock in front of us.

"Let's think for a moment about what was going on when this particular rock was being formed," I said. "A mass extinction occurred, destroying up to 96 percent of all life-forms. Its cause is somewhat of a mystery. Following that great extinction, it took about 2 million years for life to recover biological diversity. What animals were around then? What animals dominated the landscape?"

"Dinosaurs?" someone ventured. "Triassic sounds a lot like Jurassic."

"Good guess. That's the next time period. During the Triassic, fish and turtles filled the seas, and on land, we find abundant evidence in the fossil record of reptiles. During the Triassic, reptiles diversified and flourished. What did evolution bring forth in reptiles?"

Silence. I realized this was a new way for them to think about life-forms.

"The biggest reptilian accomplishment in my view was in reproduction. Up until then, reproduction occurred primarily in the sea with the female laying eggs and males battling over who gets to swish a shower of sperm over them. Most, but not all, fish reproduced in this way. And still do. Reptiles brought the sea into the female body, where the amniotic egg is fertilized by the male. As a result, they created a new and resplendent intimacy in the universe. Reptiles! In cosmology class at this point in the story, Dr. Brian Swimme remarked, 'Let's show a little appreciation for reptiles here.'

"Most significantly, something new springs into consciousness: female *discernment and choice*. Instead of giving over the next generation to the prowess of males only, the female now has some ability to determine who will fertilize her eggs and father the next generation. Think of it! Approximately 300 million years ago evolution handed the future of life to the discernment of females."

One of the teachers in the group nodded slowly. "That's impressive."

"I think about this a lot," I continued. "Clearly female choice is important to the evolution of life, to life itself. Who created the peacock's tail? The peahen did through her choices. Resplendent feathers mean health. She's not thinking this like we would, but she is looking for something, and chooses the big tail. Female choice continues through birds and mammals, determining characteristics and health of the next generation. Does this make sense to you?"

Most nodded.

"So, what could be an insight here for humans? Although it may be a big leap to make this next connection, I will. Because humanity came from and remains within the evolutionary process, I would say that any human institution or church or governing system in which women do not have proportional influence at every level of decision-making is inherently flawed, is a distortion of the long course of evolution and life itself. It deprives the future of the grace and wisdom, if you will, of female discernment, a very old and venerable life process. In religious terms, perhaps we could say that because evolution is how God creates life-forms, then to exclude women's discernment from decision-making and shared power is to go against God's way of doing *life*.

"Does this connect in your mind with the leadership skills your teachers promote in you as young women? And with your dreams for your future? Think about these things as you choose one of these bright rocks. Label it Triassic-Permian with the dates."

They were silent as they chose rocks from right beside the road and labeled them.

"When you're back home and need to focus on a decision for your future, pick up this rock and remember that female decision-making is crucial to life. Give yourself time to think deeply as you pay attention to your ideas, emotions, and dreams."

We climbed back into the vehicles and continued up the mountain. The next stop was at pale purple rock, almost the color of pasque-flowers: gypsum and cross-bedded sandstone. Someone asked what "cross-bedded" meant and I said we'd look it up when we got back. The rock was formed during the Pennsylvanian period, roughly from 318 to 299 million years ago. I told them that life brought forth trees then, and that early forests began their slow progress across rocky continents, creating soil as they went.

"For 20 million years, these lush, continental forests sequestered carbon, drawing it out of the atmosphere. They were eventually submerged in shallow seas and compressed into today's coal deposits. During this time, Wyoming and the Appalachian regions were on continental plates near the equator, ideal swamp and decomposition climate. No kidding. Imagine that. The equator."

I pulled out my Bighorn geology file to show them the Scotese map of the globe for the late Carboniferous period of the great coal swamps.

"Every seven to ten minutes, a coal train over a mile long leaves the state of Wyoming for a power plant. Interesting, how we use the word 'plant.' Coal companies like Peabody Energy (USA) and Ambre Energy and Arch Coal (Australia) want to ship up to 140 million tons of coal annually to Asian markets from Pacific Northwest ports. From Wyoming and Montana coal mines, trains will run through cities like Billings, Spokane, Seattle, and Portland, as well as many small towns. There could be as many as sixty trains a day, spewing tons of toxic coal dust from the uncovered coal transport cars across neighborhoods, schoolyards, and ecosystems along four thousand miles of rail. And, burning that much coal would produce roughly 280 million tons of CO_2 per year. That's a lot! Wind will return mercury, particulate matter, and nitrogen oxides from Asian power plants right back to us. In Washington State, the Lummi tribe protested the construction of a massive coal export port at Cherry Point, Washington, a Lummi burial ground. They based their effort on historic treaties that protect their sacred sites and fishing rights. Imagine driving cement piling through your family cemetery plot. The Lummi eventually prevailed. On May 9, 2016, the Army Corps of Engineers denied a permit to the project. In July 2021, Whatcom County, in an attempt to put an end to the proposal, passed a zoning ordinance to prohibit fossil fuel shipment facilities at Cherry Point."

I admitted to my listeners that I know more about coal export schemes than I do about cross-bedded sandstone. They chose their rocks, labeled them, and placed lovely pink-purple rocks into their cloth bags. We prepared to leave the late Carboniferous period. But before we did, I invited them to do a little reflection with me.

"I want desperately to participate in Earth's healing and recovery from climate change caused by rising levels of atmospheric CO_2, primarily driven by human activities," I said. "The effects of climate change hurt poorest people the most. It threatens the survival of endangered species. Plenty of research shows that we're devastating life as we know it, that we're on a kind of suicidal fast track. It's sad and disheartening for me to think about all this. Perhaps for you, too."

I see a few nods.

"What can I do about it, I ask myself. *First do no harm* comes to mind as a good place to start. That was a big part of my joy while living at Prayer Lodge. For several years I worked with the board to retrofit our buildings so that most of our energy use was solar and wind produced, mitigated by a ground-source heating and cooling system. To turn on a light and trace that power line up the hill to our solar panels was soul stirring and emotionally satisfying. It became daily, joyous spiritual practice for me, that doing no harm. Or, at least, doing *less* harm."

"Not everybody can afford that," someone said.

"I know, but before the federal government funded rural electric programs, not everybody could even have power," I said. "It's time

276

to think beyond fossil fuels, think nationwide, and envision and fi-
nance our way into a new, comprehensive power generation plan and
grid. Scientist and Sister of Charity Paula González taught me about
ground-source heating. She envisioned that it, along with solar panels,
would eventually be designed into every home and apartment building. There was a time when we had no indoor plumbing; now it's expected to be part of every home. Why not make renewable energy
generation part of every building design?"

I climbed off my soapbox and into one of the cars. As we continued our ascent, I was acutely aware that we were spewing carbon and
other pollutants from our vehicles into beautiful mountain air. I made
a mental note to acknowledge that at our next stop.

We rounded a bend and stopped at Sand Turn Overlook. Across
the road from us, creamy white limestone rock layers sloped gently.
First, however, we turned to overlook ranches, farms, and towns of
the Tongue River basin.

"Hang-gliders jump off here into thermals rising from the plains.
Then they glide for miles. When I come here, I let thoughts about the
future, of planet and people, hang and glide, as I try to draw lift from
the rock story," I said. "Imagine jumping off this cliff. Imagine jumping into a renewable energy future that includes clean cars."

I added that we were going back in time just in case they hadn't
noticed. As the continental plate drifted northwestward all the way
from equatorial regions, it was compressed, stretched, bulged, and
buckled by movement. Younger rock slid downward on a fault line as
land was raised, exposing older layers. Here in the Bighorns, the oldest rock is at the top of the mountains. Most people who come here
don't expect this.

Turning away from the Tongue River basin vista, we faced a lime-stone cliff.

"The limestone," I said, "is from the Mississippian period, formed between 359 and 318 million years ago. During that time, early seed plants, but not flowers, began to emerge. Seeds packed with protein helped produce larger brains in the animals who ate them. In addition, animals began to venture out of water and onto land. This was a huge enterprise, given that they lacked the ability to breathe oxygen from air. Gradually they developed organs that enabled them to do just that. The first explorers into the world of air were arthropods: scorpions, and then dragonflies, who were the first creatures to fly. And finally, amphibians evolved. They still fertilized their eggs in water, where the young hatched and lived as tadpoles. As mature amphibians, frogs, toads, and salamanders, equipped with lungs, lived most of their adult life on land.

"If they hadn't figured out how to breathe oxygen from air, you and I would be trying to figure out how to talk about all this while under water. All animal life on land depends on this achievement of amphibians. Life eventually diversified into the marvel of reptiles, the beauty of birds, and the magnificence of mammals. All thanks to am-phibians."

They chose crumpled but sturdy rocks and labeled them. "Grati-tude to the arthropods and amphibians," I said as the rocks joined the others in their bags. "Let's take a deep breath of *air*, as we think about the wonder of being able to do just that."

From here the road curved along a dramatic cliff, up and into the mountains. More red shale and white limestone on our right, a severe drop-off to the Little Tongue River far below on our left. We stopped at a view of a mountain slide, apartment-sized chunks of limestone rock in disarray. We parked in the spacious pull-off at a safe distance from two huge highway department bulldozers and a massive dump truck, their engines idling. Across the road, a landslide of rocks.

Within minutes, two men waved us farther away from the dozers, which they then drove with a roar into the rockslide pile.

"Look, Sister," one of the students yelled over the roar, "they don't even know the rocks are sacred."

Surprised, I smiled and nodded. I had deliberately not used the word "sacred" in referring to the rocks. She caught the consequences of our reflection. She saw the consequences of our worldview and the damage it can cause. I thanked her for her insight. This was the heart of my message. I almost had tears in my eyes.

Mike Flynn's nearby sign declared DEVONIAN, 360–410 MILLION YEARS AGO.

"Devonian, the Age of Fish. So, what is their gift to life?" I shouted.

We waited for the dozers to finish their noisy work.

"Well, fish further refined an inner skeletal structure, using not just cartilage like sharks and rays, but making bone. Gradually, they evolved from having armored heads and spines to sleek, finned bodies, well adapted to swimming, to both catch food and avoid being eaten. They invented the jaw, creating bite, further enhancing their ability to grab hold of, and then chew, food.

"They changed the open circulatory system of earlier life-forms to a closed system. I am most grateful, and you may be, too, for the chambered heart they developed. Fish, as you know, absorb oxygen dissolved in water through their gills, which are tissue-paper thin. Blood vessels in gills must therefore be minutely thin tubes, almost thread-like. The smaller the diameter of the tube, the more pressure it takes to force anything through the tube. Sharks and rays move blood by being in constant motion; their movement does the work of a heart. Fish needed something much stronger and created a more efficient system. They evolved a two-chambered pump, a *heart*."

Beside the road, we each picked up a pale gray rock. I invited them to hold their rock over their hearts. I offered a prayer of gratitude for the hearts that first began beating in fish. We labeled our rocks and headed to the next sign: ORDOVICIAN, 443–488 MILLION YEARS AGO.

"This far back in time, and even earlier in the Cambrian, life encased a primitive spinal cord with protective cartilage, a forerunner structure to the flexible backbone. To our best knowledge, the earliest vertebrates were small, snakelike creatures—*Pikaia*—who actually first emerged before the Ordovician period. And the juvenile phase of the sea squirt, which resembles a tadpole, also encased its spinal cord. All these animals were about six inches long or less and were either slender or flat.

"Then jawless fish with a more recognizable backbone structure gradually evolved. These animals were so successful that they are still here today, as eels and hagfish. That's more than 400 million years of surviving on a changing Earth. As a species, they survived ice ages, meteor strikes, and several mass extinction events. That's quite a record! We've only been here in our current form as a species about 2 million years.

"Eventually that protective cartilage and cord evolved into a backbone that over time enabled the diverse acrobatic movements of amphibians, reptiles, birds, and mammals. And then, one day quite recently, it supported upright walking, and right now, the feats of Olympic gymnasts. Our backbones have a long lineage."

We looked at each other, pulled back our shoulders, and straightened our posture.

"Ordovician rock," I continued, "is also limestone, formed when Wyoming was under water. It has a mild yellow cast and is worked with fine jagged lines, something like those on heart monitor screens."

As Highway 14 curved around and beneath soaring limestone cliffs, we parked beneath a prominent formation called Steamboat Rock. A favorite destination for hikers, trails wound up the steep, grassy slope. A fence stretched across the top of the cliff. We turned our backs to Steamboat and crossed the road. Here the rocks were dense, heavy, dark gray with light pink hues and flecked with glassy quartz. Granite.

"We've just taken a huge, long leap back in time," I told them as we hefted the rocks in our palms. "This rock is some of the oldest exposed rock on Earth. It is dated at 2.9 *billion* years old, formed during the Precambrian period. It is the basement rock of our planet. What was life doing way back then?"

"It was probably single-celled, huh?" a teacher ventured.

"Yes! In fact, those single-celled microorganisms, called cyanobacteria, literally changed the world. All complex life today depends on what they accomplished. What was it? They somehow managed to catch photons, whizzing at the speed of light. That's a feat in itself. Then they used all that light energy to split hydrogen out of water, combine it with oxygen and also carbon split off from carbon dioxide, and create food in the form of glucose for themselves. The waste product they left for future complex organisms . . . oxygen.

"Dr. Swimme noted in class that without brains, hands, or science labs, these microorganisms invented a complex biochemical process we humans have yet to figure out how to duplicate. Photosynthesis!

"The unused oxygen escaped into Earth's primordial atmosphere, which at that time is thought to have been 98 percent carbon dioxide, 1.9

percent nitrogen, and 0.1 percent argon. Little by little, these microorganisms drew down carbon dioxide and added oxygen to the atmosphere, changing it dramatically, making it oxygen rich. Today oxygen is 20.95 percent of the lower atmosphere. Carbon dioxide, ideally, at 0.035 percent, or 350 parts per million.

"Photosynthesis drives the life of all green plants. We humans totally depend on it, primarily for food! Without it, Earth would probably look a lot like Mars, a red, dusty place. Whatever life may be there is buried deep in a planet that itself is dead. Dramatically different, blue, glistening green Earth, awash in liquid water, is alive.

"On the other hand, all that oxygen created a crisis for life. It was a poisonous gas for those microorganisms, who were naturally anaerobic. They died by the hundreds of billions. A few escaped by adapting to life deep in water or sediments, away from oxygen. And still survive in the oxygen-free guts of animals, including us, where they help digest food. And, thankfully, some learned to use the fatal oxygen to their advantage through respiration.

"It's difficult to imagine oxygen as a poisonous gas because we can't survive without it. This is an example of life itself altering the planet in a way that was self-destructive. I think this is akin to what we're doing now by burning fossil fuels. Carbon dioxide is now way over the ideal 350 parts per million. The presence of that much carbon dioxide, combined with other greenhouse gases, is changing Earth's overall climate. This is happening in a mere few hundred years. Organisms, including humans, that can adapt that quickly to these changes will survive. Those that can't, won't.

"What about us? Most of the plant foods we depend upon are adapted to a pre–industrial revolution climate when carbon levels held relatively steady for millennia at around 350 parts per million. Forty percent of us live along coasts; and sea levels are rising. Can we be as ingenious as microorganisms? Can we adapt? Can we find ways to wean ourselves off our profligate use of fossil fuels and decide to use them sparingly to build a new carbon-free energy grid, achieving a zero-carbon process from cradle (extraction) to grave (burning)? And dismantle nuclear power as well."

Leaning against a Precambrian granite cliff, I shouted into mountain air, "Let's aspire to be at least as clever as single-celled organisms. You engineers and industrialists, design and create a *carbon-neutral* industrial revolution!"

I hopped off my second soapbox.

I told them we were finished collecting rocks. I said we now had a forty-five-minute drive up and across the top of the mountains. The land rolled and dipped. Wildflower meadows sloped to a network of streams banked with willows. Some slopes were slashed by gleaming limestone formations. We crossed an unmarked divide, stopped the vehicles, and stood at an overlook, spellbound. The central Wyoming Bighorn Basin spread below us, all the way to snowcapped Absaroka Mountains on the eastern edge of Yellowstone National Park.

I have become convinced that much of the silence of Earth pools here, deep and warm. Silence rises like thermals, engulfing us in tangible quiet. Soul laid open by quiet mystery, I teetered on the brink of—could it be prayer? Adoration?

"Better head on to the Medicine Wheel now," I said to myself, "or else I'll want to spend the night here."

This is something I dream of doing someday. I did it once at Dryhead Overlook in the Pryor Mountains. I woke up dreaming of being overrun by a thundering herd of hippopotami. I haven't slept alone on the brink of a mountain overlook since.

We curved around more rounded mountaintops, caught glimpses of the ethereal basin, skirted yet more colorful meadows. Ahead was Medicine Mountain, named for the ancient wheel-like structure of stones found near its very top. A stone circle, 80 feet in diameter and approximately 245 feet in circumference, it has twenty-eight spokes that radiate from a central cairn to the outer rim of the circle. Thanks to the dedicated work of the Crow, Northern Cheyenne, Shoshone, Lakota, and Ute, and collaborating county, state, and federal agencies, the Wheel area and the whole mountain was renamed as the Medicine Wheel / Medicine Mountain National Historic Landmark in 2011. The values and traditions of these Native Nations are written into the administration of the landmark.

All of us were soon walking the one-and-one-half-mile foot trail along the edge of the mountain to the summit. We talked about how life now teeters on the brink of the end of the current geologic era, the Cenozoic. It began 65 million years ago with the extinction of the dinosaurs. It evolved into the era of mammals, primates, and now humans. We are the dominant Earth life-form now, the equivalent of photosynthetic bacteria, dramatically changing all the great life systems and cycles of our home planet: atmosphere, soils, water, the carbon cycle, and the web of life itself, even DNA. And we're doing it in a mere several hundred years.

On top, we huddled against the wind. I shared with them what I'd learned from Native American interpreters who work for the Park Service and sometimes are here to assist with questions.

"No one knows for sure who laid this wheel of rocks," I said. "Or when. Today's tribal nations have stories that say the Wheel was here when they arrived. What could be the meaning of the twenty-eight spokes? Twenty-eight feathers in the tail of an eagle. Twenty-eight vertebrae in the backbone of a buffalo. Twenty-eight days in a woman's cycle. In addition, some of the spokes seem to point to the rise of a star on the night of the summer solstice. If nothing else, we get the sense that this place was significant to many people over a long stretch of time. It seems to have become a place of soul-searching. At this time, when Native Americans come here to fast and pray, seeking guidance in their lives, all visitors are asked to remain down at the trailhead until the ceremonies are over."

I gave each of them a pinch of a tobacco and sage mixture, telling them this was an offering they could scatter where they wished, to show respect for this place, and the spirits who dwell here. I encouraged them to walk in silence around the Wheel. And afterward, they could find a protected place to sit on a rock to absorb the vista and their own souls.

"As you walk and sit to ponder, to enjoy the beauty here, remember you are surrounded by the prayers and sacrifices of many people who have come here throughout the past. Think about this. What could be your contribution to the great pageant of life? What will be your gift? How will we together participate in the great story of creation as part of Earth, in this universe?"

We then approached the Wheel in silence, weighted not by granite and rocks but with responsibility. And awe. This is our moment.

Affairs are now soul size.

"To reinvent the human at the species level, from within the community of life, by means of story, and shared dream experience."

These words of Thomas Berry, the stories from the rock layers, reverberated inside me. I sensed the presence of ancestors, courageous inventers of new life-forms.

Fourteen young women began to walk toward the Wheel.

We silently walked clockwise around a wheel of glistening stones. I watched them make their offerings. Ravens wheeled above us. And wind.

Acknowledgments

I wrote this book from within an embrace of friendship and generosity.

Although even as a child, I felt a kinship with land, animals, and plants, as an adult that sense of kinship grew into love for Earth and passionate dedication to Earth's protection, beauty, and well-being, and to ministry dedicated to enhancing the human-Earth relationship. From this perspective, Earth wrote this book; I am simply one woman writing Earth.

A book rises from a circle of constant, generous support of the many needs of heart, soul, and body. I am indebted to these people and communities.

From my heart, I thank my family: Dad, who encouraged me to write as often as I could; Mom, who called my words beautiful; Aunt Rose, my godmother, who faithfully prayed for me; and Regina, Susan, and Monica, dearest friends and sisters, always by my side. Though not often said directly, words remain sacred in our family. We grew up with and continue to strive to the best of our ability for truthfulness, kindness, and respect with just enough humor and plenty of love.

The Sisters of St. Francis, Oldenburg, Indiana, approved my signing a contract with Riverhead Books/Penguin Random House in 2003. They have encouraged and supported me in many real ways these twenty years since. Sisters and Associates, I couldn't have written this without you and your prayers.

Jake Morrissey, my editor at Riverhead Books, a division of Penguin Random House, believed in me and my work through all the years when I had little belief in it or my capabilities.

My profound gratitude for Sister Helen Prejean, author and dear friend, who year after year encouraged my writing in her inimitable, enthusiastic Cajun way.

St. Wendel, Indiana

In a small elementary school in a rural landscape, I learned to grow minds and hearts, and cultivate my writing skills through teaching.

Kansas City, Missouri

Partnering with parents and guardians in their commitment to children's education, taught me to believe in a future of hope. And helped publish the school newspaper.

In Crow country

Gwennie and Larry Plain Bull, my Crow parents, and Laurie, Dorcella, and Fred, thank you for welcoming me into your family and clan, for sharing your wisdom, and teaching me with gentleness. And for those many good times in your home and Crow Fair camp.

George Bull Tail: for the naming ceremony and Crow name that continue to be a daily blessing in my heart.

Charlene Laverdure, generous teacher and secretary: for your guidance and invaluable assistance.

Rose Turnsplenty and family: so many gatherings and celebrations, too many to name!

Dorothy Spotted Bear, Sylvia and Fred Gone, and Bruce Spotted Bear Sr.: a school depends primarily on cooks and maintenance, as well as on the principal, who benefited greatly from your friendships, and conversations and prayer with you.

Heywood and Mary Lou Big Day: for all the sweats and meals, for being with you in your home on Pryor Creek, for all you taught me, thank you!

Father Randolph Graczyk, language teacher and good friend: your pastoring helped bring me home to life in Crow country.

All my students and St. Charles ministers, teachers, and staff: you remain a constant blessing in my life. Thank you!

In Northern Cheyenne country

Vonda, my sister, and my brother-in-law, Francis Limpy, and their children, Rocky, Brenda, Karla, and Tish: I often hear your voice, my sister, in my heart. I continue to learn how to be a better human from you. I think of you, too, whenever I peel spuds.

Marcelline Timber and Charles Little Old Man: All those sweats! Thank you for the songs, teachings, and prayers. Thank you for those visiting and cooking times at Sundance Camp.

Charlotte and Tom Rockroads: You showed me how to be brave and kind, and taught me to always remember as best I could what the old people said.

Carolyn and Larry Martin and April Martin Chalfont: for sharing a vision of a healthy place for women and providing the land. I was privileged and blessed to get to live there.

Wilhelmina Schmidt: beautiful voice rising from a beautiful heart and soul. I'm ever grateful for all the singing, and visiting, we did!

Brother Conrad Heinen, builder of Prayer Lodge greenhouse, decks, and community: for all the times and ways we broke bread, thank you!

Springbank Retreat

Sister Trina, those eight years of annual retreats with you and community helped me to nurture and hone my thoughts and words, enabled me to organize them in creative and appealing ways, and provided a supportive setting in which to launch them.

Inestimable circle of friends

Dorie Green, an excellent writer who helped finesse my words; Pat Feldsien, who did early editing and convinced me I had something to say; Rose Vines, who with loving-kindness and consummate skill did a massive amount of dedicated work finding order in my countless pages of chaos; Sister Pat Bietsch, who gently endured years of living with a struggling author; Sisters Marge Wissman and Barb Piller, for your gracious hospitality whenever I needed a refreshing, calm, and happy place; the La Claire Convent Sisters, who always welcomed me home. Each of you, your loving friendships permeate my life and work. You midwifed this book! Thank you.

All you other dear friends, visiting, hiking, camping, cooking, dreaming cosmic goodness, playing cards, going to pow-wows, gardening, driving endless Montana, Washington, and Louisiana roads to be together, being in Oldenburg for retreats and meetings and fun, planning Prayer Lodge, planning retreats and prayers, as well as cooking and sewing classes: you know who you are. I love you and thank you for nourishing these words, and walking-talking me through the tough times.

Every one of you who've shared my journey these many years, I hope I've worthily woven your goodness, influence, and teachings into what I've written. You lit the path, I walked it. Any stumbles are mine.

And, finally, with a smile in my heart:

A huge, loving "thank you" to you who provided incredible meals, conversations, and special places of beauty, peace, and security to write:

Benedictine Sisters of San Benito

Holy Names Parish, Sheridan and Story, Wyoming

Sisters of St. Francis, San Damiano Retreat Cottage, Oldenburg, Indiana

Barbara and the late Karl Fischer and family

Denny LeBoeuf

Larry and Carol McEvoy and family

the Barker family and Leigh Scardina of Grand Isle, Louisiana

Lin and Jim Roscoe and family

Rose Vines and Lillie Eyrich

Ucross Foundation writing residency: it was invaluable!